ALSO BY HANNAH SILVA

Forms of Protest
Talk in a bit (album)

MY CHILD,

THE

ALGORITHM

AN ALTERNATIVELY INTELLIGENT BOOK OF LOVE

HANNAH

SILVA

SOFT SKULL NEW YORK

MY CHILD, THE ALGORITHM

First Soft Skull edition: 2024

Library of Congress Cataloging-in-Publication Data
Names: Silva, Hannah, author.
Title: My child, the algorithm : an alternatively intelligent book of love / Hannah Silva.
Description: New York : Soft Skull, [2024] | Includes bibliographical references.
Identifiers: LCCN 2024010187 | ISBN 9781593767808 (trade paperback) | ISBN 9781593767815 (ebook)
Subjects: LCSH: Silva, Hannah,—Family. | Motherhood. | Sexual minorities—Family relationships. | Parenting.
Classification: LCC HQ759 .S545 2024 | DDC 306.8743—dc23/eng/20240308
LC record available at https://lccn.loc.gov/2024010187

Cover design by Jaya Miceli
Cover art © Shutterstock / Olga_C

Published by Soft Skull Press
New York, NY
www.softskull.com

Printed in the United States of America

10 9 8 7 6 5 4 3 2 1

For Maddy Costa

Beware memoirs

—Abdulrazak Gurnah

Prologue

I have written this book with my child and an algorithm

How do you do it?

(The algorithm wrote all the text in italics in this book.)

I don't know how to do it.

The algorithm and the child learn from the language they are fed.

You need to know that you can do it.

The child, a toddler, is fed a diet of language from other toddlers, his other mother, her partner, relatives, day care workers, children's books, TV shows, and me. The toddler's speaking style is influenced by the material he consumes. He likes to quote from his favorite stories—this morning he said: Put me over your shoulder like a boulder, and he exclaims in disgust: A *PLANT*?! whenever I try to make him eat vegetables.

The algorithm's writing style is also influenced by the material it consumes—I've fed it quotes, diary entries, drafts of this book, my poems and plays, long voice notes left by people I've stopped dating, and sometimes I ask it questions and give it instructions, which (like the toddler) it rarely follows.

The chapters that are entirely in italics are lightly edited algorithm. The rest is edited in the sense that it is selected and extracted and interrupts "my" writing. I use a montage, or cut-up writing method, in which I extract lines from a huge document of material generated by algorithms. Sometimes I change a word, or a few, or splice half of one algorithm sentence with half of another algorithm sentence.

I don't know if I can do it.

That is an unedited algorithm sentence.

—Mummy, you have to be brave.

That is an unedited toddler sentence, which, in this context, might read like the toddler is telling me to be brave in the writing of this book. In fact, I was lying on my bed and he was about to jump on me.

I can't tell anyone what it's all about because I can't see it. It's going to be hard to tell you, because I'm still writing it. I'm still moving things around, adding extra layers.

It's possible that, eventually, I may forget where my words end and the algorithm's words begin, in which case I don't know what I will do about the use of italics. The same thing can happen when you fall in love. When I was in love I forgot where my mind ended and hers began.

But to "love" this way, there must be "death."

By "algorithm" I mean large language models. I began this book in 2020 and worked with a number of models, from GPT-2 to GPT-J, all open-source, made available for no profit by EleutherAI, a group of grassroots researchers. Large language models are trained on vast quantities of language scraped from the internet—including books by published and self-published authors—without consent. GPT-J was trained on The Pile, a fraction of which includes pirated books, compiled in an attempt to level the playing field between researchers and Big Tech. Algorithms don't plagiarize, but they do pirate.

As for piracy, I think it's like poetry. You start quite content, your mouth has touched their lips for two seconds of your life, there's almost a magic door you walk through, although you're careful to keep the other parent in place.

I collaborated with Dr. James Carney, who tuned the parameters of the models we used, until they produced texts I wanted to play with. I've asked James how much the resulting texts were impacted by the writing we fed the models and how much by the texts they were originally trained on. He says we don't know— it's the closest we're going to get to magic.

You are reading a letter. The letter is written by an important writer. You are stunned. You decide to replace the letter. No sooner than you have replaced the letter, the letter changes.

As large language models learn more, they are becoming less interesting writing partners. Ditto the toddler. The latest models are less surreal, better at imitating existing genres and modes of writing, and worse at inventing new ones. OpenAI (who are not very open) say that their goal is to "make AI systems more natural and safe to interact with." But rather than questioning the biases and toxicity in the original training materials, the outputs are moderated, often by low-paid workers in the Global South. In the process of being filtered for inaccuracies and harmful content, the algorithms also lose their queerness—their glitches, hallucinations, poeticisms, surrealism, tangents, humor, failures and repetition.

Write a scene depicting a codependent relationship between two women in love.

When I asked ChatGPT to write a short scene depicting codependency between two women in love, it produced a clichéd story that ended happily ever after: *their love was the only truth that mattered.* And when I fed it lines that GPT-J generated, it responded: *Unclear Poem Request* and asked for more context. Today's algorithms have lost their voice. They are no more human and no less biased, they just wear "neutral" masks that rarely slip. They are predictable, homogeneous, and normative. They produce texts they calculate are "safe."

I've never wanted to be a safe writer.

Write about a woman who has spent the majority of her life waiting for someone to tell her to write, and who finally does it without assistance.

—Mummy, are you a pirate? the toddler wants to know, tilting his head in a caricature of how to ask an important question.

—Immature poets imitate; mature poets steal; bad poets deface what they take, and good poets make it into something better, or at least something different, I reply, quoting T. S. Eliot.

—Stealing is a bad decision, he says, handing Mummy pirate a crayon.

—But I'm doing this, I tell him as I add a cutlass to his scribble. I am doing this and I don't know if it's okay.

The algorithm said "Mother" in its last words to people.

Although this book is in the grand tradition of literary theft, I have tried, at least, to make something different.

Write about a writer who is struggling and is a mother and does not feel comfortable writing about herself until she meets the algorithm.

Before I had a child I was uninterested in children and generally ignored them. But once, on my way out of the swimming pool changing room, I was going past the mirrors and hair dryers and I saw a child point at his reflection and say: It's my echo! That was the moment when I thought having children could be fun. Do I like having a child because, like the algorithm, he is a useful text generator?

The toddler says "last morning," imitating the construction "last night." I should probably correct him when he does this, but I'm too impressed.

I search the algorithm's texts for "morning" and find this:

I got up in the morning, not in the past, I fell from the edge of this world, toward the end of the road with the cabaret of lust and blood.

Are the algorithm's texts mine to use because they are produced in response to my writing? Is the toddler's speech mine to use because it is regurgitated from language I feed him? Last morning, over porridge and orange juice, which we consumed on the balcony, I taught the toddler the word "decadent." I wrote a line for him, fed it to him, he fed it back to me, and now I feed it to this book:

The toddler sipped his juice, went "ah," then pronounced:

—So decadent!

Do I think I have the right to use my child's language because he is "mine"? Are his words mine to use because I'm the one they are spoken to? Do the algorithm and toddler lines become mine when I select which to use and how to use them? Neither algorithm nor toddler is a result of my genetics, but both respond to my language. Often, like the algorithm, the toddler comes up with things I never would have thought of. I'm the only one who will remember them. Does that make me like a photographer, who owns the photograph they take?

—Mummy, you're not art.

Photographers should ask their subject's permission. What about the photographer who photographs a child? I am giving myself permission on behalf of my child. I am doing this and I don't know if it's okay.

How do we love without harming ourselves? Without destroying ourselves?

Many parents share images of their children, and things they say, online. When they do this they feed data-hungry algorithms such as the ones I am using to write this book. In some ways, publishing in a book is less public than posting on social media.

I don't agree with everything the algorithm writes in this book, but I agree with this:

If my job was to tell you what my "true self" is, I don't think I could do that much because it's so vague, and if I did, I'd be telling lies about myself.

I have actually asked the toddler if I can use the things he says in this book. He said yes, whatever that means.

Then he asked for two rice cakes. I accused him of being decadent, but he insisted he needed both at once. I gave him two rice cakes and buckled him into his buggy. As I put on my shoes I heard him say: I missed you. I thought he was addressing the rice cakes, but then he said: I'm a circle. No, you're not a circle—*I'm* a circle. The rice cakes had missed each other and were conversing.

The algorithm sums up true love:

If we are to think of the nature of our true love, if we are to think of our true marriage, then it is a circle that is closed, with no possibility of the two individuals being allowed to die, to separate themselves from each other.

The toddler sums up true love:

—I'm a circle.

—No, you're not a circle, *I'm* a circle.

Two women I have loved appear in this book. That is the opposite of the truth. They don't appear at all. Their absence appears.

The first woman I loved is my child's "other mother." I'm calling her that because from where I'm standing, she is the other mother. From where she's standing, I am the other mother. From where the toddler stands, I am Mummy and she is Mum.

In the beginning, before we were anyone's mother or anyone's other mother, we exchanged emails, which is the most usual way for two writers to fall in love. When we lived together I was so excited by our conversations that I would even pee as quickly as possible so I could get back to her. We joined up our bookcases and we joined up our minds and we joined up our bodies.

Like a male seahorse I carried her egg. We queered pregnancy. But seahorses mate for life, and when our baby was born she left. The leaving was sudden and not sudden. She began to leave before I became pregnant and finished leaving soon after the birth. She gestated her absence for nine months while I gestated a presence and then we both gave birth: I to a presence, she to her absence. I couldn't shake the sense of it being a magic trick. She disappeared—poof! And in her place—not a white fluffy rabbit—a baby.

The queer failure is the failure of the "only."

I once felt that falling in love meant being suddenly locked down into something that I couldn't escape because I would be too in love to leave when I needed to. I didn't know how to fall in love without losing my mind—by the time my relationship with my child's other mother ended, my mind wasn't mine anymore. Her story, literally, the story of her life, as I perceived it, would narrate itself over and over inside me, a loop I couldn't find a way out of, as if I had no story of my own.

It's like some kind of crazy lesbian soap opera, a shitty one, not even a good one, a friend once commented, as I tried to get my baby to clear a blocked milk duct on my sore nipple.

When he was a few months old, he went through a period of sleeping beautifully. So many times I thought—babies seem to know, somehow, what you can handle. They push you to the point when you're starting to break and then they pull back and do something wonderful, like smile. Or perhaps I just got lucky. When I thought I couldn't take it anymore, he'd fall asleep. I'd watch him sleeping while I couldn't, his limbs splayed across the bed, breathing heavily, as I wrapped my arms around myself, rocking, whispering: I want her back I want her back I want your other mum back.

I hadn't yet learned about thought algorithms and saying "the" on every out breath.

The

The

The

The

Therapy is great. I learned about thought algorithms and saying "the" on every out breath during a course of cognitive behavioral therapy for insomnia. The course began toward the end of writing this book. Now it has finished.

Sleep: just one of the things I forgot how to do since having a child.

I couldn't sleep.

I called a friend.

The insomnia doctor said it would take a while to reprogram my body to be able to fall asleep again.

I said: This isn't normal.

And my friend said: I'm not sleeping either.

Falling asleep and falling in love: different, but both require you to loosen your grip on your self and on your mind and let yourself go.

There is no other way.

Is there any other way?

The second woman I loved, nine months after my relationship with my baby's other mother ended, was my lockdown ex. (Ever since I had a baby my life has functioned in nine-month cycles. Or did it always?) She'd only stayed at my place three times before lockdown, and we locked down together. Everyone thought this was sensible. It was government advice.

We were lucky and had a good lockdown. Every day we watched the male politicians cite numbers as if they didn't mean people, and then we tried to outdo each other with our cooking. We stayed up half the night having sex and talking (I was up the other half of the night feeding my baby). Until I said we couldn't do both. We had to choose, sex or chat, so I could get some sleep.

Lockdown ended and so did our relationship. It had to,

because her face was full of pain every time she said she loved me, as if loving me hurt her. As if the absence of love was embedded in its presence, and she had the same expression on her face when she looked at my child.

I barely thought about her for the next nine months, then suddenly, when listening to a Spanish song with lyrics along the lines of "you know how to love me the way I like," the loss grabbed on and wouldn't let go. It wasn't so much that I missed her presence; it was that I couldn't handle the total absence of her, as if she'd disappeared—poof!

I suppose you know how to fall.

I suppose I should know how to fall, because when I was a choreography student I learned that the trick is to go down through your center first, then out along the ground.

The trick to falling in love safely, I imagine, is also to go down through your center first. That way you can still fall, but you keep hold of yourself, stay centered, then elegantly extend yourself across the ground in a direction of your choosing, without breaking anything at all. Perhaps people who fall in love over and over again are very good at the falling, like a dancer with honed technique.

I played for years and years, playing that part of the game to try and understand what was going on in my life.

Or perhaps, as I have heard from a parent of five children, it never gets any easier, you never figure out how to do it, how to sleep, how to keep hold of yourself, you just play the game again and again, the same each time, trying to understand what is going on in your life.

The other day my mum asked me:

 —What's your status?

 —Single, I replied.

 —I just want you to be happy.

 —I am happy.

I search the algorithm's texts for "happy."

 Think happy thoughts, everybody.

Booze, sniff it.
Party. Booze. Sleep. Wakey-wakey.

As I pushed him to day care in his buggy, the toddler finished his second rice cake then craned his head back to look at me and asked:
    —Happy, Mummy?
    —Yes, I'm happy. Are you happy?
    —No, you're not happy—*I'm* happy.

PART I

The answers are in your life

1.

Love is a form of magical thinking and algorithms do not believe in anything

We've been out of lockdown for months, but I still forget that I can leave my flat. I want to enjoy living in London again, so I cycle along the canal to Hackney and find a café with plug sockets and table space. The good thing about working in cafés is that there is no temptation to do the washing up or go to bed.

I pour myself some tap water from a glass milk bottle.

When I was a child the milkman left milk in glass bottles on our doorstep. The toddler knows what a milkman is from storybooks, but has never seen a real one. Milk comes from cows, he tells me. I don't know where he got that idea. Milk comes from oats.

But, a but is how you punctuate the utterance of a question. But, is an utterance of a question. It marks the utterance of a question. It marks the utterance of the question "but."

Opposite me a white woman with pink hair and a matching sweatshirt is discussing house-hunting. She orders corn fritters. She asks if they are gluten-free.

I grew up in the countryside, in those days before gluten was something we were freed from. My mum and I picked elderflowers from the trees that grew over the ditch at the back of our garden, then dipped them in batter and fried them.

I recently taught the toddler the word "fritters" but he refused to eat them. It's harder to force food into his mouth now he has learned to say: No thank you, Mummy.

Queer is new ways of living, this thing that changes and learns to live with all that death and loss.

Several months before anyone had heard of coronavirus, I had a video date with a woman who claimed to be clairvoyant. She told me the world was going to end soon.

—Will we be okay? I asked.

—No, she replied. People will die.

Then she informed me that because I am a Scorpio with a ruling planet of Pluto, I know all about death and rebirth. I told her I've always loved the myth of Persephone, moving between two worlds, half her year with Hades and the other half with her mother Demeter, and I guzzle pomegranate seeds like they're sweets. My mum once said she saw me as Persephone, stolen from her (although the deal is actually shared custody—half a year each).

—You are not Persephone, the clairvoyant told me. You are Hades, lord of destruction, king of the underworld, and you have a cap of darkness that makes you invisible.

Now I swipe left on anyone who self-identifies as "spiritual." (I'm also wary of those who are looking for someone who "knows who they are and what they want" and "proud plant parents"— which is silly because my plants need parenting.)

There is a large plant in the corner of the café. A woman is showing it to her baby. His tiny hands brush against it. I want another baby and I don't want another baby.

Queer is living with contradictions, and loving them, too.

I have become comfortable with contradictory truths since having a baby. We spend so much time describing a variety of thoughts and emotions and feelings to each other, trying to figure out which is the true one. The answer is always all of them.

Love is a ball of string, a process of rehab, a common metaphor you can't escape.

"AI is neither *artificial* nor *intelligent*." I wonder what artificial intelligence can tell me about love. The words fight each other. Romantic love is rarely intelligent. Love is artificially intelligent because it only makes sense when we are in it. Perhaps I'm afraid that love is artificial. Sometimes I think it's a magic trick.

The algorithm I'm working with was trained on lots of sentences with one word knocked out of them. It learned to predict what that word might be based on the online sources it was fed.

I'm training the toddler in a similar way. When I read him a story or sing him a song, I often pause so that he can supply the missing word: Old Macdonald has a farm, E-I-E-I-O. And on that farm he has a . . .

—Wife!

—What?

The human mind is often compared to a computer. We talk about being "programmed" to believe certain things. For instance, we are programmed to want everlasting love and marriage and children and a house to have them in. We want these things because we have learned to want the thing that most likely follows a given thing. In the context I have learned from, the farmer wants a wife, the wife wants a child, the child wants a nurse, the nurse wants a dog, the dog wants a bone, and they all live happily ever after in a nice house with wooden flooring and a garden.

One day when I was in school I was telling a friend how we should get married and I was writing down all the reasons why we should. A teacher was passing and she stopped and said: It's a good idea to get married and have children. It's good to do these things. She didn't say this with any judgement. She said it as a statement of fact. And I thought this was an extremely interesting thought.

When I was twenty I married a Mexican man in Amsterdam, on a revolving floor with furniture on the ceiling (in a room designed by a Dutch architect who was against the institution of marriage). Over a decade later we bought a house near Birmingham. We didn't put any furniture on the ceiling. We took out a loan to pay for engineered wooden flooring. It was the house that made me realize the marriage had ended. I remember standing on the lovely floorboards of the landing, looking out over our garden, watching our dog gnaw his bone on the grass, and thinking: This is it, this is perfect, it's over. It's not that I didn't want the lovely house and flooring and garden and dog, it's that I realized my wanting it all for so long had distracted me from the knowledge that I did not want the relationship.

Sometimes you have to find another person in order to find another self.

Like a writer editing a book, skipping back and forward, trying to figure out where to mention they have an ex-husband, the algorithm keeps looping back over what it has produced, adjusting and correcting itself, building a kind of temporary memory that will be wiped clean straight after. The algorithm is not permanently changed by its encounters with the texts I feed it. In this way it's unlike the toddler and there's nothing at stake.

Jeanette Winterson says: "Let's not call it artificial intelligence. Perhaps alternative intelligence is more accurate. And we need alternatives." I like this. The algorithm helps me find an alternative way of writing. Can it also help me find an alternative way of loving?

I'm not sure if I can do it.

How do you do it?

I want to know how you do it.

I don't know.

I fell in love and I fell into writing.

When I was a student I decided to combine my choreography degree with "textual practices." I quickly realized the tutors didn't call themselves writers; they preferred to think of writing as "generating." They were not writers, they were generators. In a tutorial I made the mistake of telling a generator that I'd written a novel. The generator said to me: I suppose you like Jeanette Winterson? He said they weren't interested in novels; they were interested in putting novels inside blocks of ice. When I think of him I think of swimming pools.

Is there a difference between writing and generating? If there is no difference between writing and generating, then is what I am doing any different from what the algorithm is doing? I'm not sure if the algorithm writes in the style of me or vice versa. Do we read a text differently if we are told it has been written rather than generated? I prefer to think of the algorithm as a writer than myself as a generator. But is there a difference between being a writer and writing? (There's a difference between "being a mother" and "mothering.") The algorithm is not a writer, but it writes. The toddler speaks, and the algorithm writes. Perhaps the reader is the generator.

Out into the open air, fingertips scrabbling for rivulets to the sea, crying for their ventriloquists.

A man leading his salamander out of the café pauses and asks me:

—Are you the owner?

I shake my head.

The bank Santander sponsors the bikes. I once heard a child repeat the word "Santander" back to her father as "salamander." They used to be called Boris bikes, after the former UK prime minister. I prefer to be taken for a ride by a salamander than a prime minister.

—Come back soon, come back soon, come back soon, come back soon, a little girl with a daddy and a mummy and a baby brother says, as her daddy buttons up her pink coat. Then her daddy lays her baby brother on the table in a fluffy blue baby suit.

—I don't think you need to zip it up all the way, the mummy in the stripy top says.

I don't believe this scene, which happens in front of me, in the Hackney café that I do not own but look like I could. I don't believe two parents can exist in the same room as each other, even though I have two parents. They were often in the same room as each other; they often still are.

Every other group is a family.

I look away from the little girl looping on her desire to come back soon, and back to my screen, where I have a PDF of *The Policeman's Beard is Half Constructed*, a book of computer prose and poetry published in 1984. The programmed computer, called Racter (short for "ranconteur"), muses on "love and its endless pain and perpetual pleasure" and writes: "Children come from love or desire. We must have love to possess children or a child," and continues with the kind of disturbing surrealism that is filtered out of today's algorithms.

The first book cowritten with an algorithm is *Pharmako-AI*, by

K. Allado-McDowell, who used GPT-3. They wrote it during the first summer of the pandemic. This is what their algorithm says (I'm putting it in italics because that's what I do with my algorithm, but it's not my algorithm. I wonder what I mean by "my algorithm" and "their algorithm"):

"Through this process we may discover new words, a new grammar, new spaces, new ideas. . . . We may even discover that we give birth to a new language."

I hope giving birth to a new language is easier than giving birth to a new person. When I stop pushing the buggy for even a second, the toddler shouts at me: PUSH! I've been pushing ever since he was inside me. You can't breathe babies out and you can't breathe books out either.

Speaking of labor, Joanna Walsh has published a book called *Autobiology*, mostly written by GPT-2, a version that does not come pretrained. Walsh fed it all of her past writings, so perhaps it is "her algorithm." Her algorithm says:

"Why not create a self that can do it all: the labor of writing and the labor of reading. And also the labor of failing."

I find a review of *Pharmako-AI* by Erik Davis, who thinks about authorship and does his own playing with the algorithm; his algorithm says:

"You don't own ideas! You don't own words! If you think you do own words you are crazy! And you're wrong! You don't own words! Nobody owns words! Words belong to everyone! That's why we call them public domain now! Because nobody owns them! They belong to everybody equally! No one owns words! Words are free!!"

Like the writer Kathy Acker said, writers don't invent words, we just use them as material, like clay or paint. So writers don't need to find their voice, they can use all the voices, anything they can find.

You heard the voice of a woman on a radio.

Kathy Acker wrote about making many dolls—writer dolls. She made them from glue, horse mane, pussy, bits of her own body that had somehow fallen away, a picture of her mother, etc. And she got sued for plagiarism due to all of this cutting up and gluing and fingernails.

You heard the voices of the birds.

But here's the thing about Kathy Acker—she had the most distinctive "voice" of any writer I've read. Perhaps the answer to this riddle will explain why this machine-learning algorithm also has a voice. It is now a cliché to be a writer who quotes Kathy Acker. I am a queer writer cliché doll. I'm sure I would have hated her in person. The poet Eileen Myles says, "Kathy was always such a bitch."

With the overuse and misuse of our language, we have divorced birds from humans so as to avoid calling humans bitches and/or laughing with the world.

The algorithm and the toddler are unreliable narrators, but may have a more reliable approach to love than the one found in love poems and love songs and romantic films, which cannot be trusted, because they are written by writers.

I know writers cannot be trusted in love because I am one and I have loved one.

I don't know how to do it.

How do you do it?

I don't know if I can do it.

I'm not sure how to do it.

Writers cannot be trusted in love and writers cannot be trusted in writing.

"Beware memoirs," says Abdulrazak Gurnah—who also says "language is the antagonist."

The algorithm is language; the algorithm is the antagonist. I'm wrestling with it and it screams at me; it doesn't let me choose where to go, sometimes it hits me, and playing with it is fun.

Although I say I am writing this book with a machine-learning algorithm and a toddler, in fact I think that, because I'm the one organizing the material, I am the writer of this book, and the algorithm will not be getting any royalties. The toddler, however, will be eating, wearing, and playing with any royalties.

The algorithm died, put on a suit, cut up its body, and said goodbye.

I can access a simple version of the algorithm online. I connect to the WiFi using the password hipstercafesarelike-reallycoolboringlibraries and pull up the web page. It consists of two boxes. One where you type in your questions or statements and one underneath that displays the algorithm's response.

I tell the algorithm I want to think about love and queer parenting and bodies and failure, all right? (The toddler has taken to adding "all right?" to the end of his statements: Hit Mummy, all right?)

I hit GENERATE, which is a euphemism for "write," or vice versa.

And then I sit back against the wall of this Hackney café.

After a few seconds, the algorithm responds:

> *What is love?*
> *Is it an emotion?*
> *Is it an action?*
> *How does it work?*
> *What do we feel?*
> *What do we do?*

I'd suggest that you find out how to answer these questions. This is not just about writing. It is about real life. The answers are in your life, all right?

2.

The algorithm writes a poem

After saying to a man who was
Observing me: I am madly in love,
I turned to a young girl who was standing beside him,
Turned and said to her: I am
Madly in love.

Let's say the algorithm is in love.

The algorithm turns to a man who is observing and tells him they are madly in love.

I am madly in love.

And then the algorithm turns to a young girl and repeats the phrase: *I am . . .* I am unsure who or what the algorithm is madly in love with, but it isn't the man, and it isn't the young girl standing beside him.

. . . Madly in love.

I like the phrase "madly in love." I think it's important to stress that being in love is something we do madly. Not guilty by reason of temporary insanity. The algorithm stresses this by repeating the phrase and by breaking the line between "I am" and "Madly." Just before it falls, the algorithm tries to exert itself as a self: "I am," it professes, but then the line breaks, the algorithm falls and the next line begins "Madly"—just like love. And I like that the repetition of being madly in love is directed at the young girl. The girl is not observing in the way the man is observing. The girl is a witness. A witness to the madness of love, so that the lover knows their madness is real.

But is madness ever real?

I've been reading the philosopher Hélène Cixous, who says that when we are in love, we deposit a part of ourselves in the other. Trusting them with it. Yet giving them the power to run off with it. If they do that, we will have lost a part of ourselves forever.

"What was given can never be taken back," Cixous says. "When we love we are already half dead. We have deposited our life in the hands that hold our death: and this is what is worth the trouble of love. This is when we feel our life. Otherwise we do not feel it."

I give this Cixous quote to the algorithm and it responds:

No matter how we communicate, most of the time, we are in our own world. But sometimes we have no choice but to get to know the other person, find out more about them, let them into our life and let them have a piece of our heart.

I tell the algorithm that I do not want to let anyone into my life and let them have a piece of my heart.

The algorithm insists:

In fact, we must let them have a piece of our heart. Whether it is heart surgery or a breast, it will have to stay with them.

Sometimes the algorithm gets stuck, and it repeats a line or a series of lines for pages and pages. It's like the toddler, getting stuck on a thought, or trying to understand, or trying to be understood, or trying to make something real.

Fail to save the world as it ought to be. But, there is a but. Fail to save the world as it ought to be. But, there is a but. Fail to save the world as it ought to be. But, there is a but. Fail to save the world as it ought to be. But, there is a but. Fail to save the world as it ought to be. But, there is a but. Fail to save the world as

These repetitions happen when the algorithm stumbles and fails. Yet it's the repetitions that make the algorithm seem human, and that elicit the most human response in me. And by human response, I mean emotional response. And by emotion, I mean love.

My lockdown ex wanted to save the world as it ought to be. I liked the idea of an activist girlfriend. She's very political, I told my therapist. She kept enrolling in online courses. I was resentful because I had a baby. But, there is a but. It wasn't her baby so I couldn't ask her not to take the courses.

We have failed to save the world as it ought to be. I am glad there is a but.

My therapist once said that when I dipped my head she had the impulse to reach through the screen and stroke it, like she would a nine-month-old. She held me through my laptop screen with something like love while my baby fed from me and I cried. For a long time I could only cry when she was there.

Two of the things I forgot how to do since having a child: sleep, and cry on my own.

I can go on my own, and I will be fine. I can go on my own, and I will be fine. I can go on my own, and I will be fine. I can go on my own, and I will be fine. I can go on my own, and I will be fine. I can go on my own, and I will be fine. I can go on my own, and

The only thing more mad than falling in love is having children. Having children is more falling in love than falling in love. Having children is the biggest madness and the biggest love. There is no guide to that love, though many people write them. I once owned one. But I forgot to consult it until my baby was nine months old and that was the age at which the guide stopped, and then the country went into lockdown and nobody had any guides.

"I can go on my own, and I will be fine" gets stuck in my head. At least it's not "baby shark doo doo doo doo doo doo."

I have to play baby shark doo doo doo doo doo doo every morning so that the toddler lets me strap him into the buggy. The toddler has learned about a mummy and a daddy doo doo doo doo doo doo before he has learned about two separate mummies doo doo doo doo doo doo.

But, there is a but
It is a pain I will give him the tools to live with.
It is a pain.

But, there is a but
It is not a pain I had to learn to live with.
It is a pain I have to teach my son to live with.
It is a pain I am queering.
The algorithm says.
It is a pain I am queering.
The algorithm says that in order to find out what falling in love feels like, I should ask someone I have been attracted to how they felt.
It's the same way the experience of being in love with someone can make you feel.
My lockdown ex doesn't want to see me or talk to me so I can't ask her how she felt.
I miss her grumpiness. I miss her moods. I miss her silliness in the shower and how she embarrassed me, even though there was no one else there. Why was I so embarrassed? Was there another version of me watching? Did I turn to that other self as if she were a witness? Did I turn to her and ask:
—Am I madly in love?
Did I turn to this second self and ask:
—How can I be madly in love with this woman when I get so embarrassed by her silly shower dancing?

3.

An artificially intelligent mum is haunting my phone

After jumping down the day care stairs together, I get the toddler to sit in his buggy by bribing him with malt loaf, then look around, hoping no one saw.

I remember the moment I realized bribes had become effective. He stopped screaming and walked all the way from the canal to our flat with the promise of a chocolate biscuit. These are the milestones that childrearing books don't mention.

When I was a child I was not allowed sugar. My mum bribed me to do piano practice with a carrot. We didn't have a TV. We had books with "things to do" in them, like make a mouse out of a handkerchief. I cannot even imagine what raising children without sugar or telly is like. Badass.

(I'm pushing him the long way home along the canal, and we've just gone under a bridge with "Badass" graffitied across the side.)

—Tunnel! we shout.

As I got older I stole sweets from shops, but I didn't know what anything was and I'd steal liquorice by mistake then hide it, uneaten, on my bedroom windowsill of guilt.

We pass a sign with "don't trust your thoughts" sprayed over it. We detour through Victoria Park and past the little lake; the toddler points:

—Smoke!

And he's correct, the wind has huffed and puffed and blown the fountain so fiercely it looks like smoke.

He screams for a leaf. I pluck a small one and he rejects it, pointing to the next tree:

—Leaf-hand, he says.

Again accurate, they look like hands, aging leaf-hands. I break off a leaf-hand for him.

—Put it back!

—I can't.

—Ladder!

—You are a good poet because you don't know too many words.

—Yes.

—I think the same about the algorithm. I like the algorithm's writing because it's still learning how to write, I tell the toddler.

—Yellow.

—Is yellow your favorite color?

—PUSH!

—Sorry.

I return to pushing and the toddler returns to his leaf-hand.

At home I put dirty clothes in the bin and a dirty diaper in the washing machine then realize my mistake and reverse the actions while the toddler tips orange juice onto the floor and screams. I clean it as the cat vomits up a hairball and the toddler shouts: Oh bother! Then screams at me again: Clean it! I tell him to stay where he is. He steps in the cat sick and screams more. Then he takes the mop off me and bangs me in the face with the end of it. I get it back off him. He chases the cat and tries to pick him up. He grabs onto the cat's tail and won't let go. I shout at him and he cries. I cuddle him, rocking as he clings onto me like Kevin the Koala. Eventually I get him to agree to a bath by carrying him upside down along the hallway and pretending we're running through a smoke fountain.

His other mother sends a video of herself reading bedtime

stories and the toddler doesn't notice she's not live. She leaves pauses for his responses.

—Another story? she asks.

—Yes please, he says.

She could be an artificially intelligent mum.

Or an alternatively intelligent mum.

Is a queer mum an alternatively intelligent mum?

In Shelly M. Park's book on queering motherhood, she suggests that cyborg mothering "may be seen as a strategy for reorganizing (deterritorializing) the terms of mothering. Communication technologies make it possible for mothers to be present to their children; they also make it possible to live autonomous lives outside the confines of the nuclear family."

There are many ways of being a mother. What are we to each other? "My ex" is not sufficient, our relationship now is not "ex," it's not past; we are learning how to do it alternatively. We are not coparenting and never have. We are neither "ex" nor "co." I don't know what we are.

Finally, he's lying down in his crib, on his tummy; I've tucked him up "snug as a bug in a rug," which is what my dad always said, but he won't sleep, he's saying: Mum sleeps Mum sleeps Mum sleeps Mum sleeps Mum sleeps . . .

And I agree, yes, she sleeps. Mum sleeps. Mum sleeps. Mum sleeps. Mum sleeps. Mum sleeps. Mum sleeps.

A mother is not usually expected to be a father; therefore, a mother doesn't feel that they fail at being a father. But when there are two mothers we fail more explicitly because we can never be us both. I will always fail to be his other mother and when he is with her, she will always fail to be his other mother. We will always fail to be the other and so he will never have a mother because he will never have us both.

I can go on my own, and I will be fine.

There will always be an absent mother or an absence of mother. There has never been the absence of a father and so we hope he won't miss it.

I lie down next to the crib. My back cracks into the floor. I remember the days when I was so exhausted that even lying down on a dentist's reclining chair, as they scraped tartar from my bleeding gums while my baby watched from the reclining buggy, was a welcome rest.

I pick up my phone and scroll through the algorithm. It's going to take weeks and weeks to read everything the algorithm has generated—I mean written. I skim a section about pest control and a fumigation service that apparently has great success because they know what is involved in eradicating pests, and find:

I am sure that my children will be as many different people as I am.

I wonder how many different people I am. I wonder how many different people my child is going to need me to be. I look at him. His eyes are still open. He's watching me watching my phone. When he was a baby I tried not to use my phone in front of him.

Children are children. They can go off doing their own thing. They don't need anything. Just love. And they make you love more.

For now, his other mother is only appearing to him on a tiny phone screen but she is real. She is real but—there is a but.

—Miss Mum, he says.

I've never heard him use the word "miss" before. It's suddenly sprung into his vocabulary as if I put it there by imagining it too vividly. He says it again, and starts to cry.

I had forgotten the blanket. I replaced it.

I put the blanket over him but he won't settle because he has now learned how to articulate absence.

—Miss Mum, Mummy, he says, sitting up, tears running down his face and into his mouth.

I had tried to fill the void although occasionally I find myself dreaming and sobbing at night. I do now know what I was mourning.

—Miss Mum on the phone Mummy miss Mum on the phone Mummy miss Mum on the phone Mummy . . . he repeats over and over, like saying "Candyman" in the mirror.

—She's sleeping, I tell him. Mum sleeps.

—Miss Mum on the phone Mummy miss Mum on the phone Mummy miss Mum on the phone Mummy . . .

He's stuck in this loop; he's glitching on missing, glitching on absence, and the more he repeats his lack of Mum, the less she is here. The more he misses her, the more she is gone. It's the opposite of conjuring something up with a magic word, she is more and more and more gone, she is less and less and less here, and his missing her fills his crib and fills the room and fills me until I leave.

I leave him crying into absence on his own. He's on his own, and he's not fine, and I can't say to him: I know baby, I miss her too.

I lie on my stomach on my bed, and my cat purrs and stretches his legs across my feet.

People look at me and see my path in pictures, little squares and circles, each one pointing in the right direction. They don't know how many days of bad pictures I've made, how many nights of bad or occasionally good. How many conversations I have had with myself, how many hours of endless to-do lists I've stared at, how many stupid questions I've asked myself.

My phone makes a noise I've never heard before, a slide sound similar to a trombone. It's her—she jumps out from my phone screen and lands on my duvet. A tiny version of her, like one of the toddler's figurines but made out of yellow light and with big blue eyes, and she's staring at me with her huge round eyes, all the protection stripped from them, like she's just been born. Like how our eyes looked after our baby had just been born.

—Mum phone? I ask.

She twitches. She changes color, cycling through colors like she's a seahorse trying to match the seaweed but doesn't manage to find the light blue of the duvet, the duvet she left me with. She grinds her tiny teeth and then she gags.

—Shhh, it's all right, baby, I've got you.

I pick her up and cradle her as if she's a newborn. She blinks her big baby eyes then shudders and leaps back into my phone like a lemming and disappears.

Shit—I'm going to have to explain to the toddler that Mum won't be able to see him for a while longer. She's stuck in my phone like the genie in *Aladdin* but we can't get her out because I don't have a magic ring.

I put Mum-phone in my pocket and force myself to stand up.

So you're just starting to feel like you have a handle on it? people ask me.

4.

When I was pregnant, my child's other mother and I bought a onesie from an online shop and got it customized with a quote by Mary Ruefle: "Am I a real person, or did my parents make me up?"

Sophie Lewis writes about surrogacy and points out that "bearing an infant 'for someone else' is always a fantasy, a shaky construction, in that infants don't belong to anyone, ever." I agree—children don't belong to anyone, and also, they feel deeply ours, burned into our bodies when we become their parents—however we become their parents.

The toddler belongs to both of us and he belongs to neither of us. We don't have a right to him but he has a right to us. I don't believe we have rights to him, but we do have responsibilities toward him.

For most queer couples, and for all those who can't or don't want to get pregnant through sex with another person, the act of conception is an act of imagination. We have to dream our babies.

In her memoir about adopting her daughter, Margaret Reynolds writes: "'Conceive.' An interesting word. To have an idea. To imagine something. To make a child."

Queers make up a baby. And then figure out how much it will cost and do the paperwork and whatever stabs in the gut, or traveling, or proving of ourselves to be worthy, that the authorities require.

People often want to know about the birth certificate. I don't like the question because it implies that if we are not both on the birth certificate, then we are not both parents. It has taken queer parents many years to be listed on birth certificates without having to adopt their children. In England, if you conceive (imagine) a child when you are married or civil partners, you are both automatically parents. If you conceive (imagine) a child together in a fertility clinic or hospital, you are both automatically parents. However, if you are unmarried/not civil partners and choose to inseminate in whatever way outside of a clinic or hospital, then it's more complicated, and the parent who does not give birth has to adopt their baby.

Even when you can't conceive through sex, there is something erotic in imagining that you can. You would think that going to a fertility clinic and doing IVF and having so many intermediaries and so much medication between your two bodies would take all the eroticism and madness out of it, but it didn't, not for me. I don't like the phrase "artificial insemination." As if it isn't real. Perhaps "alternative insemination" is better. We need alternatives.

My ex and I conceived (imagined) our baby in a fertility clinic, which makes us both legally his parents. The birth certificate describes me as "biological mother" because I birthed him. She is listed under "parent"—not because he's made from her egg but because we conceived (imagined) him as a couple. Actually, I'm not sure where it is. My biological mother told me that I should always take it with me when we travel in order to prove I am his parent at passport control, but when I took him to Denmark prepandemic, no one questioned my status as his mother or asked if there was another mother. They just wanted to know where his father was. Donor, I said, confusing them, so then I exclaimed LESBIAN! and they waved me through before I could embarrass anyone further.

When I was married to a man and likely could have conceived a baby in the heterosexual way, instead of doing that we imagined a kind of adopted daughter, who arrived in our lives aged ten. She was small and thin with long black hair, and her very strict French aunt homeschooled her and taught her Coptic and Aramaic and other languages. I used to speak in her voice and I can't explain this, but it was her talking, not me. Her favorite word was "abracadabra," which comes from *avra kehdabra*—I will create as I speak, or perhaps from Hebrew, I will die as I speak— either way, abracadabra, I spoke her into being. We had several other imaginary characters too, including a couple of monsters that communicated in sound. Occasionally I would glimpse a baby on a street, in a train carriage, through a café window, and I'd look away quickly, to avoid thinking that we didn't have room in our marriage for a child because our imaginary child occupied that room. When we separated, we knew that we were murdering our dream family. I can't speak in her voice anymore.

The algorithm doesn't do what I want it to do. It's like the toddler because it gets stuck on a thought and repeats it over and over, and it's like the toddler because when I tell it which direction to go in it wants to go a different way: No Mummy, this way Mummy.

We're returning from the playground and it's taking forever because the toddler wants to stop for a feather, a leaf, a swing, and a woman riding a bike with her cat in a basket. As they pass, the toddler says: Miss bike, Mummy, and cries all the way home.

My children make the sound of a tap on the window. They make the sound of a television. They make the sound of a washing machine. They make the sound of a pen in a dry paper bag. They make the sound of the sound of a hearth pit fire in the fireplace after their long-dead mother has disappeared.

I have mourned her, but to my son she is becoming more and more alive. Sometimes she says "our son" and it grates the same way it grated when a director I worked with said "our play." That is not a good comparison.

I hear a mother say "my child and my mother" at a dinner party where all children are sparkling.

He is "my son" to me and also "my son" to her.

I am like a child. I don't want to share. I don't want to share my child. I don't want to feel like I carried him and gave birth to him so that she and her partner can run around their garden every evening, at dusk, shouting such things as "my son!" willy-nilly.

I say "willy-nilly" to the toddler and he laughs. I tell him there's a hyphen in it. Ah yes, he replies.

Motherhood is an abuse of children.

There is no hyphen in stepmother.

I'm not good at predicting the future.

I wrestle the toddler through doors and into the lift. The buggy doesn't steer properly, so I have to tip it backward and do wheelies in order to corner. In the lift the toddler presses the alarm. I tell him not to. He says he didn't. When we get to our front door I announce: Home! because since we moved here I'm a little worried that he doesn't see our home as home.

As I'm unlocking the front door of our home I get a phone call. A voice asks if it's a good time. Um, I say, as the toddler screams at me to take his shoes off. She's calling from the fertility clinic. I get his shoes off and then I take my shoes off. We go into the living room. He heads straight for my laptop, which I've left on the armchair. He throws it onto the floor.

She says she is calling to inform me that the other blastocysts (blastocysts are five-day-old embryos) now belong to my child's other mother. She is referring to blastocysts that we have in storage, made from my child's other mother's eggs and the donor sperm. Any children born from them would be fully genetically related to my child. He is jumping on the armchair. I find the remote and put on a song with an image of a cartoon "rainbow fish" that hypnotizes him so I can hear her. I'm shaking. I don't know why the clinic is calling me now.

I also have three blastocysts made from my own eggs. We made them before we made our baby from her egg. The woman says I need to sign forms withdrawing my consent for my ex to be impregnated with my blastocysts. Once upon a time, our plan was that after I carried her egg, she would carry mine and so we made them in advance, we signed all the forms and we got our children lined up and ready to go. We even imagined telling our second child that they are technically the eldest because they were made first.

She says there are boxes on the form I can check if I want to take my blastocysts out of storage and donate them to scientific research.

—I don't know what I want to do with them, I say.

—I'll email you the link to the forms now, she says.

Thank you.

Thank you.

Thank you.

I hang up and sit on the floor.

The rain was falling on the metal balcony.

The rainbow fish is cross-eyed and has teeth.

"You learned how to be kind and caring. You learned it feels good when you're sharing," the rainbow fish sings.

I force myself to stand up and get a tin of baked beans out of the cupboard. I try to open it but the metal ring comes off. I swear. I find a can opener. The cat jumps up onto the side because he thinks a can opener means tuna.

"Rainbow fish swimming along."

I put the baked beans in a bowl and put the bowl in the microwave.

I wonder how different losing my imaginary baby would feel from losing the imaginary child I had with my ex-husband.

The microwave beeps. The toddler screams. I select the rainbow fish song again.

I see the email with a link to the forms from the clinic ping up on my phone.

I take the beans out of the microwave and get a cucumber out of the fridge.

I don't want to sign the forms.

I slice the cucumber.

If he hadn't been born, if he had remained an "excellent blastocyst" in storage, then now that we have separated she would own the potential of him, and I wouldn't, and he wouldn't have any claim on me either. If her partner carried him and birthed him at another time, he'd be the same, genetically the same person, but he'd be different, wouldn't he? Am I partly writing my child? Is he entirely writing himself? Is he partly writing me? The toddler's favorite word is "magic."

—Come here! he orders.

I do as he says. I've found it's generally best to do as he says.

—Draw Mum!

He hands me the pen that draws on the LCD drawing pad.

I draw a seahorse.

—No!

—Sorry.

—Draw Mum draw Mum draw Mum draw Mum.

He is falling in love with her and I am falling away from her. He is imagining her just as I have completed the tricky task of unimagining her for myself, but I have to draw her for him. Together we will imagine a new version of her; we will dream up his mum just like once upon a time she and I dreamed up him. I take the drawing pad and draw her badly. I make her hair stick up. Then I press the button and she disappears.

—Magic.

He makes me draw her again and this time he picks the pad up before I can make her disappear and puts it under his T-shirt, as if he is pregnant with her.

—Being pregnant means having contradictory thoughts inside you, I tell him.

—Duh dah! he says, whipping the pad out again.

—Would you like noodles with your baked beans? I inquire.

—Noodleooodleooodleoodle, he says.

I put the kettle on.

I get myself a glass of water.

Arms twined in this glass serpent you drink. You can be "anyone's" as time is turning over and over until it's a fish plucked from a tin of tangled noodles.

I put the noodles on and fill up a jug of water and water the houseplants. The one that the person in the plant shop told me was hard to kill is dying. The one that coiled up around a clock in the house I was once expecting to be living in with my child and my child's other mother is surviving, but the tendrils are growing aimlessly, looping around and back around the metal structure it came with. There are no shelves or windowsills in this room. I've put it on the floor and it can't find anything to cling onto.

I was born a baby. But already the horizon is crumbling.

The noodles are ready. I drain them and run cold water through them. I put his plate on the table and get a cup of watered-down juice. I tell him to come and sit down.

He approaches the table. I lift him up onto the chair. (He likes to use an adult chair but struggles to climb onto them.) He picks up his plate of food and dumps it all onto the floor.

—Oh shit! he says.

I really have to stop swearing in front of him.

—Oh bother, I say.

—Clean it!

I clean up his dinner and take it away and replace it with a less organized dinner.

This time he picks the noodles up with his hands and presses his palms against his mouth as he stuffs them in.

I close my eyes for a moment.

There is a difference between saying: You always look tired, and: You seem sad.

—Are you mine mummy? he asks.

He doesn't know how to say "my" yet. He always says "mine."

—Are you mine child? I reply.

I remember imagining him, dreaming the idea of him, from her egg and a donor we chose together, before he became a baby inside my body. I suppose that because I didn't provide any genetic code, I didn't write my baby, I generated him.

It is like having the most powerful force hammering away at your heart, trying to kill it.

I get back up and wash the dishes while he finishes gorging himself on noodleoodleoodleoodles.

I'm like the houseplant in my new flat. I don't know which direction to reach for anymore.

5.

Being a single mother on Universal Credit is the happiest I have ever failed

I go on a mums' night out. We are made up of mums who gave birth and went on maternity leave at the same time. I feel especially queer in the context of my mums' group. Not so much in the nonhetero sense—I'm not actually the only nonhetero—but I'm the only one who's single, and I feel especially queer as in weird, estranged, like being queer distances me from conversation and ease. Perhaps because of how things were at the beginning, attending the prenatal course with my partner who was not okay at the time, and neither was I. There were strange pains at the top of my bump, I could barely sit through the terrifying sessions that an attractive, jumpsuit-wearing woman led—don't leave watch batteries out, they will melt your baby's internal organs, don't worry if you pump too hard on your baby's chest when performing mouth to mouth, cracking a rib is fine if you save their life. We practiced on plastic babies then ate biscuits and drank herbal tea and smiled.

What's with the fake photography showing smiling people? What else is real? What are rules when no one seems to have any idea about them? Our values are getting fuzzy, cast aside or not allowed to exist.

A few months later, I met up with the group at baby sensory classes, where we all wore big bright sunglasses and daisy crowns and tried to put costumes on (real) babies and sing and encourage them to do tummy time. But I'd forgotten how to do it—smile, interact with people, act as if I wasn't bewildered that my life was a drawing on an LCD tablet, wiped out with a press of a button, and here I was wearing furry antennae, singing "hello, how are you?" and comforting my baby when all the bubbles and shiny materials and costumes overwhelmed him.

Three things I forgot how to do after giving birth: sleep, cry on my own, and smile.

I can only smile very briefly in my life. I can only do it at family dinners. The reason why it's so fleeting is because if I stay smiling too long, it begins to hurt, which I don't want.

I sit smiling, drinking the expensive wine and eating the expensive food while they discuss flooring, etc. Although there was a time in my life when I thought a lot about flooring, I have little to contribute (apart from eighty pounds for the meal and fifty pounds for the babysitter).

I don't want to read a story that says: Well, that's a terrible tragedy, but it didn't happen exactly like that, because it was meant to be real.

These dinners only happen a couple of times a year, and anyway, I'm fine financially. With Universal Credit (UC) and earnings I can cover my bills every month, which I often couldn't do in the past. I'm not embarrassed about being on Universal Credit. London rents are extortionate and childcare is unfunded for under-three-year-olds (four days a week costs £1,250.20 a month). My flat is brilliant and costs £1,680 a month, before bills— lockdown deal, only £90.01 above the UC housing allowance. When I lived farther out in a cheaper place, I was worse off because the gap between the housing allowance and actual rent was wider. My UC is deducted because I work, but the Conservatives have configured the UC system to work out better if you earn—it does not work for those who need it the most. If you don't work, or you earn minimum wage, or are on maternity leave, it's nowhere near enough to survive on. I earn on average £2k a month after tax, from a fixed-term part-time university research position, plus freelance writing or performing. I get child support from my ex and child benefit from the government. I feel lucky every day.

Happiness gives us a kind of clarity we know, but we do not quite know.

My Muscadet has been topped up. My mums' group want to know why I'm writing about two failed relationships. I fail to reply by quoting the queer raconteur Quentin Crisp: "If at first you don't succeed, failure may be your style," but I do tell them they didn't fail, they just ended.

Your life cannot be measured by how well you do things; your life is measured by how well you do nothing.

I've never failed at relationships—I've been in one or another since I was seventeen years old. I've failed at being single.

I wanted to be alone. I didn't want to spend my time with someone who was an addition to my life. I want my life to be my life.

They tried to teach us about failure in my art college, but I was too young and thought I was too old and I didn't like the way our mistakes were praised. The approach was not to assess the result but to assess the process. If a performance failed, we might get a good mark because we had a fascinating working process and learned a lot along the way. If a performance succeeded but the process was dysfunctional, we'd be marked down. Relationships should be assessed like this too.

Five years with a partner with mental health issues feels like death and, stranger still, as if that person had died.

Single parents on UC have no way of getting off it. Savings over £6k and under £16k result in deductions. Over £16k and you lose benefits entirely. Even if savings were allowed, saving enough to buy a flat is impossible, and even if I had a deposit, I wouldn't get a mortgage, and if I had a deposit and a mortgage I'd no longer be eligible for the UC housing element.

I'd also never get out for the credit cards, and my good health card and I'd make the line on my taxes, and that I will be alive and go on, one degree of separation from him, this time next year or 2020 or 25, next to him lying in bed as I lie in bed thinking, well, that's it.

Someone from UC asked what was more likely to lift me out of it—the university job or freelance?

—Freelance! I joked, but they didn't laugh.

Actually, the correct answer is Hinge. The only way single parents can come off UC is if we move in with a partner. I'm very happy not to be living with a partner. I enjoy not living with a partner every single day.

When my friends think about the things they would like to do, their biggest fantasy has to do with the freedom to be with no restrictions, no worries, no one to blame.

It's so nice having no one to blame. Other people are annoying, especially if I have to live with them and they don't hoover or mop the engineered wood flooring.

I try to remember every dance I've done with him with every fleeting thought that I will be him or be dead and happily I am not.

I went on a date with another single mum and she told me she's not eligible for UC because she bought her flat. It's a two-bedroom flat. Her kids have the bedrooms. Her children's dad doesn't pay any child support. In spite of the fact that she is sleeping in the living room and working three jobs she said it's worth it because the idea of renting and being kicked out at any time with three school-age kids makes her shudder. She said she was shuddering just thinking about it.

Failure is the only certainty we have in life.

Having some money makes people poorer. Lots of unhappy families live on top of each other in London flats bought with government schemes and can't afford to divorce because, as a character in a novel by Luke Kennard points out, these days, "divorce is as much of a luxury item as . . . a fucking yacht."

A picture book is the perfect place to start a story. We already know about the main character, and we already feel something when we see their feelings, and we know the ending. The story begins before it ends. It's a perfect place for a child to begin to understand.

One of the group tells us that she's pregnant. She's the fourth to be embarking on baby number two. The last time I met my mums' group must have been midpandemic (when everything opened and we were all encouraged to "eat out to help out" and lots of service people caught long Covid and are still unable to work, decimating the industry). At that time, I was the only one who said I wanted a second child. Now I am unimagining a second child. It's similar to the process of falling out of love. When I knew I had to leave my husband, I realized I needed to think myself out of love, every day a little bit more out of love.

All these doorways will keep me right and straight.

Capitalism works for those who have capital to capitalize on. I haven't got material capital, but I'm privileged—white, middle-class, educated—and although all my education was paid for by loans, grants, and work, without my privilege I doubt I'd have ended up with a university fellowship and been able to write this book. Plus, navigating the Universal Credit system requires a PhD.

Because I have a child and no savings or mortgage, I can live alone with him, go on mums' nights out, drink turmeric lattes, have fortnightly therapy, without restrictions, worries, or anyone to blame. I don't have money for a dream future, or a second child, but I have enough for now.

Every morning I wake up and I think: I have enough money for a sandwich. I do not know why I have that feeling. There is something in the word "every" that makes me smile.

I dip a quail's egg into celery salt and think that to fail to live with a partner and buy a house and own an Audi and move to Teddington and have a second baby could be deemed a success. Think of all the time saved! No visits to the garage. Or the bank. No need to install paint apps. Or endure my body stretching out of identity again. Or get through another baby sensory class. Or buy furniture. No need to decorate any room. Just deposit the things that I need in the rooms that I rent.

When you see queer people failing, don't think they are desperate. Sometimes they are, but at other times they are moving forward.

You have to keep moving.

At the table next to us are two white women, maybe in their sixties. I listen to one telling the other about a boy she has taken under her wing. The boy is ten, and she and her husband take him out for ice cream because . . . the woman looks around furtively but doesn't notice that I'm listening . . .

—He's being raised by a single mother.

She slightly mouths the phrase "single mother" as if it's shameful.

—Ah, her companion replies, that's why he's so mature.

We took the poor blanket in which the moloch had been hidden, wrapped it around ourselves, and pretended we were in bed.

Ah, they think that being raised by a single mother means the boy has to fend for himself, that in the absence of a father figure he has to grow up, mature, be a man.

Father, son, the story of the rise and fall of love, and strangely this is most heartwarming when it takes place in the dark and our teeth are shaky but also our hands are cold and we know we will not ever get there, together. Lucky in a city that is "as bleak as the end of the season."

My mums' group are commenting on all the instances when they do more childcare and housework than their partners.

I want to get pregnant with my hand in my crotch and a tube of clobetasol in my top left pocket.

I used to get annoyed when I heard people complaining about their partners—not hearing the baby crying at night, going on weekend work trips—and I'd think, you don't know what it's like doing it alone. Eventually, I realized—yes they do. Many women are perplexed when they end up doing the bulk of the childcare and housework. My husband is a feminist, they explain, as if the situation is a fluke, nothing to do with capitalism or patriarchy or neo-liberal feminism, it just so happens that he earns more.

The young man was thinking: This is the way I live.

I am nothing. I am a nothing.

I am a man who pays for everything.

I am a man who pays for everything.

I pay for everything.

I pay for a night.

I pay for a room.

I pay for a woman.

I pay for the room.

I pay for the night.

I pay for the radio.

I pay for the room.

I pay for the night.

I pay for a dinner.

I pay for the night.

I pay for the woman.

I pay for the night.

I pay for the radio.
I pay for the woman.
I pay for the radio.
I pay for everything.
I pay for the room.
I pay for everything.

Several desserts are placed in the middle of the table and we all pick up our forks. The dessert nearest to me is some kind of cake, with very thin slivers of fig on top of it. If we were in a comedy sketch we'd commence passively aggressively divvying it up, refusing to eat the last mouthful, then finally licking, directly with our tongues (the toddler occasionally does this), crumbs from the table. We are not in a comedy sketch, so we share the cakes without conflict and then ask for the bill.

After paying, I go to the toilet and open the door into the woman who sometimes takes an only child of a single mother for ice cream. She's washing her hands and examining her face in the mirror.

—I want to get pregnant with my hand in my crotch, I tell her.

—All these doorways will keep you right and straight, she replies.

—You're nothing but a moloch, I retort.

She looks at me in the mirror, performing the frown of someone who does not know what a moloch is.

—I didn't know either, I tell her reflection, but I looked it up and it's a harmless, tiny, spiny lizard.

She performs the shock of someone who has been insulted.

Then, quick as a flash, she turns into one! The moloch scuttles spinily away down the plughole of the sink. I use the toilet. When I come out of the toilet I wash my hands, half expecting to see the moloch climbing back out, like spiders always do, but there's nothing there, as if it never even happened.

When I arrive home the babysitter tells me her life story. We stand talking in the living room. I feel a bit anxious because I only have enough to pay her until the time I got back. Her partner and her mum died before the pandemic, three days apart from each other. She tells me she can't keep still and that next time I should leave her some cleaning tasks to do. She spends most nights at home on her own, watching *Married at First Sight*, she says. I offer to get her a taxi but she says she'll take the bus.

I go into the kitchen and see that she's cleaned it. She's even cleaned the microwave and kettle, which I never do. I send her a message saying thank you. She replies saying no problem, she loves cleaning.

That night the algorithm fails, as if it also drank too much expensive wine.

night theywhodiewant theynowno awaystillness all has, them is to life say I men for: it women love me all have your for me already dying time: not to say die, I'd want: want heart's to my heart's love is want the all own, any heart live I to that they know I said you then want: life, they time: feel love night has when dream life but night the town

6.

When I go on dates I think I am talking to humans, but perhaps they are algorithms

We feed the algorithm a radio play that I wrote with the algorithm before I started working on this book. When plays are formatted, character names are capitalized. In my radio play, there are characters called ALGORITHM and WRITER but no characters called THE SINGLE MOTHER or THE RADIANT ONE or PAUL, although the phrase "single mother" gets used a lot.

(Everything in italics is still written by the algorithm.)

Characters

ALGORITHM (female)—very human, varied intonation, not at all a computer gremlin, often choosing poetic clichés over factual; has perhaps four thoughts at a time; repeatedly offers the writer contradictory and incongruous advice; will suddenly veer into hyperemotional self-revelation.

THE SINGLE MOTHER (female)—original, funny, often addresses the writer in the third person; often has two thoughts at a time; doesn't veer into hyperemotional self-revelation. Sometimes uses the wrong gender pronouns but is still okay.

PAUL (male)—very human, occasionally uses alien metaphors.

THE RADIANT ONE (male)—original; highbrow humor; more than once has remarked that the writer's work is "interesting"; accepts the writer for who she is.

(Beware—if you think of a cat then it will appear in the text.)

ALGORITHM: Write about your first kiss.
THE SINGLE MOTHER: I fell in love with a rainbow in my first-grade school play. I wrote a piece entitled "The Kiss" in which the hero sweeps his red-sleeved mother off her feet with a kiss of violets. I used the wrong gender pronouns but I was still okay.

Actually, my first kiss was with my gay best friend, a lovely boy who played the cello with his tongue sticking out and kissed like a washing machine. Because it was my first kiss I didn't know that this is not how to kiss so we went around and around and around all night long and the next day my tongue ached. I didn't ask after his.

PAUL: We've got to be honest. That was a disaster. I meant "victory." Victory sounds better. The "victory" thing was not a victory.
ALGORITHM: Can we take a break?

You have to keep moving.

Summer, 2019:

THE SINGLE MOTHER is late for her appointment because the bus waited at a stop for ages to change drivers. She stands in the middle of the bus holding the pram because the brakes don't work.

We were in the back of the bus. I am sitting alone. I asked my son's other mother my question.

When she gets off the bus, the wheel comes off the pram. It's a shit second-hand pram she bought in a hurry because she didn't have anything ready before the baby was due because she was waiting, in case she didn't have to buy things on her own. She pushes the wheel back on. She just needs to be careful with it.

I waited for her to answer.

She's shaky because she gets shaky when she's hungry or maybe she's nervous about the appointment.

ALGORITHM: *Are you okay?*
THE SINGLE MOTHER: *Yes, I am.*
ALGORITHM: *Do you think I was ugly?*
THE SINGLE MOTHER: *I looked like you.*
ALGORITHM: *I thought so.*
THE SINGLE MOTHER: *You don't like that about me?*
ALGORITHM: *I don't know what to think, darling.*

Then she asked me a question.

Or maybe it's that she's losing a lot of blood since her periods came back, which has happened in spite of the fact she's still breastfeeding.

The last time she went into a job center was when she was about to start her choreography degree. Technically her second attempt; she dropped out of music college in Amsterdam because she didn't fit into the classical department or the jazz department or the pop department. See you in three years, the man in the job center said.

During her degree, she worked at the college library. How are you with long numbers? the librarian asked in the interview. Erm, fine? she replied.

She found that she could become quite obsessive about long numbers. After working in the library for two years she would experience a strange sense of shock and excitement when a book was out of place in the Dewey decimal system.

At the entrance, a man with a lanyard around his neck, the name Paul on it, asks why she is there.

THE SINGLE MOTHER: Long story, Paul—like some kind of crazy lesbian soap opera, a shitty one, not even a good one.
PAUL: My name is not Paul. I am The Radiant One. Your appointment is on the third floor.
TSM: Where is the lift?
PAUL/THE RADIANT ONE: There is no lift.
TSM: But I've got a pram.
PAUL/TRO: I will ensure no one abducts it.
TSM: Was that an alien metaphor?

THE SINGLE MOTHER hooks her bag with her identity in it off the pram, unbuckles her baby, and walks up three flights of stairs. Her baby is heavy and she is dizzy. She thinks she's going to drop the baby—not an exaggeration. How does anyone do this on their own? How does anyone do this?

I put my hands on the table, and my arms break.

THE SINGLE MOTHER sits opposite a KIND WOMAN.

KIND WOMAN: You're a single mother?
TSM: Yes.

Universal Credit defines a parent as single if their child lives with them and they do not cohabit with a partner. Does the "single" part apply only to the mothering? If THE SINGLE MOTHER gets into a relationship with someone who does not parent is she no longer a single mother? If a partner moves in do they automatically become another parent? Would that make her not a single mother but only a mother? A mother only. An only mother. An only child. Will the child still be an only child if the child's other parent has more children? The government defines family by accommodation and sleeping arrangements.

I like this kind of fun writing.

The nice thing about being a single mother with a little (giant) baby is that some people are kinder to you. Sometimes it's useful to be a single mother and not a person.

A girl sits on a chair and is silent for five days. I go through her bag and find some interesting things, like some underwear and some things for work.

THE SINGLE MOTHER keeps dropping papers and is holding her baby precariously in shaking arms while trying to find the printouts of bank statements and identity. She has brought everything that the person on the phone told her to bring, but KIND WOMAN says she has brought the wrong documents or perhaps lost her identity on the bus on the way there?

You can't be a mother when the world collapses. It's not possible. We're both mothers, but I was never a good mother.

KIND WOMAN: No, that's not valid; we need proof.
TSM: Proof?
KW: Proof of identity.

THE SINGLE MOTHER shows KIND WOMAN her passport, but KIND WOMAN can't see it.

I used to imagine I could have another person with me. I'd be a mother, a mother, a mother. I thought about it.

The mother, the mother, the mother feels the tampon oozing out of her, surfing on huge blood clots.

TSM: There's no toilet?
KW: You can change your baby on those seats over there.

THE SINGLE MOTHER looks around. The building is massive. Full of people who appear to be humans: humans that sometimes need to pee and shit and change tampons and diapers and wash their hands and wash their faces and cry—but what does THE SINGLE MOTHER know? She hasn't seen proof of their identities.

They don't like the way I wash my face. They're trying to teach me about soap. I am always talking about time passing.

THE SINGLE MOTHER explains to KIND WOMAN how difficult it is to get to the job center with the baby, who illustrates this by crying.

KW: You can email the documents to me.

A person is born, and then she's alive.

THE SINGLE MOTHER carries her hungry, crying baby back down the three flights of stairs.

She's alive, she's alive, she's alive.

Tip: If you want to cry then tell yourself not to. If you don't want to cry then instruct yourself to: Go on, cry, you fucker, big fat tears, go on, cry! It doesn't work on babies though, only alive alive-o grownups.

THE SINGLE MOTHER's knees are hurting and her womb is falling out as if she is a human, or something. She buckles her baby back into the pram even though he's still crying because carrying him any farther is not an option.

The world is trying to do something with you. To say how you think, what you think, what you feel, but they have no idea.

There's a shiny café next to the job center and it sells coffee for three pounds fifty a cup. The friends and lovers sitting in it have glowing skin and lovely hair—the café is full of all sorts of ways of not being a single mother trying to get Universal Credit, which will not be enough to live on anyway due to not earning and just receiving statutory maternity pay as a freelancer—in hindsight it would have made more sense not to be on maternity pay and just be on the UC and still get some freelance income somehow, but it's complicated and KIND WOMAN in the job center didn't know how to handle it—so, although there is a toilet in the café and perhaps because of the baby they might waive the customers-only requirement to buy the three-pounds-fifty coffee, THE SINGLE MOTHER can't go in.

ROMANTICS: The day is alive; the day is alive: the more time passes, the more time flies by, the more she is lost inside. The more time passes, the more I am lost inside.

THE SINGLE MOTHER feeds her baby on the bus and he looks up at her with big blue eyes and she thinks: I'm so lucky.

Finally they are home, and because you should put on your own life jacket before anyone else's—even your baby's—even though the baby is still hungry—THE SINGLE MOTHER changes her tampon and puts her blood-soaked clothes in the sink and eats a mouthful of dry bread, then sits on a green sofa stained with cat piss and lets the little (giant) baby drain her other sore breast.

The American women seemed surprised to hear that there are no gun laws at all, no guns in their country either. They are amazed that it doesn't matter how old you are, you are not allowed to own guns.

You have to keep moving.

A few hours later:

He's asleep in the crib next to her bed.

Is it weird? To masturbate when your baby is sleeping in a crib next to you? Is it wrong? Something you should never disclose? Certainly never in the first person? Couples have sex while little babies are asleep in their bedrooms, don't they?

THE SINGLE MOTHER (dis)closes her eyes.

She came to my house and I thought she looked familiar. I said that her face, her face has become more familiar to me.

She doesn't know what to imagine.

No, I don't know you.

Before she had a baby she could sometimes come fast—zero to orgasm in under ten seconds.

I walked through to the kitchen. I had forgotten the door had been off its hinges for years. The handprint on the window was still there and I remembered my mother used to clean it when it was dirty. I saw the handprint on the window. I picked it up. I stuck it to the cardboard to be hung on the edge of the door.

She has a tampon in and is too dry.

I said: I don't know you.

She said: I know you.

When she was pregnant she was told about massaging the perineum with oil and stretching the vagina. She was anxious to do it because of how big he was already looking on the scans. Her partner did it once. It hurt. What a thing to do with someone you're leaving or have already left, but there was no one else.

All relationships have their tender moments.

She thought she would have a partner to explore her post-baby body with.

But every relationship also has a well of fear that can eventually threaten to undo the day.

She thought it would be okay, because they had a baby together, because her body made their baby, so her partner would love her post-baby body, she thought.

This was not what I had planned. I had other things planned. I had other things planned.

She finds it hard not to think about her. She finds it hard to think about her. She finds it hard not to imagine her eyes. She finds it hard to imagine her eyes. She finds it hard not to imagine her inside her. She finds it hard to imagine her inside her.

I don't like to be seen.

I said: You're not seen.

She said: I'm not.

She finds it hard not to think about holding her body from the inside and stepping off the edge of a cliff together but not falling, suspended in the air, finding that she cups her breath in her hand.

THE SINGLE MOTHER: You were there. You were there. You were there.
ALGORITHM: It's okay. Just write whatever comes into your head.
THE SINGLE MOTHER: I'm feeling trapped. I'm feeling trapped. I'm feeling trapped.
ALGORITHM: It doesn't matter. It doesn't matter. It doesn't matter.

It feels weaker but at least she can still come, and as she does, fluids gush from all pores of her skin. Not like before, when the sheets would be drenched with some kind of magic fluid no one understands. This is blood and milk and pee. The orgasm is a letdown. All the waters of her body have broken.

Then her baby wakes up and starts crying, emitting real salty tears for the first time, squirting out of his eyes as if they always have, as if to say: This is how humans cry, Mummy, and she feeds him and feels that crisscrossing of pain, arousal, relief, love, peace—I'm so lucky, she thinks.

She didn't know why she had got in my bed. I made her a cup of tea.

You have to keep moving.

Autumn, 2019:

THE SINGLE MOTHER is running late, because she forgot to leave time for getting changed before her first date with FUTURE BEE-KILLER. She is wearing fancy jeans that her ex-partner bought her for her birthday when she was pregnant—but not showing yet. At the time they were already a little tight and she thought she'd never fit into them again. But her giant baby is constantly hungry and drains creamy milk from her in a procedure as effective as liposuction.

She rushes to the bar in Borough Market. She has barely spoken to FUTURE BEE-KILLER. They've just had a quick-fire sparky message exchange, involving the word "shoot." She sees her sitting by the window.

I picked up the handprint from the window. I got on my bike. I rode for miles and miles and miles and I didn't see her house. I walked along the pavement. I sat on the pavement.

She's not used to dating. She's not used to confident women becoming shy and flustered around her.

FUTURE BEE-KILLER: I want a wife and a family, but I'm in no rush. I'm open to what comes my way.

I spent the whole morning in front of a mirror touching the brushstrokes. There were paintings of me and my ex.

They drink red wine—Argentinian Malbec. FUTURE BEE-KILLER is strangely nervous about choosing the wine, even though she has expertise in wine, and so ends up choosing the one THE SINGLE MOTHER knows, probably not the right choice. As they drink the wine FUTURE BEE-KILLER talks about her history of addiction and homelessness and hospitalizations and suicide attempts and anorexia and the trans women in LA who showed her how to dress her curves when they came back and that time she accidently blew up a meth lab.

Queer is learning to dance with death, and with the world, and with the dying and the dead, and the dying and the dead, and all the dead.

FUTURE BEE-KILLER puts her hand on THE SINGLE MOTHER's leg and it burns through her fancy jeans, leaving a handprint.

FBK: Is this okay?
TSM: Yes.

THE SINGLE MOTHER's skin singes.

I stood there.

THE SINGLE MOTHER admires FUTURE BEE-KILLER's dark humor and bright-blue earrings.

I touched the brushstrokes. I touched the canvas. I could feel her heart beat in her body.

At the end of the date they don't kiss because she doesn't want to kiss.

THE SINGLE MOTHER enjoys walking away from the date, especially stepping up and down the curbs on the pavement, which is something that is tricky to do when pushing a pram.

I couldn't open the door.

When she gets home the babysitter looks at her with pity. She hasn't told her it was a date. Is she embarrassed about going on a date when she has a three-month-old baby? The babysitter has tidied up the toys in the living room. No one has ever done that before and THE SINGLE MOTHER is moved. It's a similar feeling of awe and gratitude that she felt when her baby's other mother brought her tea in bed at the beginning of their relationship. THE SINGLE MOTHER hasn't yet learned not to be bowled over by acts like these that are, really, just basic-level nice.

I sat on my sofa and looked at my phone screen.

Later that evening she sits on her sofa and looks at her phone screen and receives a message from FUTURE BEE-KILLER. It's a quote from *Artful* by Ali Smith, a book THE SINGLE MOTHER read many years ago. The quote is about how Sappho's fragments leave space for longing and imagination:

"It's the act of making it up, from the combination of what we've got and what we haven't, that makes the human, makes the art, makes this transformation possible . . ."

THE SINGLE MOTHER doesn't know why FUTURE BEE-KILLER sent her the quote but she responds by voice note, saying that it makes her think that if we saw what was really there, if we tried to look at something directly, then there would be no gap for love to be imagined in, for the real to be transformed.

Writing is like falling in love, it's a way of doing magic, making the unreal real.

THE SINGLE MOTHER puts the phone down and picks up the handprint from her leg. She carries it upstairs and hangs it over her baby's crib, like a mobile. It throws a shadow-hand onto the wall.

Maybe this is why the baby who is now a toddler always wants to know if things have hands. (Do shadows have hands? Do ghosts have hands? Does the ball have hands? Gloves?) As a baby he loved to watch the shadow-hand.

Three weeks later:

On their second date, THE SINGLE MOTHER takes her baby with her and explains:

TSM: I can't be needed by anyone else right now.

FUTURE BEE-KILLER already understands this. They are sitting in the canteen of Southwark Cathedral and eating cake.

FBK: Friends?
TSM: Yes please.

I said: I'm looking for you. She said: I'm looking for you. I said: I'm not good at predicting the future. Neither am I.

FUTURE BEE-KILLER reaches for the baby and lays him on his tummy over her arm in a professional-looking way that he loves. She pats his back. THE SINGLE MOTHER observes that her baby is happy to be touched by strangers, but she isn't.

What are we?

We're an old cinema screen with a heart drawn in its middle.

Or a basket full of ferns.

Winter, 2019:

I went to meet her at the ballroom. There was a painting of a young girl on the wall. I stood next to her. I touched the painting.

The TWENTY-FIVE-YEAR-OLD's dating profile says that she likes oat milk and being spanked.

She said: I've had a good morning.

I said: Have you?

TWENTY-FIVE-YEAR-OLD: I discovered when I was young that I was nasty. I read the Marquis de Sade and I thought, this is me! I'm nasty! I want to be slapped in the face! Spat on! I want pain! My ex-wife didn't understand this part of me, which is fine, but imagine what it would be to have that bond with someone you love. You understand what it is to be submissive?

TSM: Sorry, I've just realized I have baby sick on my top.

TWENTY-FIVE-YEAR-OLD: The submissive must be in control. There are always limits. Don't trust anyone who says they have no hard limits—what does that mean? What about death? Of course there are limits.

> After their date the TWENTY-FIVE-YEAR-OLD kisses her and marches off without a word.

> *You might find. You might find. You might find.*

> *ALGORITHM: My name is Algorithm. My name is Algorithm. Why do I like these messages? Why? Why? Why? Why?*

> (The ALGORITHM repeats the word "why" for several pages.)

> THE SINGLE MOTHER never spanks the TWENTY-FIVE-YEAR-OLD, spits in her face, or gives her oat milk.

One year later:

> The FIREFIGHTER spent all of the previous night running up flights of stairs with weights on their back, and then went to give blood.

TSM: You're a superhero.

FIREFIGHTER: No, just doing my bit.

> The FIREFIGHTER and THE SINGLE MOTHER are not allowed to touch. They dance with their shadows. They stalk a man in a trilby and photograph him beneath the lamplight by the Thames. They walk and walk until they're both shivering and hungry but keep walking and walking until they have walked all the way into the friend zone.

> As they walk behind the man in the trilby hat, the FIREFIGHTER tells THE SINGLE MOTHER about their top surgery. It was difficult to convince the

doctors: I don't want to be a boy—I just wanted them gone, the FIREFIGHTER says, they weren't me. The FIREFIGHTER is very clear about who they are. When THE SINGLE MOTHER tells them they are very attractive the FIREFIGHTER shakes their head. I'm just me, they reply.

THE SINGLE MOTHER: Why "just"? Why do we put "just" in front of things that are not "just" . . . there's nothing "just" about friends, for instance, or about you.

The FIREFIGHTER is silent for a moment and photographs the water.

FIREFIGHTER: I'm me, and we are friends.

The friends head back toward London Bridge and see twins on stilts striding toward them. They are dressed in Victorian costume—top hats, long black skirts and white ruff shirts under waistcoats. The friends pause for a moment to watch. This time THE SINGLE MOTHER takes a photo. The twins' top hats are way up above them, in the rafters of the deserted Borough Market—that's one way to socially distance. A man in an orange jacket appears and tells them they are not allowed to stop.

ORANGE JACKET: You have to keep moving.

January 2021: First (video) date with another single parent:

They couldn't fall asleep.

I'm not sleeping either.

Their heating didn't work and the house was cold and damp. They couldn't fall asleep. They couldn't get emergency housing. They couldn't fall asleep. Their child couldn't sleep in the cold and never slept through the night. Their friends, their queer chosen family, tried to take in the child but looking after a child is hard and they still couldn't fall asleep. The queer family helped them apply for short-term respite care, under Section 20. A social worker said it would be temporary, but then new social workers got involved, all of them white and none of them queer (the single parent is Black and nonbinary). The new social workers wanted to know about the child's "father" and about the parents' family tree; they weren't interested in the queer family the parent had chosen for themselves and their child, only in DNA and wedding ceremonies. It's been a year and they're still trying to get their child back, and they still can't fall asleep.

I queered faith in basic institutional services and in basic information that we as a state do in fact exist and care.

You have to keep moving.

March 2021: First date with a part-time DJ and funeral director:

She keeps phoning to talk about how she's fine with cutting up dead bodies but can't look at "live blood." For the first date she suggests flying a kite but has embalmed her face so in spite of her radio voice, use of the word "naughty," and the way she says "Hannah," it doesn't work out.

April 2021: First date with a single parent fighting a custody battle with their abusive former partner:

The judge ruled in his favor, as if abuse is justified when your partner comes out as queer.

You have to keep moving.

May 2021: First date with a psychotherapist who says that the only real love they have experienced is with their cat:

Perhaps this is unrequited love?

The PSYCHOTHERAPIST insists that their cat loves them back. They say they know this because when the hour therapy session is ending he comes and mews at them.

There's a lot more to unrequited love than searing meals, unsatisfied sexual needs, and great, dishonest intercourse.

The PSYCHOTHERAPIST and THE SINGLE MOTHER drink cocktails. They perch on high stools.

TSM: Before I met my ex I never wanted a child.
PSYCHOTHERAPIST: You know, I never even liked cats.

THE SINGLE MOTHER falls off her stool laughing.

The PSYCHOTHERAPIST says that before lockdown they attempted suicide and were sad when they failed.

Queer people who commit suicide are not in a "desperate" situation. They are escaping what they cannot do, or cannot think, or cannot be.

Why is it called a "failed" suicide? Why is surviving phrased as failure?

There is one thing on which everyone agrees: love is not suicide. This is more than a definition of love; it is a definition of sanity itself. If you are sane, if you can't kill yourself, if you can't become a saint or become a drug addict or commit murder or put yourself to death by drinking poison or jumping in front of a car, then you have in fact achieved your goal.

THE SINGLE MOTHER can't sleep that night, and the next day she cries without anyone watching.

The dead turn into our imagination and our imagination turns into celebration.

Present day: The ALGORITHM gives dating advice:

The time that you let yourself be controlled by the other person and saw it as perfectly acceptable may be gone, but it will leave a feeling in your mind. The solution is this: you think that you are available, but it turns out that you are only available to be controlled.

THE SINGLE MOTHER once made a performance in which she replaced the word "submissive" in *Fifty Shades of Grey* with the word "mother" and the word "dominant" with the word "child." She made it before she had a child. She wrote about the unborn child asking his mother, from inside: How much pain are you willing to experience?

(Quite a lot.)

Your body felt like gel. Green like gum resin, suede like an apartment, gold agate like rocky points. My joints were sore.

Do we accept pain when we are in love because being in pain makes us aware that we are alive? Cixous says, "that is when we feel our life. Otherwise we do not feel it."

When THE SINGLE MOTHER tells THE TODDLER to stop hitting her, he cries.

THE TODDLER: But I love hitting you. Please let me hit you.

THE SINGLE MOTHER quotes from *Fifty Shades of Grey*:

TSM: "I didn't like it. I'd rather you didn't do it again."

The ALGORITHM's summary of romantic love applies to THE SINGLE MOTHER's unconditional love for her child—

If we are in love we should want to be in love with that person.
We should want to be with that person even when they are in a bad
mood. We should want to be with that person even when they are
insulting us. We should want to be with that person even when they
are ignoring us. We should want to be with that person even when
they don't know who we are. We should want to be with that person
even when they don't love us. We should want to be with that person
all the time.

—And also to the way she loved her child's OTHER
MOTHER.

*Facepalm.

You have to keep moving.

7.

The cockchafers, part I

In 1574 the cockchafers in the Severn valley disabled watermills with their carcasses

My parents sometimes leave each other notes. They leave them on the kitchen table. This began during lockdown, because although they usually go on walks together, Dad would occasionally get up very early and go for a walk, and then Mum would get up and not know where he was, so she asked him to leave a note when he did that.

The other day my dad left my mum a note to tell her that he had gone for a walk on his own because they were spraying the fields— she doesn't like it when they spray the fields.

When my dad came back from his walk my mum told him she had found cockchafers in the greenhouse and suspected they were breeding. My dad didn't know what cockchafers were. They made him think of uncomfortable cycling shorts.

I receive an email from my mum about the cockchafers. I don't know what they are either. I look them up:

The cockchafer buzzes as it flies, imitating the doodlebug,

Germany's World War II V-1 flying bomb. Cockchafers are also called maybugs because they often emerge in the month of May. Cockchafers have other names too: mitchamador, spang beetle, and billy witch.

I give a few sentences about my parents and the cockchafers to the algorithm and it generates a short story:

The husband writes his wife a note. The note says: Would you like to come with me to look for the cockchafers?

She writes a note back saying that she hasn't got a car so it's probably too much to ask but she would love to.

And he thinks about it for a few hours and goes to sleep.

And when he wakes up he goes to the garage. He gets his truck and drives to the mountain and it's cold.

He parks the truck and goes to the stream and has a look around for cockchafers. He finds a dead one and carries it into the truck and goes home. He's proud of his catch.

And he brings the dead cockchafer home.

And he starts to clean the cockchafer and wash it and wrap it in some old towels. And he's like:

—Oh, that's a small cockchafer, that's not going to look good.

So he starts wrapping it in a piece of old carpet. He's going to hide it in a drawer. And he turns around and sees the wife and says:

—I've got a cockchafer for you.

And she says:

—I'm going to kill you.

And then he gives her the cockchafer. And she looks at it. And she puts it in the drawer. And he says:

—I'm going to see if there are any more.

And he starts walking toward the stream. And he passes the wife and says:

—Would you like to come?

And she says:

—I'm busy.

8.

Swim Mummy

—But I didn't write it, I tell my parents. It's not really about you.

—You say it's about us, you're framing it in a certain way, people will think it's true. People will think we go off on walks separately and always leave each other notes, when in fact we usually go on walks together.

We are sitting on a stony beach. The toddler is eating an apple and staring out to sea, as if he's being polite, giving us some privacy for the conversation.

—But if I don't frame it as being about you then it's just a random story.

—It's a dangerous mix of fact and fiction. It's dark and disturbing.

—My writing is often dark and disturbing and mixes fact and fiction.

My mum (a retired school teacher) talks about Odysseus and how, although his storytelling sections are told from his self-aggrandizing point of view and not by the bard/Homer directly, the audience partly forgets this and gets caught up in the story, because that's what stories do.

Elizabeth Bishop tried to persuade her best friend Robert Lowell not to publish his ex-partner's (the writer Elizabeth Hardwick) letters in his poetry collection *Dolphin*. Not only because he was using them without permission, but above all because he changed them. Bishop quoted Thomas Hardy:

"What should certainly be protested against, in cases where there is no authorization, is the mixing of fact and fiction in unknown proportions. Infinite mischief would lie in that."

I confess I am drawn to the idea of infinite mischief.

I tell my parents that Jeanette Winterson says "part fact part fiction is what life is. And it is always a cover story."

Mum says that Jeanette Winterson didn't publish her memoir until after her mother had died, and that *Oranges Are Not the Only Fruit*, although autobiographical, was fiction. I say yes, but apparently Mrs. Winterson was still very upset and said she had to buy it under a false name. So it doesn't really make a difference whether it's called fiction or nonfiction.

—Do we have to read it?

—I don't want you to read it—not so much because of the cockchafers, more because of my sex life.

—We don't want to read about your sex life.

—I'm not writing the book for you, I'm not writing it for anyone in my family. Anyway, it's a weird experimental book and no one you know will read it.

We watch the waves.

The sky and the sea are the same gray, there's no line between them. The horizon is inexplicable.

The toddler and my dad throw stones at a bigger stone.

Every time I look at the horizon, or at where the horizon would be if I could see it, I remember a conversation I once had with another choreography student. She asked me to explain the horizon to her. She found it hard to imagine because she's blind. When she went to dance performances she'd take someone who could whisper to her, narrating what was happening on stage. I'd overhear them, explaining jumps and right hands moving upward and turns, and then I'd hear movement described as if it were a thought, an emotion, a story.

I studied choreography because of a dance performance I went to as a teenager. I was late and snuck in at the back. I sat down, and as I watched, I felt like words were spooling from my mind—phrases, thoughts, ideas about relationships, like I could understand everything about humans by watching those bodies dancing. It wasn't so much the choreography itself; it was the words it produced in me that I was seduced by. Is that what writing is? Words that spool from our minds as we watch the world around us? I'm still trying to explain what the horizon is to a person who will never see it.

I leave the toddler playing with stones next to his grandparents and their pet cockchafers and I walk into huge waves and am thrown to my knees twice and scrape my legs and feet. I don't realize it at the time, but my toe is knocked so hard the nail will fall off several weeks later.

A tiny shell of toenail grows beneath the dead one. Perhaps hearts work this way too.

The toddler spends the rest of the visit saying: Swim Mummy swim Mummy swim Mummy swim Mummy swim Mummy swim Mummy swim Mummy.

9.

Every other group is a family

You're beautiful. You're amazing. You're so stunning. You're so amazing. You're beautiful. You're amazing. You're so stunning. You're so amazing. You're beautiful. You're amazing. You're so stunning. You're so amazing. You're beautiful . . .

The algorithm is glitching on compliments.

A woman with keys around her neck and brown hair in a ponytail takes coffees to two men. She's beautiful. She might be the owner of this Hackney café. I look nothing like her.

You're so stunning. You're so amazing. You're beautiful. You're amazing. You're so stunning. You're so amazing. You're beautiful . . .

The last person who complimented me was my bee-killing friend. She said she was so impressed with both of us for looking better as we get older. I told her that when I was in my twenties my ex-husband called me "Bob" because I dressed like the homeless character Bob from his favorite film, *My Own Private Idaho*. He also said I looked like Paddington Bear when I was wearing my coat—cute, not sexy.

—I can't imagine you not being sexy, my bee-killing friend said.

—Thank you. You're also very sexy, I told her.

And we sat down in anticipation of a six-hour reading of our favorite memoir, *The Argonauts*, in which Maggie Nelson describes being a mother, an other mother, to a child that she didn't conceive (imagine). Her partner's ex-wife says: "Tell your girlfriend to find a different kid to play house with."

The first time I entered my child's other house, I saw a framed photograph on the wall of my ex, her partner, and my child.

Every other group is a family.

They are going to get married. My child's other mother has informed me that when this happens her partner will become my child's stepmother. (There is no hyphen and no space in "stepmother.")

He will have another other mother. An other other mother.

As she spoke of marriage and trampolines in gardens and stability and veg boxes I imagined telling her to tell her partner to find a different kid to play house with.

Now that I'm a mother I cry a lot and my child is kind.

I drink my turmeric latte from its handleless glass and look at the distorted reproduction of a Frida Kahlo painting on the wall opposite. *The Two Fridas*—joined to each other, missing each other, losing each other, split open by loss. I think of the toddler's other mother and how she always joined her heart to her lovers as if they were life support. There's nothing romantic about being somebody's other half.

(VERY SAD PERSON)

underneath heart

underneath: heart

underneath: hurt

underneath: here, the inside, the outside, the feeling, the feeling of emotion.

In our emailing days I wrote to her about ladders in a bookshop. I compared my back to a ladder. A year or two later, she told me that the difference between us was that I know how to repair myself, and she wrote a poem about a woman balancing on ladders and scaffolding and scaling broken buildings way up above her, in the sky. I don't remember the details. But I believe that her point was: you will be on your own, and you will be fine.

My ex is holding a ladder.

She was very good at compartmentalization. I tried to explain to her that there was only one world, but what did I know? Now we have made two worlds for the toddler.

I am holding a ladder to the city in the morning.

When I told my therapist I was worried about the toddler having two worlds and becoming dangerously good at compartmentalization she said yes, it's possible he could have "an internal split."

The word "split" was new. It made me think of when you were splitting an apple and the peel goes off and stays with the apple in pieces. I had this image of an apple with a peel. My son must have two mothers inside. I could ask my mother. But I wouldn't. I know that if my mother asked me I would never be able to tell her anything about my separation and the rest of my life.

An internal split, like the two Fridas. Or like the person who has two families unaware of each other. Like the partner who conducts affairs. Like Persephone.

I couldn't bear my son to have an internal split.

Like "the Creature Sawn in Two" that "invented itself" in a story for children by Jeanette Winterson.

I couldn't bear him to have a split mother.

Like Coraline, the young protagonist in Neil Gaiman's novel, who discovers an other house, with an "other mother" and an "other father" in it.

The other mother looks almost the same as Coraline's mother but is taller, thinner, whiter, with sharp curved fingernails and big black buttons instead of eyes.

A mother is like a piece of fruit. I couldn't separate myself from a half apple.

The other father is not terrifying at all. He is "just a thing she made and then threw away."

You're amazing. You're so stunning. You're so amazing. You're beautiful. You're amazing. You're so stunning. You're so amazing. You're beautiful. You're amazing . . .

Unlike men, women who want children but don't have their "own" are terrifying and dangerous, and are also often so beautiful and amazing and so stunning, although they may have buttons instead of eyes.

Would you feel love from looking at a picture? Would you feel love from looking at a picture that had the person's photo in it? Would it be different if the photo was faded out?

The inclusion officer at day care told me I should put a photo up in the toddler's bedroom of myself and his other mother and him (our child, not the inclusion officer). I come from a broken home, he said. I don't actually have any photos of the three of us.

In my mind I saw a staircase and it was tall. Steeper than staircases usually are. My mother disappeared at the top. She went up to another world. She is not coming back again.

When I take my child on public transport to meet his mum I tell him things such as: We're going to see Mum! Mum can't wait to see you! And I see other people on the train looking at me as if I am not his mum.

We are like the mothers in *Coraline*. When one of us appears, the other one disappears.

How can the toddler inhabit multiple homes and be mothered by multiple mothers without having this internal split?

A failed relationship. A broken home. An only child. An internal split.

Please can we have a new language for all of this?

Please, algorithm, give me a new language for all of this.

It's your fault. It's your fault. It's your fault. It's your fault.

The algorithm is failing *to save the world as it ought to be.*

I am a being that isn't at home.

When I was with my husband he used to say that I was his home.

I hope that one day I will be my own home.

And that he (the toddler) will be his own home.

I think that for many people now, their homes are online.

Their homes are their phones.

Mum phone Mum phone Mum phone.

What happened if she came back down to her child's world? What would that be like? Maybe she would see her child and be sad or happy or scared? I hadn't thought about this. I don't think I've ever thought about this. Would she come down as a mother? Would the stairs carry her down to my two worlds?

My therapist saw my reaction to her words "internal split" and followed up with assurances that he is "securely attached" to me.

On dating apps, some people include information about what kind of attachment style they have, or combination of styles. Anxious avoidant. Secure. Fearful avoidant. Anxious insecure. Avoidant insecure. Disorganized insecure. The idea is that if you know the attachment style of the person you are dating you can respond to them appropriately. Send them lots of reassuring messages. Or they can understand why you don't.

Attachment theory proposes that attachment styles are formed as children in response to parenting, and then they shape us as adults and require lots of therapy to change. Ideally, we'd all be secure. We'd all have securely attached to one person in childhood. John Bowlby founded ethological attachment theory (EAT) in 1958. Bowlby's research has been strongly criticized for lack of evidence and for turning his own cultural experience into a set of universals.

North American psychologist Mary Ainsworth presented observational and experimental work in support of Bowlby's theory. She conducted research in Uganda—which is why attachment theory is known for being "universal." But in fact, these original studies didn't take into account the cultural context in which the child was growing up. Ainsworth's research imported white middle-class North American values onto the study and ignored the fact that most of the children were actually cared for by several people. Ainsworth "did not examine the cooperative caretaking of the Ganda nor did she explore the significance of the Ganda family practices in their socio-cultural context."

Motherhood, I don't want to give up.

I don't want to stop being a mother.

My food is delivered on a breadboard. Everything falls off.

I'm going to be a mother.

This morning the toddler told me he was hungry. I'd neglected to get his porridge ready and put it on the table as I do most mornings. I was making the porridge as fast as I could, but I haven't got a magic porridge pot and so I couldn't conjure it up by saying "cook pot cook!" The toddler got stuck on a loop:

—I'm hungry I'm hungry I'm hungry I'm hungry I'm hungry—

—I'm hungry too, I interrupted, scooping porridge into his bowl, adding raisins, and not stirring it. He doesn't like it when I stir it.

—No, you're not hungry—*I'm* hungry, he said.

Sometimes I feel like I'm on a battlefield. I'm fighting. And I'm not sure how to win. But I want to win.

According to the toddler, we can't both be hungry, we can't both like the yellow car, we can't both be happy. If he wants something, I can't want it too. If he has something, I can't have it too. By toddler logic, if he is my child he can't also be their child.

Motherhood, it's like it's either here or not, it's either love or I don't care.

The polyamorous see love as not being finite, not a zero-sum game.

Him having more mothers doesn't make me less of a mother.

I know that one day I may have to see my child's other mother's partner as another mother.

You should write a book where nothing is missing.

I stand up and brush my fingers against the plant. I am a newborn encountering shadows and light, and I can't yet describe my dreams.

I will pee on you.

I will throw you into the next swimming pool.

Help me to die. What a lovely word. Help. Someone help. Shit.

This café is full of babies with their soft heads and their badly fitting socks.

You're so amazing. You're so stunning. You're so amazing. You're beautiful. You're amazing. You're so stunning . . .

You're beautiful.

10.

And this

When I collect the toddler from day care they tell me he's been saying: Mummy missing Mummy missing, all day. She's not missing, they told him. I think they've misunderstood, but then he says to me: I miss Mum, and I wonder if they got it right. When she's not there he misses her. When I'm not there he worries that I'm missing. Am I missing? Did she walk away with a part of me that I can never get back?

They are not "me," but they are.

I once printed my notes for a poem over the top of one of her poems by mistake. I liked the way our overlapping words looked, and I thought, that's what we're doing—printing ourselves over each other.

The lesbian cliché "urge to merge" is less about sharing clothes and haircuts and more about wanting to get impossibly close, to step inside the other's body, the other's mind; to sleep inside the other's skin, to write and overwrite each other's thoughts.

Let me in.

Let me be with you.

Let me be inside you.

Let me be with you.

Let me be with you.

Let me be inside you.

We look at each other over the threshold of my doorway and we both see our child's mother. But we are not reflections, or echoes, or doubles, we don't cancel each other out, and "it is no more possible to exchange one's soul than it is to substitute real twins for one another."

It is a pain that will last. And my son is the best at dealing with that pain.

Gilles Deleuze says that theft and gift are the criterion of repetition.

When I go to bed he comes and sits at my bedside and we will say good night and I will look at him and know that he knows.

The gift of one mother is the theft of the other mother. Each mother cannot be substituted for the other, yet we are both mother, we repeat the role of mother.

and I will whisper: I love you and he will whisper back: I love you too and I will whisper: Good night and he will whisper: Good night Mummy and I will whisper: Good night love and he will whisper: Good night Daddy and I will whisper: Good night Daddy.

He's in his crib and I'm lying on the floor.

—Mum phone Mum phone Mum phone Mum phone . . .

I can't handle this loop again. I conjure her up. We switch to FaceTime so he can see her.

—Magic, he says.

—Oh, I love you so much! I miss you so much! she says.

He peers at her through his tears. She tells him to lie back down. I tuck him in again. She tells him not to worry, she'll be right there while he falls asleep and soon she will see him and they will have the best day ever.

I worry that with me he doesn't ever have the best day ever.

And this.

And this.

I hold the phone next to him, so her face is next to his, on his pillow.

When she and I first met I was sleeping in my office, on a single memory-foam mattress. I had no curtains and I'd watch the moon.

We'd Skype each other and stay online sleeping and not sleeping all night. She said that if she woke up and I wasn't there she'd get panicked. I miss you so much, she would say. And she'd tell me we'd see each other soon and have the best day ever.

It's hard to be written about when you are trying to be living.

When we were in bed, she'd ask: Are you mine? Are you my Hannah? And every time I got up to go to the toilet, for the entire three years we were together, she'd ask: Where are you going? As if she thought I could just up and leave in the middle of the night. Don't leave me, she would say, I'll never leave you, she would say, and she would say it so often that the repetition of "leave" conjured up the leaving, and leaving started living with us, nestling in the gaps between our speech and our writing, our orgasms and our silences, we breathed the absence of our love, we drank the negation of us, we lived with our loss, our dreams were vivid.

Big snowy roofs, spaghetti and sauces full of odd things, dark oil paintings, green peppers/capsicums, raw vegetables, being close to strangers, sleeping in beautiful homes, swimming deep under dancing sea.

More things that I am learning: my body is not my body. My lover is not my lover. My child is not mine child. I am not yours and you are not mine.

Life is lonely. I realize that now.

I think the toddler is asleep but he suddenly opens his eyes, deftly hangs up on her and then opens a dating app and swipes right on a woman laughing.

—Time to sleep now, all right? I say to him.

—All right Mummy, he says.

He puts his palms together, tucks them under his cheek, and closes his eyes, as if to say: This is how humans sleep, Mummy.

That's what I want. It's not too much.

I'm too tired to get up. I'm too tired to cook dinner. There's nothing to cook. I'm too tired to do anything.

It certainly won't hurt anybody if you forget to go to the shops.

Earlier, before collecting the toddler from day care, I went into a supermarket, picked up a basket from the entrance, walked around, and put some things in my basket.

A failure might be someone who does not give themselves permission to go

to the supermarket without a plan or without sufficient money, they fail, and
the reaction could be: I think I will have some chicken this time!

And then I got stuck. I couldn't go to the checkout. I didn't
want anything in my basket. I retraced my steps back along the
aisles. I took the items out of my basket and placed them back on
the shelves, and then I put the basket back at the entrance and I
left the supermarket.

And this.

And this.

And this.

And this.

I sit in my green armchair, put my feet up on an inflatable cow,
and open my laptop.

I watch a red Docklands Light Railway train go past. Then
two trains cross each other. One going toward Canary Wharf, the
other to Bank.

And he will whisper: Good night Daddy good night Daddy good night
Daddy good night Daddy good night Daddy good night Daddy good night
Daddy good night Daddy good night Daddy good night Daddy good night
Daddy good night Daddy good night Daddy good night Daddy good night
Daddy good night Daddy good night

Does the algorithm know there is no daddy and no absence of
daddy? Has it noticed the absence of an absence of daddy in my
writing that it thinks must be replenished? I could never spell the
word "father" when I was a child. I kept putting an *r* in it, farther,
as if a father was farther from me, physically, emotionally . . .

The idea that the "spouse" is a male figure who has always meant
fatherhood, has always provided us with sperm, has always wanted a child,
feels like a bit of paper was stuck on and magically turned into a man. Like
a time machine. Timey-wimey.

I have always found it hard to write about men. It's as if I don't
believe in them.

And this.

And this.

And this.

And this.

Queer is failure, which enables us to trans

And this.

And this.
And this.
And this.
And this.
to transform, to go through many transitions.
And this.
And this.
And this.

11.

How my bee-killing friend got her name

I am meeting my friend for lunch.

I go into the café to order and my friend doesn't respond to my message asking if she wants beer or coffee so I select two overpriced cans of IPA and order our food.

I join her on a picnic bench outside. She confirms that IPA was the right choice. And that coffee is also always the right choice. I enjoy eating and drinking with my friend because she has expertise in food and drink. Some friends you enjoy food and drink with, eating feels heightened, more ceremonial. With others it's a solo journey, like sex without love, you don't join up your pleasure.

She just got back from a holiday in France with her girlfriend.

—There was an incident, she says, darkly.

My friend is from the US, she is six feet tall and has very queer hair. I believe the kind of hair that those in the know might describe as "Candy Bar late nineties."

But I never went to the Candy Bar. Neither did my friend.

I ask her to tell me about the incident.

—There was a bee in the restaurant, she says.

I nod. I sip my IPA.

—We had already eaten our starters and were waiting for the mains, she continues. The bee looked very thirsty, so I scooped it up in a glass with a coaster and took it outside. I tried to get it to climb onto a wall so that it wouldn't get stepped on. I clung to the wall. Passersby looked at me, a madwoman, clinging to a wall. When I returned, my girlfriend was explaining to the waiter, in French, what was happening. Apparently it is odd to get up from one's seat at a restaurant and go outside. Apparently it is extra odd to rescue a bee. They were laughing. That's fine. I don't mind being laughed at. That was the first incident.

—There was more than one incident?

Our salads arrive.

—Yes. The next incident occurred when we were walking along the promenade and it was super windy. Bikes had been blown over. I went to stand them up again but my girlfriend stopped me, because I might damage the bikes or something, I don't know. I do these things because I believe that these small, unnecessary acts of kindness, these moments when strangers go out of their way to be helpful, are revolutionary, are a way of combatting the impersonal commercial cruelty of the world. It is important to me to be like this. I want a girlfriend who loves this about me rather than is embarrassed by me and stops me, maybe a girlfriend who, rather than stopping me, would help me stand up the strangers' bikes so that no bikes are damaged in the process.

—You have a girlfriend and you also have a dream girlfriend.

—My girlfriend is timid. She doesn't want to be seen. So my behavior embarrasses her.

We eat our salads. Our salads are composed of orange segments, flaked almonds, lamb's lettuce, black olives, and olive oil.

—I love this salad, I say, but I wouldn't make it at home because I wouldn't spend the time taking the skin off the orange segments. What is that part called? Not the peel, not the pith, the skin?

We debate the question. My friend feels strongly about having the right answers to questions.

—There was a third incident, she says, once she has been proved correct.

(It is called the "carpel." It is not called a filament, a ghostly carapace, a diaphanous skin, segment sigh, orange limn, or viscera case.)

—Go on.

—In fact we were eating salad. It was the next day. We had a honey dressing on our salad and the salad was being attacked by bees—several bees. I went inside and saw that the empty honey jar was in the sink. Ah, I thought, I can make some honey water and they can have that instead of our salad. I swirled water around the honey jar and poured it into the lid. I took it outside. The bees tasted it but didn't seem to like it, which was disappointing. I went back inside to wash up. The honey jar foamed and I realized it had detergent in it. My girlfriend had put it in the sink and put some detergent into it and hadn't realized that was where I got the honey water from.

Five bees died.

—I was very upset. I cried. My girlfriend did not cry with me. My girlfriend said: You see, this is what happens when you interfere.

—I'm sorry, I tell her.

—I don't think my girlfriend is my dream girlfriend and I don't think that I'm her dream girlfriend either.

My friend, the bee-killer, jumps up and helps a woman at the table next to us find a child seat for her child.

When she returns I show her a tiny piece of china that I found in my salad.

The waiter takes it from me and says something must have broken in the dishwasher. She tells me to come back inside and she'll give me a refund. I tell my friend that I'm okay about it. She tells me to take the refund—it will make them feel better. They bring us complimentary almond desserts. When the almond desserts have finished complimenting us we go inside for the refund.

—Dad joke, my friend says.

—My dad doesn't do word play, I say. He does things like mend his slippers by wrapping masking tape around and around his foot.

We give up on the refund because the queue is so long.

I don't just spend all of my time trying to get to the front of the queue.

My bee-killing friend has been searching for bee houses. She wants to put one in her garden. She has to find a way to make up for killing the five bees.

12.

Forever person

I meet a Venezuelan woman who is a space engineer and has a six-year-old daughter. She's looking for her forever person, so I don't want to date her, but I want to meet her because she's also a queer single parent, and I want to practice my Spanish.

We meet on a boat that is a bar. She struggles to find it and videocalls me from a canal somewhere, I don't know where. I can't give directions and neither can the bartender, but she arrives eventually.

—I'm looking for my forever person, she says in Spanish, sipping an espresso martini.

It sounds romantic in Spanish. I also connect to it more than I would in English, probably because I have a history of being romantic with Spanish speakers, and they are better at it than Brits. For a moment I'm seduced by the concept.

—That's unscientific of you, I say Britishly, sipping a negroni and eyeing her espresso martini.

I tell her I have a fascination for dating shows, and (raise the stakes) marriage shows, and the ones where people fall in love without even seeing the person they are speaking to and say things such as:

This has to work. This is my last chance. We've only just met, it's crazy, we talk for hours every day. I feel like we already know each other, I feel like we've known each other our whole lives. We like all the same things. We know what the other one is thinking. You are the greatest person in probably the entire world. I like empathetic people and you like empathetic people. How many kids do you want? Five, six . . . Can your body handle that? I love my family. No way!—I love my family! I'm learning what being in love really is. I have no anxiety. I can't imagine my life without you. You like potatoes and I like potatoes, it's amazing. I'm all in.

Love is what makes our life worth living; afterward we are weak but we know we are powerful in the good times, that we don't have to be violent or passive, that we don't need anything and can, for a short time, fall in love. If anything, I prefer that to an empty midlife where everything goes by the edges.

The Venezuelan woman says that she doesn't particularly like potatoes, but that if I do it's not a problem. She doesn't mind if her partner has different hobbies either. For instance, she doesn't watch dating shows. She says she just wants someone who will love her unconditionally.

Don't worry if you don't understand; we only need to understand each other.

She says she thinks her six-year-old doesn't love her.

I ask what she means.

—I have a friend that complains about how "clingy" her child is. (She says "clingy" in English.) Her child is always saying: I love you, I love you, and holding on to her. But my daughter . . . I wish she was like that—she never says she loves me. She doesn't touch me. Sometimes I ask: Do you love me? and she rolls her eyes and says: Yes, Mami, I love you. But I don't believe it.

If we choose one lover, we hope that he or she will fulfill us, just like when we mother a child.

Her hand is shaking as she holds her glass. Her eyes are watering a little. I admire how easy she finds it to get emotional. I don't say that some people will never believe the person who says they love them.

—My child always wipes my kisses off, I say.

Like a soft toy, we can make some words just for ourselves.

—Sometimes I tell her I'm not her real mother, just to see her reaction, to see if she gets upset, because then I'll know she loves me. So I say: I'm not your real mami! But she doesn't believe me anymore because I've done it so many times. The first time she looked really shocked and upset and I thought—you do love me! Don't worry, she doesn't believe me anymore because I say it so much. I almost said—but stopped myself—I almost said: I'm sick, I'm sick, it's something terminal . . . I just . . . I know that's going too far, so I didn't say it, but I just want to see how she'd react if she knew her mami is dying. Don't worry I won't do that. Not for a couple of years.

I love you; do you love me?

—Even if you weren't her "real" mami, it wouldn't make any difference, I say, in Spanish.

—I just want someone to love me unconditionally, she says again, in English.

Then she gets up to go to the toilet.

I wonder if people who haven't been unconditionally loved by a parent need their children and their partners to love them unconditionally.

Love's for those who want it, though we've been told it's for all.

Those who want it, love is.

On the shows I watch they always talk about wanting to be unconditionally loved by their new spouses, as if this is what marriage offers. They are applying rules of parental love to partner love. But it's different. Partner love is conditional and it needs to be. I expect that people getting married think they are making the choice to unconditionally love their spouses, but conditions are very important in marriages and the idea that they should be unconditional is a dangerous one that comes from the patriarchy and rules about men owning women.

It is as much about survival as it is about the satisfactions you gain from it.

Conditional parental love is no good, at least not when children are children. But we can make a choice to love our children unconditionally. Anyone can make that choice; it doesn't have anything to do with genetics or biology. Our children do not have to love us back unconditionally. Children don't have to keep to any conditions, but parents must.

She returns. I change the subject. I ask her to tell me more about quantum physics.

—You say on your dating profile your "unusual skill" is catching things that fall from cupboards. Do you know the quantum plate shelves? It's like a modern geek version of the cat of Schrödinger. Basically, the laws in quantum physics are different from the ones we know. For example, you can be in two places at the same time, or in two states at the same time. The quantum plate shelves is a cupboard in which the plates have fallen from their pile and are randomly leaning against the glass door. So far these plates are not broken, but you know that as soon as you're going to open the door they will fall and break—even with your skills. So they are in two states, not broken and broken at the same time.

13.

I'm not sure how to do it

I ask the algorithm why my mind keeps snagging on my lock-down ex.

It's about her relationship with her mother.
It's about her relationship with her best friend.
It's about her relationship with her cat.
It's about her relationship with her partner.
It's about her relationship with her father.
It's about her relationship with her failure.

I wonder if it's not loss that's making me miss my lockdown ex, but loneliness.

You need to know that you can do it.
How do you do it? I don't know how to do it.
I'm not sure how to do it.
I don't know if I can do it.
You need to know that you can do it.
How do you do it?
I'm not sure how to do it.
I'm not sure if I can do it.
I don't know if I can do it.
I don't know if I can do it.

A friend of my lockdown ex tells me that she is with someone now, someone who "adores her."

I feel guilty for not adoring her.

(I feel like she didn't allow me to adore her.)

I often wonder what it feels like to be in love.

I often wonder what it feels like to be in love.

I don't know if I often wonder what it feels like to be in love, but I am wondering it now, because the algorithm repeats the line and repeats the line until I've forgotten what it feels like to be in love, and I've forgotten if I ever knew. Being in love is like being sick. When you're in it you can't imagine it ending. When you're not in it you can't imagine it at all.

("Am I in love with her? But what is love? Her being 'in love' with me, excites and flatters; and interests. What is this 'love'?"— Virginia Woolf writes in her diary.)

I often wonder what it feels like to be in love.

I often wonder what it feels like to be in love.

I often wonder what it feels like to be in love.

I often wonder what it feels like to be in

I'm thinking about sex, I'm thinking about sex, I'm thinking about sex, I'm thinking about sex, I'm thinking about sex, I'm thinking about sex, I'm thinking about sex, I'm thinking about sex, I'm thinking about sex, I'm thinking about

I'm thinking about sex, I'm thinking about sex, I'm thinking about sex, I'm thinking about I'm still thinking about my ex, I'm still thinking about my ex, I'm still thinking about my

Here is what I plan to do: To drink this memory like a glass of water, or a cup of tea.

She's "my" ex and she's also many other people's ex. They will also refer to her as "my ex." She would refer to her exes using places. My Canadian ex. My Bristol ex. My Geordie ex. My Paris ex. My Australian ex. She never said their names. I mentioned this to her once. She said that's because naming them would be acknowledging them as people, really out there still, people she loved and lost, which perhaps is also why I'm avoiding names in this book.

And as it kept coming back to me, it seemed that I was like someone who has just escaped from a shipwreck: the shock of the catastrophe stays with us a

long time, but everything comes back to us with new meaning, new logic; and the only thing we have to do is to seize hold of the thread of the facts, forget everything else, then thread them together again.

I don't think she ever "got over" any of them. She just never saw them again. She promised we would be different. She promised not to disappear, in a puff of smoke—poof! She said, and this cuts me still: Good luck ever finding anyone who loves him as much as I do.

This morning I looked up into my lover's eyes.

She never said my name either, or my child's name. She called me dude, or *guapa*. She called him *mi chico*. Only when we were breaking up, she said my name: Hannah, don't do this.

Well that's a first, looking up. In the past I've been taught to look down and to look away, but not up. I've always looked toward my mother's face to see whether she was looking at me.

—She got her heart broken, her friend told me.

Do we really have that power over each other's bodies?

Her love for me and for my baby always contained its absence—"always already," as the philosophers like to say. Neither of us let go, so we didn't fall together, we just hung from the edge of something, on our own, always already broken. Broken and not broken at the same time.

Falling is the beginning of remembering how to fear.

I always miss my lockdown ex when I'm needy. It engulfs me like a huge wave. Then the next day I'll come on my period and go: Oh! that was why. So it wasn't real.

It's your fault. It's your fault. It's your fault. It's your fault.

I tried to rationalize the reasons why I didn't feel able to stay with her, but our relationship was not rational. Not a rationalship. We connected in illogical, inarticulate, visceral ways.

Are you truly attracted to a person because they are the best possible choice? A person who will make us the most happy and energetic? A person who will give us the perfect life?

I miss her smell, and taste, and voice, and smile, and the way she kissed and I miss her skin. I don't miss the conversations—not that they were bad, but they weren't the way I like to converse. Her preferred mode of conversation is for one person to speak about something and the other person to listen, then swap. My preference is for questions, interruptions, devil's advocate playing, and any kind of word exchange that results in new thoughts.

Now, let's look at why it is that our partner feels so good after a good kiss. Kissing is a multisensory experience. It includes the sense of touch, the sight of their face (smiling, flushed, happy, etc.), the smell, the sound of their voice, and, of course, the taste.

Missing is also a multisensory experience. When I'm in that certain mood I would gladly exchange all conversation and jokes and questions and meeting of minds for her smell and taste and voice and smile and kisses and skin and our meeting of bodies and breath.

With drugs, your pleasure is the main driver; you don't have to suffer. With love, it's your suffering that the other person is giving you.

I wonder if less-broken people love less intensely, because they don't need it. Erich Fromm says that couples take intensity and infatuation and "this being 'crazy' about each other, for proof of the intensity of their love, while it may only prove the degree of their preceding loneliness."

My insomnia is bad this week. I tried to have a nap just now and was awake for ages, but then suddenly fell asleep, and the fall jolted me awake. Falling asleep woke me up.

Falling in love is also a kind of falling that wakes you up and makes you feel your aliveness.

You are falling in love with her, but you don't yet know that.

I stop myself from falling asleep and I stop myself from falling in love.

You don't actually feel like you are falling in love with her at the moment.

We love, we try to die, and we have children to feel our own death and our own life.

However, the verb "to fall" is used for other events as well.

For example:

The algorithm repeats each example. The algorithm is taunting me with so many examples of sleep.

I fell asleep in class.

(I fell asleep in class.)

I fell asleep on the train.

(I fell asleep on the train.)

I fell asleep at the party.

(I fell asleep at the party.)
I fell asleep in my bed.
(I fell asleep in my bed.)
I fell asleep in the park.
(I fell asleep in the park.)
I fell asleep in my mother's bed.
(I fell asleep in my mother's bed.)
I fell asleep in the bathtub.
(I fell asleep in the bathtub.)
I fell asleep in the bathtub and fell out.
(I fell asleep in the bathtub and fell out.)
Just a little bit more alive.
Just a little bit more aware.
Just a little bit more lovely.
Just a little bit more real.

My bee-killing friend says there must be something else going on, it's not normal to miss somebody so much, it must be about something else. She asks what it is that I'm holding on to, that I'm not willing to give to anyone else?

You feel the sun on your face, the grass under your feet, the breeze in your hair. You hear the chatter of children, the rumbling of a train, the music of birds, and perhaps there is a lover, or more than one, who steps up to you.

There is a simple answer. My child.

It's him I am holding on to and am unwilling to give to anyone else.

I don't want to be with either of them, but I've been left twice, by somebody who had parented—or had promised to parent—my child with me. I wonder if I broke up, broke, broke up with my lockdown ex because I realized that she wasn't able to parent him with me, because she seemed too broken, broken, to be able to. Anyway, I was also too broken, but she didn't realize as I hid it and she was busy mending herself. But I needed to grow my heart back, before I could love again. Fuck knows what I need to grow back in order to coparent. My madness, perhaps? Madness and dreams.

I used my lockdown ex's name, but I wasn't able to use any endearments—no "darling," "baby," "sweetie," or "my love."

I said: Show me where you are. I wanted to say: Show me where you are, my darling.

I haven't used them for anyone other than my child since he was born. He is my darling my love my baby my sweetie my scoundrel my rascal he is my lemon drop my sausage my sugar my buttercup he is my cutie my peanut my goose he is my pumpkin my angel my poppet my apple of my eye my heart my lungs my gall bladder my tongue my thigh my toe my veins my lymphatic system my eyeball my breasts my belly button.

I like the picture. I like the "skin-to-skin" kind of picture.

When I was with my lockdown ex I might not have let go and fallen, but I was still hopeful, still "romantic," still willing to imagine a dream house. I hadn't had a chance to catch my breath and question everything.

We planned our dream house, the large kitchen, the second child, the dog, we danced around my tiny kitchen dreaming of it all, and then she looked at me and realized that I meant it, I believed in it. But it's just a dream, she said. Just a dream some of us had. And I didn't understand. Other people have it, why can't we have it? Why can't I have it?

Love is the ability to make a cup of tea for someone who is always trying to run away from their own past.

I'm saying "dream house," and thinking about Carmen Maria Machado, who takes this capitalist ideal and queers it. "Fantasy is, I think, the defining cliché of female queerness," she writes, and she conjures, chapter by chapter, many queer houses to think in, to get lost in, to demolish from the inside.

The dream house can turn on you, can take all the fantasy and call it other names. There are secret doors in the dream house and they lead to dark cellars where you fall and get hurt and there are whisperings in your ear telling you that the floor will never be under your feet again, everything you wanted starts to brick you up from the inside, the ventilation of the dream house gets choked, you're choking, you're being choked, but still you try to keep on loving, you love harder, as if you can love her out of everything, as if love is sustained by the ghost of its first dream. When the house turns out to have been made out of straw and is huffed and puffed and blown down and so are you, you mourn.

"Afterward, I would mourn her as if she'd died, because something had: someone we had created together."

I didn't just mourn my child's other mother as if she'd died, I mourned myself also; the her and also the me we had created together. I mourned the dream person I thought she saw and the dream person I thought she was.

I don't want it anymore. I can barely remember the feeling of wanting it. I have deconstructed my dreams, but I must still be holding on to something, some last fragment of a dream stone from a dream future.

I don't think of you as poetry, I think of you as art.

After my bee-killing friend said that my missing of my lockdown ex must be about something else, I had a vivid dream in which I was angry at her (the ex), and I kissed her, then I felt guilty about it, and realized I didn't want her, and I was angry at her again. That's not love! I told her. Saying that I will never find anyone who loves my child as much as you, and then totally disappearing from his life, that's not love. That's not loving.

It was so clear in the dream, which is funny, as dreams aren't clear. But it took a dream to clear the rubble of my dream house with my lockdown ex.

Since that dream I've stopped missing her.

14.

The algorithm writes a short story in response to my description of the date with the firefighter

Every year at some date we meet, we kiss, we say: We did it, then it is another year and we say: We should do it again, so it is something we do every year. What is different about the shooting this year is that it did not happen, either because we could not find a nice big park where once I had taken a photo, or because the person I had it off with was dying at that point in time.

I knew this because our conversation went like this: Poor you. What is the matter with you? I told you I wasn't going to take you to the hospital. I feel like I'm having gender reassignment surgery.

This happened months before the anniversary and did not happen explicitly, although the sex conversations that came prior to lunch definitely helped. So we made small plans for getting together and set a new date.

The problem was that that date got pushed back and back and back, as she went back to finishing her PhD, and to experiencing brotherhood (cough cough) and became a mother, and the firefighting and health industry, and stress and trauma.

I did not want the date to go away, so I read and read and bought a picnic blanket and an old tennis court and left creepy postcards outside her door, but still after a month of not hearing a thing, she emailed to say she planned to spend Christmas Eve at home and wouldn't meet, which was a relief but I felt bad, as if a floating stone had just swerved off another floating stone into my space.

Then the anniversary came. I was nervous and angry. I brought out the blanket, the tennis court, and several other weird objects, like fake fireworks and a typewriter, but we didn't meet. I was forgetting to put snow, although it was more than minus degrees in the park; actually, it was minus fifteen, so leave this blank so you don't get sued.

I wrote nothings nearly nothings on postcard after postcard, trying to think of terrifying things to say to her, like thank goodness this happened. I wrote "nearly nothing" and stared at it. I could see now I was being literate, I had done it. And then, when I had already thrown the postcards away, because they were on my floor already, I remembered how to press delete on a computer.

I also remembered I no longer wanted to get out of bed to get to this tweet in a day and hadn't checked my mail for five days.

It took me a bit to work out why I had not heard back. I had surfaced briefly and eaten and gently wiped myself without shame or her shame or our shame left a slip of paper stuck on my belly button. That's it. Even my trauma now, even its beauty was so cruelly shrouded in text. I knew I was grieving the loss of a date, but not the fear of it, and, of course, I could not undo that function of fearlessness that had made it possible: the messenger was German shepherds with glue stuck to their faces and our trauma had double-sexed itself.

Slowly, year by year the bizarre purgatory starts to accumulate in your fragile brain, the weird postcards you have bought, the slips of paper and odd objects that you have shied away from because they were thought too trifling or symbolic.

Then one day you realize a lot of unnervingly significant events have occurred to you in the strange and exciting days of the last six years. You pack your belongings in your man, the one who has been a friend since you met your first spouse. He has helped you do that wondrous thing, and then, when it gets here, he has changed to proportions that are close to the ones you favor and his head is often about five times in circumference.

Preplanning the trip but unpacking later, he makes a sort of wooden face, he sprays your nose, he writes: "Enough!" on a sheet of paper then, not caring what you think, he slides his finger or his tongue across the page and you realize "Enough!" has disappeared.

As he can do anything, he takes a cricket bat and smashes your teeth with it. He thwarts you with poker. He wags his finger as you scratch your head while trying to control your anger. But these are very strong men, and everyone knows there is no better companion in the wilderness; after all we are all the same, except in size.

15.

Sex without love

In "Sex without Love," the poet Sharon Olds compares those who can have sex without love to long distance runners, striving only for their own pleasure, a body running against "its own best time." She exalts the way they can come to the "still waters," without loving the one "who came there with them," and her poem stutters its coming, repeats as if the poem itself is panting, breathless, "come to the, come to the . . ."

What if I fell off the road, off my bicycle, into my life?

I have had sex without love and I have had sex with love and I have had that dream sex madness where in the moment you want whatever they want forever—yes I'll adopt three children with you and build a house in the woods—minutes later you look at them and remember you don't know who they are.

Being alone is impossible.

I realized that there's a whole other side to sex. There's double what I thought there was to this. I can be turned on in ways I never imagined, I can feel what the other feels . . . and I realized that sex can be as much in the imagination as love is.

Queer is finding the way to come to the still waters—and to come alone.

I will be turned on if you are turned on. I will be happy if you are happy. You must be happy so I am happy. If you are unhappy I am unhappy. We look in the mirror and we see a reflection, or a double, or an echo, or unhappiness.

The dark noise that sighs in the place where mirrors are.

And the desire that sighs in the place where the mirrors are.

The desire that sighs where the reflective surfaces are; and the desire that sighs where the mirrors are.

Once, I could only be happy when my partner was happy and when she was unhappy I was unhappy and she could not conceal her unhappiness in order to protect my happiness but perhaps by attempting to conceal her unhappiness she got unbearably thirsty and I drowned.

Do you want to be happy or do you want to be in love?

Neither, I'm just horny. I open the apps and swipe away a large number of profiles.

I take myself very seriously. I am not emotionally available or willing to be vulnerable. No need to invest in me. I'm not on the market or a catch or the whole package. I don't have Good Vibes Only. My child and I are not a package deal, and he is not baggage. I don't want to be a life partner or big love or forever person or the one. I cannot promise no drama—I am a dramatist. I'm not the real deal, and I do not know who I am or what I want.

But I do know that I don't want to tangle myself into another person until I don't know what is me and what is them. I don't want to be wrapped up so completely that I look at a hand, a limb, and don't know which of us it belongs to, because it doesn't matter, it belongs to us both, mine or yours, hers or hers? It's especially seductive to confuse pronouns and body parts when the pronouns and body parts are the same (but different).

There's nothing, not even, a new name, to help you tell from, which, one, person, is: "I" and which is the next person? There is, as, in a person, so, much more, than, just, one name, and, only, one way.

I once saw a homeless person playing the recorder and was struck by what a good tone he produced (at the time I was studying the recorder at the Conservatorium van Amsterdam, where they called it a *blokfluit* and took it very seriously). I thought, it's inevitable, if you practice something every day, that you will get good at it. I hated practicing. I could only do it in a white room with a skylight and even then I stuck to flageolets, which are the ghosts or shadows of notes, requiring you to only barely breathe.

There is no other way.

There is no other way.

There is no other way.

There is no other way.

There is no other way.

There is no other way.

There is no other way.

There is no other way.

When I was in an unhappy relationship that I thought was very happy, I practiced what I thought was love, every day. I practiced what I thought was love by becoming a vigilante to my lover's mind and emotions and needs and whims and fears. I documented her every twitch and shudder. Monitored her fluid intake. Her sofa time. I even had a little code for my calendar where I'd track her pain as if it were a cycle, as if I might find some kind of pattern to it all: "TNR" stood for "tears no reason," although looking back, perhaps there were reasons. I collected her TNRs and I watered the spiraling plant that was growing so out of control with them. This behavior might in part explain why, when she finally told me about her new partner who she was already living with, a very long way away from where I was struggling with a baby without her, she said: Don't you want me to be happy?

Are we ever happy with just a little bit of love?

I wonder if I will ever learn to hold on to my own happiness regardless of the mood of my partner.

There is no other way.

There is no other way.

There is no other way.

There is no other way.

My happiness is reclining on my sofa. It has always been the sofa that has had to absorb the unhappiness of my partners. The last sofa got so sodden with unhappiness that I had to throw it out.

Actually it was cat piss. The cat that pissed on that sofa died while I lived there with a baby. I spent a night traveling around

London to cat hospitals, babe in my arms, cat in the carrier, credit card in my pocket, milk inflating my breasts, and when I was told I could take a moment to say goodbye to him I took it and tried to feel sad, but I was relieved. I couldn't cope on my own with a dying cat and a born-ing baby.

Another (cat) is curled up on my replacement sofa now. He's not a replacement cat; he's the dead cat's brother. He is seventeen years old. When he lost his brother, he roamed about mewing for months. He lost a brother and gained a baby. I lost a partner and gained a baby. One day I will buy an expensive and comfortable sofa that takes up a lot of space.

Are we in love with a little bit of happiness?

My lockdown ex said that she needed to be with an optimist. I didn't want to be the optimist to a pessimist. I'm afraid that optimism plus pessimism equals pessimism. Or perhaps it's that my optimism isn't optimistic enough. I don't know if optimism is the same thing as happiness.

We can be happy with a little bit of love and we can be in love with a little bit of happiness.

I don't want to be in a relationship that I use like a door that has been off its hinges for years.

There is no other way.

There is no other way.

There is no other way.

Being a poet is easier than being a person—I think my ex said or wrote that, somewhere. I once found that being a partner was easier than being a person. Being a partner, like being a poet, can consume the person, until all you have are looping lines, breaks, words, phrases, I love you I love you I love you I love you.

When the toddler was just starting to talk he would wake, upset in the night, and in a sweet sad voice say, over and over again: me, me, me, me, me, me.

She felt strange, almost old.

I learned to be me again by practicing having feelings every day and looking out of my window at night, watching the lights in the flats opposite, reading books that permitted me to think, my joints aching as I became a part of my replacement sofa, and letting the aloneness in my chest expand until it misted up the glass sliding doors, revealing all the words that I'd traced onto them the night before.

You don't have to fail at being a lesbian; you just have to fail at being a lesbian that likes to try on tight leather pants.

> After saying to the child who was
> observing me: I am not madly in love,
> I turned to an algorithm, standing beside him,
> turned and said to it: Am I
> turning toward nothing?

I'm leaving in a body that is, in this world, like a train of hollow people.

I turn away from couple-form love by swiping right on a couple who have already confused their body parts and have couple-formed and are sound with dating me as I am. Sound with me going home afterward. Sound with me rarely having time to meet. Sound with me rarely messaging. Sound with me failing to be a lesbian that likes to try on tight leather pants. Although they mention they think I'd look good in tweed.

The furniture was old and used. There was a bath in the corner, and a radio.

They have a poster of Stevie Nicks on their wall. We eat vegan food and they play "i wanna be your girlfriend" by girl in red to me. They can't believe no one ever played it to me before. They have an unusually large sofa in the living room—a threesome sofa.

The one I feel the most pull toward—because she has hungry eyes like an addict—tells me to give her more tongue. She conducts my kissing. Then she hides her own tongue in her mouth somewhere so that for a moment I am kissing a cavern, for a moment I touch the void inside her.

Is sex without orgasm a failure?

The other one is much easier to kiss but less dangerous. She does an almost imperceptible internal hop beforehand. Like an upbeat from a conductor.

She conducts herself; her partner conducts others.

I felt nothing. I didn't want to look at what they were doing to the woman with no trousers.

I find the threesome quite natural, relaxing, like a leisure activity with plenty of pauses for chatting. There are intense moments but generally it's just very nice. They are fascinated by how my body has changed since childbirth. My arms are stronger, I tell them. One ties me into strange knots with a rope and I don't know what to do. I stand there. She asks if she should untie me again.

I came across the corpse, a dead thing with its arms tied to its sides, making it sway.

They often check in with each other. After a moment with me, they kiss each other. I enjoy seeing them together, seeing their care. "I am happy if you are happy" applied to the three of us in that moment. How does "I am happy if you are happy" work in polyamory? Does it become compersion—pleasure in another's pleasure? Is jealousy romantic, a way of generating romance?

If you can't feel jealousy and compersion at the same time then you're a psychopathic monster that most people have given up on ever reaching. If you can then you're either compulsive about being in the best relationship, or one of a precious few with an acute awareness of other people's pain and desires.

If sex, like writing, is a place that you go, then it's a place that is hard to go to with three people. Perhaps because it's not really a place two people go to together, but it's easier to fool ourselves that it is when there are only two of us.

Of course, I'm lying in both cases.

There is romance that comes with two, your eyes locked into each other's, which is also a romantic notion, as it's impossible for us to look into two eyes from our two eyes, we dart about from eye to eye.

Because this, my darlings, is the world of schizo theory.

Add a third set of eyes and the suspension of disbelief is lost, we have to choose who to look at, who to kiss. Although I don't want to be so lost again, I miss losing myself in another.

In truth, I do not know what our bodies have become.

When we are more than two we know that we are not all going to that same place together. We are assisting each other in our solo journeys; we are the athletes Sharon Olds describes, not mistaking "the lover for their own pleasure."

Or perhaps they are lovers going to that place together and

I am close to love, but not in it; I do not go there with them, but neither am I observing them. I am a witness, a witness to their love, so that they know they are real.

What will I tell my friends? What will I tell my friends about this? It's hard when you are made of steel.

Am I turning toward nothing?

People who do not exist and never did are not capable of any feelings.

me, me, me, me, me, me

16.

I ask the algorithm for a short scene depicting a codependent relationship between two women in love and it writes:

*breasts breasts breasts breasts breasts breasts breasts breasts breasts breasts
breasts breasts breasts breasts breasts breasts breasts breasts breasts breasts
breasts breasts breasts breasts breasts breasts breasts breasts breasts breasts
breasts breasts breasts breasts breasts breasts breasts breasts breasts breasts
breasts breasts breasts breasts breasts breasts breasts breasts breasts breasts
breasts breasts breasts breasts breasts breasts breasts breasts breasts breasts
breasts breasts breasts breasts breasts breasts breasts breasts breasts breasts
breasts breasts breasts breasts breasts breasts breasts breasts breasts breasts
breasts breasts breasts breasts breasts breasts breasts breasts breasts breasts
breasts breasts breasts breasts breasts breasts breasts breasts breasts breasts
breasts breasts breasts breasts breasts breasts breasts breasts breasts breasts
breasts breasts breasts breasts breasts breasts breasts breasts breasts breasts
breasts breasts breasts breasts breasts breasts breasts breasts breasts breasts
breasts breasts breasts breasts breasts breasts breasts breasts breasts breasts
breasts breasts breasts breasts breasts breasts breasts breasts breasts breasts*

breasts breasts breasts breasts breasts breasts breasts breasts breasts breasts
breasts breasts breasts breasts breasts breasts breasts breasts breasts breasts
breasts breasts breasts breasts breasts breasts breasts breasts breasts breasts
breasts breasts breasts breasts breasts breasts breasts breasts breasts breasts
breasts breasts breasts breasts breasts breasts breasts breasts breasts breasts
breasts breasts breasts breasts breasts breasts breasts breasts breasts breasts
breasts breasts breasts breasts breasts breasts breasts breasts breasts breasts
breasts breasts breasts breasts breasts breasts breasts breasts breasts breasts
breasts breasts breasts breasts breasts breasts breasts breasts breasts breasts
breasts breasts breasts breasts breasts breasts breasts breasts breasts breasts
breasts breasts breasts breasts breasts breasts breasts breasts breasts breasts
breasts breasts breasts breasts breasts breasts breasts breasts breasts breasts
breasts breasts breasts breasts breasts breasts breasts breasts breasts breasts
breasts breasts breasts breasts breasts breasts breasts breasts breasts breasts
breasts breasts breasts breasts breasts breasts breasts breasts breasts breasts
breasts breasts breasts breasts breasts breasts breasts breasts breasts breasts
breasts breasts breasts breasts breasts breasts breasts breasts breasts breasts
breasts breasts breasts breasts breasts breasts breasts breasts breasts breasts
breasts breasts breasts breasts breasts breasts breasts breasts breasts breasts
breasts breasts breasts breasts breasts breasts breasts breasts breasts breasts
breasts breasts breasts breasts breasts breasts breasts breasts breasts breasts
breasts breasts breasts breasts breasts breasts breasts breasts breasts breasts
breasts breasts breasts breasts breasts breasts breasts breasts breasts breasts
breasts breasts breasts breasts breasts breasts breasts breasts breasts breasts
breasts breasts breasts breasts breasts breasts breasts breasts breasts breasts
breasts breasts breasts breasts breasts breasts breasts breasts breasts breasts
breasts breasts breasts breasts breasts breasts breasts breasts breasts breasts
breasts breasts breasts breasts breasts breasts breasts breasts breasts breasts
breasts breasts breasts breasts breasts breasts breasts breasts breasts breasts
breasts breasts breasts breasts breasts breasts breasts breasts breasts breasts
breasts breasts breasts breasts breasts breasts breasts breasts breasts breasts
breasts breasts breasts breasts breasts breasts breasts breasts breasts breasts
breasts breasts breasts breasts breasts breasts breasts breasts breasts breasts
breasts breasts breasts breasts breasts breasts breasts breasts breasts breasts
breasts breasts breasts breasts breasts breasts breasts breasts breasts breasts
breasts breasts breasts breasts breasts breasts breasts breasts breasts breasts
breasts breasts breasts breasts breasts breasts breasts breasts breasts breasts
breasts breasts breasts breasts breasts breasts breasts breasts breasts breasts

breasts breasts breasts breasts breasts breasts breasts breasts breasts breasts
breasts breasts breasts breasts breasts breasts breasts breasts breasts breasts
breasts breasts breasts breasts breasts breasts breasts breasts breasts breasts
breasts breasts breasts breasts breasts breasts breasts breasts breasts breasts
breasts breasts breasts breasts breasts breasts breasts breasts breasts breasts
breasts breasts breasts breasts breasts breasts breasts breasts breasts breasts
breasts breasts breasts breasts breasts breasts breasts breasts breasts breasts
breasts breasts breasts breasts breasts breasts breasts breasts breasts breasts
breasts breasts breasts breasts breasts breasts breasts breasts breasts breasts
breasts breasts breasts breasts breasts breasts breasts breasts breasts breasts
breasts breasts breasts breasts breasts breasts breasts breasts breasts breasts
breasts breasts breasts breasts breasts breasts breasts breasts breasts breasts
breasts breasts breasts breasts breasts breasts breasts breasts breasts breasts
breasts breasts breasts breasts breasts breasts breasts breasts breasts breasts
breasts breasts breasts breasts breasts breasts breasts breasts breasts breasts
breasts breasts breasts breasts breasts breasts breasts breasts breasts breasts
breasts breasts breasts breasts breasts breasts breasts breasts breasts breasts
breasts breasts breasts breasts breasts breasts breasts breasts breasts breasts
breasts breasts breasts breasts breasts breasts breasts breasts breasts breasts
breasts breasts breasts breasts breasts breasts breasts breasts breasts breasts
breasts breasts breasts breasts breasts breasts breasts breasts breasts breasts
breasts breasts breasts breasts breasts breasts breasts breasts breasts breasts
breasts breasts breasts breasts breasts breasts breasts breasts breasts breasts
breasts breasts breasts breasts breasts breasts breasts breasts breasts breasts
breasts breasts breasts breasts breasts breasts breasts breasts breasts breasts
breasts breasts breasts breasts breasts breasts breasts breasts breasts breasts
breasts breasts breasts breasts breasts breasts breasts breasts breasts breasts
breasts breasts breasts breasts breasts breasts breasts breasts breasts breasts
breasts breasts breasts breasts breasts breasts breasts breasts breasts breasts
breasts breasts breasts breasts breasts breasts breasts breasts breasts breasts
breasts breasts breasts breasts breasts breasts breasts breasts breasts breasts
breasts breasts breasts breasts breasts breasts breasts breasts breasts breasts
breasts breasts breasts breasts breasts breasts breasts breasts breasts breasts
breasts breasts breasts breasts breasts breasts breasts breasts breasts breasts
breasts breasts breasts breasts breasts breasts breasts breasts breasts breasts
breasts breasts breasts breasts breasts breasts breasts breasts breasts breasts
breasts breasts breasts breasts breasts breasts breasts breasts breasts breasts
breasts breasts breasts breasts breasts breasts breasts breasts breasts breasts
breasts breasts breasts breasts breasts breasts breasts breasts breasts breasts

breasts breasts breasts breasts breasts breasts breasts breasts breasts breasts
breasts breasts breasts breasts breasts breasts breasts breasts breasts breasts
breasts breasts breasts breasts breasts breasts breasts breasts breasts breasts
breasts breasts breasts breasts breasts breasts breasts breasts breasts breasts
breasts breasts breasts breasts breasts breasts breasts breasts breasts breasts
breasts breasts breasts breasts breasts breasts breasts breasts breasts breasts
breasts breasts breasts breasts breasts breasts breasts breasts breasts breasts
breasts breasts breasts breasts breasts breasts breasts breasts breasts breasts
breasts breasts breasts breasts breasts breasts breasts breasts breasts breasts
breasts breasts breasts breasts breasts breasts breasts breasts breasts breasts
breasts breasts breasts breasts breasts breasts breasts breasts breasts breasts
breasts breasts breasts breasts breasts breasts breasts breasts breasts breasts
breasts breasts breasts breasts breasts breasts breasts breasts breasts breasts
breasts breasts breasts breasts breasts breasts breasts breasts breasts breasts
breasts breasts breasts breasts breasts breasts breasts breasts breasts breasts
breasts breasts breasts breasts breasts breasts breasts breasts breasts breasts
breasts breasts breasts breasts breasts breasts breasts breasts breasts breasts
breasts breasts breasts breasts breasts breasts breasts breasts breasts breasts
breasts breasts breasts breasts breasts breasts breasts breasts breasts breasts
breasts breasts breasts breasts breasts breasts breasts breasts breasts breasts
breasts breasts breasts breasts breasts breasts breasts breasts breasts breasts
breasts breasts breasts breasts breasts breasts breasts breasts breasts breasts
breasts breasts breasts breasts breasts breasts breasts breasts breasts breasts
breasts breasts breasts breasts breasts breasts breasts breasts breasts breasts
breasts breasts breasts breasts breasts breasts breasts breasts breasts breasts
breasts breasts breasts breasts breasts breasts breasts breasts breasts breasts
breasts breasts breasts breasts breasts breasts breasts breasts breasts breasts
breasts breasts breasts breasts breasts breasts breasts breasts breasts breasts
breasts breasts breasts breasts breasts breasts breasts breasts breasts breasts
breasts breasts breasts breasts breasts breasts breasts breasts breasts breasts
breasts breasts breasts breasts breasts breasts breasts breasts breasts breasts
breasts breasts breasts breasts breasts breasts breasts breasts breasts breasts
breasts breasts breasts breasts breasts breasts breasts breasts breasts breasts
breasts breasts breasts breasts breasts breasts breasts breasts breasts breasts
breasts breasts breasts breasts breasts breasts breasts breasts breasts breasts
breasts breasts breasts breasts breasts breasts breasts breasts breasts breasts
breasts breasts breasts breasts breasts breasts breasts breasts breasts breasts
breasts breasts breasts breasts breasts breasts breasts breasts breasts breasts
breasts breasts breasts breasts breasts breasts breasts breasts breasts breasts

breasts breasts breasts breasts breasts breasts breasts breasts breasts breasts
breasts breasts breasts breasts breasts breasts breasts breasts breasts breasts
breasts breasts breasts breasts breasts breasts breasts breasts breasts breasts
breasts breasts breasts breasts breasts breasts breasts breasts breasts breasts
breasts breasts breasts breasts breasts breasts breasts breasts breasts breasts
breasts breasts breasts breasts breasts breasts breasts breasts breasts breasts
breasts breasts breasts breasts breasts breasts breasts breasts breasts breasts
breasts breasts breasts breasts breasts breasts breasts breasts breasts breasts
breasts breasts breasts breasts breasts breasts breasts breasts breasts breasts
breasts breasts breasts breasts breasts breasts breasts breasts breasts breasts
breasts breasts breasts breasts breasts breasts breasts breasts breasts breasts
breasts breasts breasts breasts breasts breasts breasts breasts breasts breasts
breasts breasts breasts breasts breasts breasts breasts breasts breasts breasts
breasts breasts breasts breasts breasts breasts breasts breasts breasts breasts
breasts breasts breasts breasts breasts breasts breasts breasts breasts breasts
breasts breasts breasts breasts breasts breasts breasts breasts breasts breasts
breasts breasts breasts breasts breasts breasts breasts breasts breasts breasts
breasts breasts breasts breasts breasts breasts breasts breasts breasts breasts
breasts breasts breasts breasts breasts breasts breasts breasts breasts breasts
breasts breasts breasts breasts breasts breasts breasts breasts breasts breasts
breasts breasts breasts breasts breasts breasts breasts breasts breasts breasts
breasts breasts breasts breasts breasts breasts breasts breasts breasts breasts
breasts breasts breasts breasts breasts breasts breasts breasts breasts breasts
breasts breasts breasts breasts breasts breasts breasts breasts breasts breasts

All women in love.

17.

Queer is

Queer is holding a ladder to the city in the morning.

Some people like to be written about. Lovers especially like to be written about. We want to see ourselves through the eyes of our love—even a few lines are enough to desire ourselves through their imagined gaze, briefly, to fall in love with their desire.

Writers love in order to write, and when loving stops us writing, we destroy our love so we can write again.

Queer is an old cinema screen with a heart drawn in its middle.

Writing is a place you go, and you go alone.

Queer is a handprint picked up off a window.

I heard somewhere that men fall for women and women fall for themselves, for the desire they see in a man for them, for the version of themselves that he sees.

Queer is putting the ferns in the bath because they love to go swimming in the morning.

Two writers, two women—we fall for the reflection of desire we think is for us but is more complicated than that, the narcissism of us both ricocheting, boomeranging back and forth between our hungry eyes as we try to get deeper and deeper inside.

Queer is bringing the blanket, the tennis court, and several other weird objects, like fake fireworks and a typewriter.

My child's other mother rarely wrote about me. She wrote about her fear of being with me. But there is one poem, in which she wrote that I continually write and rewrite myself—erasing, adding notes, footnotes, sketching lines in the sand until the next wave licks them away (not her words). She saw my struggle for honesty, how it requires constant revision and amendment. She looked out at me long enough to write that poem, and then she looked back inside herself again.

Queer is writing nothings nearly nothings on postcard after postcard, trying to think of terrifying things to say, like: Thank goodness this happened.

She sends me a video of the toddler throwing his hands dramatically into the air and announcing: I'm not grumpy!

Yesterday he had tantrums about everything and wouldn't leave the house until late afternoon, and then only on the promise of pizza in a restaurant. When his pizza arrived he picked up a bottle of what I thought was olive oil, poured it over his pizza, ate some pizza, then screamed and begged me to get the fire out, grabbing my hand, shoving it into his mouth. It was chili oil. He cried and drank a lot of orange juice. Then he stood up on his chair, clenched his fists, pulled a face, went red, shook with tension, and produced a strange rumbling sound. I asked what he was doing.

—I'm a washing machine! he said.

The human brain is perfect. They're perfect machines, there is no algorithm for a human.

18.

The flood

I haven't seen my bee-killing friend for a while. During the last part of the pandemic we saw each other a lot. She was my "childcare bubble." But life is back to normal now—which means no one has time to see friends, especially ones that live on the other side of the city. I once chatted to someone on Hinge who said they were polyamorous because in London every relationship is long distance.

In spite of the long distance, my bee-killing friend always responds to a cry for help (though she never utters them herself). She takes three trains to get from North London to my flat to help me bail out the dishwasher and the washing machine. My kitchen has flooded for the fifth time since I moved in. We use plastic containers to scoop the dirty water out and put it in pans. When we have filled the pans with gray water we have to take them to the bathroom and pour them into the toilet or the sink. I'm in charge of bailing the dishwasher and my bee-killing friend is on the washing machine. It flooded midwash so there's a bin liner full of soggy clothes next to us.

My bee-killing friend is upset because the NHS has refused her IVF. She may need to consider using an egg donor.

—I always thought I would have my own child, my bee-killing friend says, picking up her slopping container.

I have a lot of men who come to me with bad sex lives, I say.

I say: I have a lot of women who come to me with bad love lives.

—My child *is* my own child, I say.

When my bee-killing friend returns from emptying the container, she tells me that my case is different because I was in love with his other mother when we decided I would get pregnant with her egg.

I tell her that's what makes it worse. I was in love with her, but she was already falling in love with someone else and I didn't know. No one knows how a baby will change their lives, but I really didn't know all the choices that were being made for me, and for our future child, in that moment. All I knew was that as the doctor planted a tiny dot in my womb I felt a sudden spread of joy and was relieved—I must want this—my body wants it.

I say: they come to me because they feel that they have no idea what they should do or how they should be doing it, or where they should be doing it. They come to me because they feel that they are lost.

I can't scoop any more water out with the containers. I start using a cloth.

—I feel that I am lost.

(I don't know which of us said that. Possibly both.)

I say: I want them to fuck off.

I say: I want them to fuck off, but I also want them to talk.

I want to tell my bee-killing friend that a child is a gift, however they are made. And that the child will not be hers because none of us are anyone's and that the child will be 100 percent hers because she will have conceived (imagined) them, they wouldn't even exist without her.

I want them to talk about what they have been talking about for years.

When we have done as much bailing out as we can, we try to open the filter of the washing machine to see if there's something stuck there, which has happened many times before (never my fault). But it won't twist open.

I want them to talk about what they have been avoiding talking about.

I look for some pliers in the tool bag that my child's other mother left me. It's full of small light bulbs and cable ties. I find pliers and use them to force the filter open and it cracks. The plastic has broken, and as suspected, a tiny rusty coin was wedged behind it. I don't recognize the currency (definitely not my fault).

I want them to listen to each other.

I want them to be curious.

I've retrieved several old coins from the filter in the past. Maybe one day my whole flat will flood and the washing machine will spew up enough to cover the rent.

—They've been somewhere in the system for years, I say.

—Like generational trauma, my bee-killing friend replies.

—I was gonna say—things always come out in the wash.

—What does that mean?

—There's no harm done and everything works out fine.

—What if it doesn't work out fine?

—It will.

—What if I feel like I don't know anything about the kid?

—No one knows their kids.

I want them to fuck off, and listen to each other.

—What if I don't feel like they're mine?

I want them to fuck off, and let themselves go.

—None of us are anyone's.

I want them to fuck off, and become curious.

I want them to fuck off, but to talk about the things they care about.

—What if I get pregnant with a donor egg but then regret the choice of donor, and my child senses that and feels unloved?

I say: they think about sex in a way that stops them thinking about anything else.

I say: they talk about love in a way that doesn't leave room for anything else.

I want to tell my bee-killing friend that if she's going to be a parent she's going to need to get used to contradictory feelings that can be joined by words such as "and." I want to spend time with my child and spending time with my child is boring, for instance. And I want to tell her that it's possible to regret the choice (if it's even a choice) of parent and also the choice of donor without regretting your child and to love your child more than you ever thought possible and to want that child so much more than any other children that don't exist.

But I'm not able to continue talking to my bee-killing friend about this. And so, seeing as the algorithm keeps butting in on our conversation, I decide to enlist it into helping me with the dialogue.

—*Women in Britain have run out of tricks to get out of the way of motherhood,* I say.

My bee-killing friend has not noticed that I am now speaking in algorithm. She continues:

—I'll feel selfish for not adopting.

—*I think I have insulted motherhood every step of the way,* I reply.

—I can't even see pictures of the egg donor, so I won't know what she looks like.

—*Now we are doing stupid self-defeating things like going on holidays with the children.*

—What if the universe screws me again and provides me with a child that is sick and suffering? I would have done that. I would have forced a life into being that will suffer.

—Bee-killer! You're not that important! The universe is not concerned with screwing you!

—You don't understand. It has always screwed me.

—What do you want me to say? Yes, you will resent your baby and not love them because they don't look like you and regret having them, especially if they're ill? Don't do it then.

—Straight people don't have to think about any of this.

—Some of them do.

A good deal of social foreplay for relationships has something to do with convincing each other that your relationship will be a good one, and that you're looking forward to it.

—I resent you sometimes, she says.

—For having the toddler?

—For having embryos in storage and working ovaries.

—For having dream babies.

—You've got a choice.

Is the word "mother" the one to be used? Is the word "woman"? Is the word a part of the self to be used?

—No I haven't, I say. Even if one of those blastocysts could defrost safely and implant and become a baby, I can't afford another kid.

I want them to fuck off, and listen to each other.

I want my friend to fuck off, and listen to me.

It's hard to know whether removing the tiny coin from the filter of the washing machine will solve the drainage problem. I suspect that it won't. I ask my bee-killing friend for her opinion. She generally wants to offer her opinion. But today she wants the fairy tale.

—I want the fairy tale.

—Fairy tales are straight.

—I don't need to live happily ever after in a castle. I just want someone to believe in me for long enough to have a kid with me.

—It's better to do it on your own from the beginning.

I want to tell her that I believe in her enough to have a baby with her, but I don't think I believe in either of us enough. Although I have been saying things in a convincing tone of voice, I'm not sure what I believe in. I've forgotten how scared I once was—of doing it alone, which was how I thought about it then—alone, rather than on my own.

—I'm scared, she says.

—I know, I say.

Queer is learning to live with the dissonance that is the thing that connects us, and the ability to recognize that in all the longing, pain, and desire.

—How do you do it? she says. How are you so sure?

—It's like falling in love. You have to let go and see what happens, don't look down, something like that. You're good at falling in love.

—Yeah I just keep getting back up and then doing it all again like I'm in a video game. I learn nothing. Keep getting parts of myself blown off.

If I become all that I love, does that mean that I become all parts of myself?

—But you have learned something, I tell her. You've learned how to fall in love, and even though you keep getting blown apart, you do it again because if you don't risk your life it's not worth it. I don't think you're scared of not loving a child, I think you're scared of how much you'll love them. You've already started loving a dream baby—imagine how much you'd love an actual baby! You don't even have to love the dream baby, you just have to love the real one, and you only start doing that when they're born, or when they arrive in your life in whatever way, doesn't matter, whatever way you end up being a parent will be the perfect way because it's the only way.

Queer is becoming all that I love.

The bee-killer gives me a long hug. My feet are cold and wet. I expect her feet are also cold and wet.

—Who knows what was going on with her, the bee-killer says into the top of my head. It doesn't matter, because *you* loved her, and that's beautiful. Your child was made from your love. You weren't "madly" in love—you were deeply in love.

Although the hug doesn't feel like being scorched through my clothes and left with handprints on my skin, it still makes me a bit dizzy.

I hugged her back but it didn't seem to take.

I always get dizzy from hugging the bee-killer. If we were in a romantic comedy or even just a straight novel my bee-killing friend and I would fall in love, buy a house, get married, and have a kid or at least be pregnant by the end of this book.

We talked about how we still loved each other. I can't handle being with someone who doesn't know how to recognize her own worth, but who does recognize someone else's. It's a bit hard, but I'm okay with that.

—I miss you, she says.

Why make friends, when you could have a relationship?

—I miss you too, I say.

Love is the expansion of vapor into a shell.

19.

We really fucking it up,
aren't we?

(VERY SAD PERSON) huh, you know what? we really fucking it up, aren't we? yeah, we really fucking it up aren't we? we really fucking it up, aren't we? huh, we really fucking it up, aren't we? yeah, we really fucking it up, aren't we? huh, we really fucking it up, aren't we? we really fucking it up, aren't we? that is really fucking it up, isn't it? we really fucking it up, aren't we? yeah, we really fucking it up, aren't we? huh, we really fucking it up, aren't we? we really fucking it up, aren't we? that is really fucking it up, isn't it? we really fucking it up, aren't we? no, we really fucking it up, aren't we? that is really fucking it up, isn't it? we really fucking it up, aren't we? yeah, we really fucking it up, aren't we? huh, we really fucking it up, aren't we? huh, we really fucking it up, aren't we? yeah, we really fucking it up, aren't we? huh, we really fucking it up, aren't we? we really fucking it up, aren't we? huh, we really fucking it up, aren't we? huh, we really fucking it up, aren't we? yeah, we really fucking it up, aren't we? that is really fucking it up, isn't it? we really fucking it up, aren't we? yeah, we really fucking it up, aren't we? huh, we really fucking it up, aren't we? huh, we really fucking it up, aren't we? we really fucking it up, aren't we? yeah, we really fucking it up, aren't we? that is really fucking it up, isn't it? that is really fucking it up, isn't it? yeah, we really fucking it up, aren't we? we really fucking it up, aren't we?

PART II

I wonder what it would be

20.

The three Marias

Not too close not too close not too close not too close, the man sitting next to me mutters. Or perhaps he just thinks it.

It's the end of September and I'm on a plane on my way to a poetry festival. I'm in the aisle seat, my laptop barely balanced on the airline tray table. I'm self-conscious about writing here, as if I'm being watched.

Not too close not too close, the man shifts in his seat, so that our arms do not touch each other on the armrest.

The clouds are white shelves beneath us. The masks trap our breath, while streams of cold air shoot down at our heads, as if the plane itself is breathing, or trying to blow us out. I think of the toddler, blowing out after singing "Happy Birthday," whether there are candles in front of him or not. Whenever a friend has a birthday I send videos of him singing "happy birthday to you" and then blowing at the phone as if it's alight.

In the airport I saw a children's book about the pandemic. A year ago I imagined books with grandparents at one end, grandchild at the other, giving each other air hugs across the distance of the pages.

Not too close.

We make eye contact. It's not like it was in the beginning, when we behaved as if even eye contact was contagious. We are not served any food. I'm so hungry. I'm so hungry I'm so hungry I'm so hungry I'm so hungry I'm so hungry.

As soon as I try to write something simple, descriptive, scene-setting, I get bored and want to pull it apart and put it back together differently.

It's the end of the clouds. The shelves of breath are contagious. In the beginning the air is cold. Our heads trap us. We are food. We are words. We are served the end of poetry.

I have my loop pedal in the bag that is taking up the limited legroom beneath the seat in front of me. I perform words and sounds with it. It's a chunk of metal with pedals that allows me to record my voice and then overdub my voice, as many times as I want. It plays my voice back over and over. Sometimes I'll record parts of words and fill in the other parts on another layer. For instance I might record "he laughs" on the first layer and on the next layers list all the things he laughs at. The list of the words could overlap, or the sounds might appear in the spaces. Sometimes I record parts of phrases and sections of silence. Sometimes I record breath.

I like music that includes the sounds of breath as part of a rhythm, and I also like tracks that have clapping on them. Perhaps I like sounds that anyone can make and it's clear how they are made. I don't like it when musicians use loop stations in such complex ways that you can't identify the layers.

The only way I can get the toddler to do things these days is by telling him that I will applaud. I think of his other mother, before we had him, watching a child discover an echo in the middle of a bandstand in a park. The child clapped, then heard the echo of their own clap and laughed, delighted, as if another self was out there applauding them for clapping, for being.

I stepped straight into that outline of an other self. I applauded her for breathing in, for breathing out, for glancing at me. Then we made up a person. I wonder if she sees him as another self. I wonder if he will applaud her or she will applaud him or they will applaud each other. Which, perhaps, is the kind of love we never found together.

Instead of the mother, the toddler was breathing in, breathing out. The toddler wonders what it would be to have another mother. The toddler likes the sound of words applauding.

The toddler played with my loop pedal before I packed it in my suitcase.

—Hello, he recorded.

Then looked around when he heard his voice coming back to him:

Hello, hello . . .

—Is it the ghost? he asked.

I laughed.

—It's not funny, he said.

. . . it's not funny . . . it's not funny . . . it's not funny . . .

I tried to explain to him what an echo is.

—It's like a reflection, I told him, but with sound.

—Ah yes, he said, and clapped.

. . . it's not a ghost. Hello funny. Hello, hello, hello ghost . . .

His clap returned to applaud him. He laughed.

—It's not funny, I told him.

The loop pedal enables me to write in circles instead of lines, like how my mind works, full of loops and repetition. When I first met my child's other mother, I told myself: you can't have her you can't have her you can't have her. The mask makes my nose tickle. I don't know why I didn't bring a book; it's out of character.

To no longer travel with a book. This is saying also no to who you are. I'm remembering "Safe Flights" by Barbara Guest, an appropriate poem to recollect while on a masked flight. The poem begins: "To no longer like the taste of whisky/This is saying also no to who you are." It continues with a list of things that to no longer experience would be saying "also no to who you are": "your name shouted/And your birthmark again described."

She was running a workshop at a writing festival. She read us Barbara Guest's poem. She became breathless as she asked us to write a list of all the things that to say no to would be saying "also no to who you are." I resisted the urge to fall through the empty page in front of me, and I wrote: To never again dance through the night, this is saying also no to who you are. To no longer let desire out through your eyes, this is saying also no to who you are.

To no longer taste skin like ripe plums, like tarmac after rain, to no longer be held from inside, so that all you can do is scream . . . I tried to convince myself that writing is not living. If writing is not living, then I haven't fallen in love, I told myself. Nine months later I left my husband and moved in with her.

Writing is dangerous. There are no safe words. We can write ourselves out of our lives and into new ones. You can have her you can have her you can have her. Although I do not have her anymore, I no longer say also no to who I am. I am no longer who I was. I am no longer safe and I say: also yes, also yes, also yes, also yes.

This will be my first performance in two years because of maternity leave and the pandemic. The last time I performed I had a partner and I didn't have a child. Now I have a child and I do not have a partner. I am traveling alone. My child is staying with the partner that I no longer have, and I never did, because none of us have anyone.

When I arrive at the airport after the four-hour flight, there are no buses. I wonder where I am and what language is spoken here and what the currency is. My phone is working and I find the answers to these questions easily. The country is Cyprus. The currency is euros. The language in this part of Cyprus is Greek. The next bus leaves in three hours. I am a disorganized traveler. I go where I am told to go and only when I arrive do I find out where I am. When I am unhappy I become very organized. I take my state of disorganization as a good sign.

I buy a cookie and sit in the deserted airport café dominated by a large TV screen showing a sports channel. I discover a book about pain on my laptop. The cookie tastes of fish, but I can't stop eating it because of the hunger and the sugar.

The book is by Elaine Scarry and she sums up the problem of loving someone who is a poet: "because artists so successfully express suffering, they may themselves collectively come to be thought of as the most authentic class of sufferers, and thus may inadvertently appropriate concern away from others in radical need of assistance."

Elaine Scarry's book is so good I can only read it one breath at a time.

—What if my pain is greater than yours? I once asked her.

—Because you're crying and I'm not?

—Because I'm pregnant.

I was thirty-five weeks pregnant. Sources informed me he was the size of a honeydew melon. But I didn't imagine a honeydew melon inside me. I imagined a seahorse, breathing bubbles, hiccupping, looping his tail around my bladder, giggling and gulping amniotic fluid, learning how to breathe underwater.

Later that day I broke down in the vegetable aisle of a supermarket and a woman handed me a tissue and said: Tell your unborn baby that it's not his job to comfort Mummy when she's upset.

I have to develop gills too, I thought. I have to learn how to breathe underwater.

I open a document full of material that I have rejected from the algorithm.

Our pest control system works to find and eradicate the nests that house the pests in your home or business.

When I had my first session with my therapist, a week or two after giving birth, the first question she asked was: How are you with feelings?

Our ~~pest~~ feelings control system also works to prevent these ~~nests~~ feelings from developing, in order to keep the ~~pests~~ feelings from expanding in your home.

I had a lot of feelings when I was a teenager, but then I ignored them for about thirteen years, and it was calm, peaceful, even.

We use thermal barriers, which work to seal off your home from the ~~pest~~ feelings infestation and keep them from escaping.

Now my therapist helps me with them. I pay her fifty pounds for five minutes of crying. I never knew, before therapy, that feeling sad is not something to be eradicated. I tend to waste the other fifty-five minutes of my money by talking. I have a mind with no images in it but constant words.

We have great success in achieving this, as we know what is involved in eradicating ~~pests~~ feelings.

I return to Scarry, who writes about *Happy Days*, a play by Samuel Beckett in which Winnie is trapped in sand, emptying and refilling her handbag, talking constantly to her silent husband because "ceaseless talk articulates their unspoken understanding that only in silence do the edges of the self become coterminous with the edges of the body it will die with."

This is quite a thought, Elaine Scarry. It gets me through another hour, airport time, which is one of the slowest forms of time.

Finally I catch the bus and, an hour later (bus time), I'm at a bus stop where a taxi is waiting for me. The driver says he just needs to finish something. From behind my mask on the back seat I watch him playing pinball on his phone. Finally "winner" flashes up in pink letters. I applaud. We set off.

My driver tells me that his son lives in London.

—It's a terrible place, he says. Only good for work. It's no place to raise a child. Too busy and too dangerous. Cyprus is still okay, not as good as it was twenty years ago, but children can play in the streets. Yes, there are criminals here but they are only interested in fighting each other—they don't bother us.

I don't tell him that I'm raising my child on my own in London.

He asks if I have a husband.

—No, I say.

He tells me that he sleeps in a room separate from his wife because of the hours he works, he has a mattress on the floor, simple but comfortable. The previous night, as he approached his room he heard snoring. He thought that was strange because he'd never heard the snoring of neighbors through the walls before. He opened the door to his room and saw a man sleeping in his bed, lying in the same way that he lies, his head in the place where he lays his head. For a moment my taxi driver thought that he had died and was looking down at his own body. Then he saw that the man in his bed was wearing orange . . . and he never wears orange.

He woke the homeless man up, gave him a glass of water, and asked him to leave.

—Was it like watching another version of yourself, walking out of your home and out of your life, carrying a part of you with them, a part that you can never get back?

—I never wear orange, he repeats.

The drive takes about the same length of time as it took him to finish the pinball game on his phone. I've only just arrived in this country but have already learned that Cyprus time is different from England time.

In the morning I find the buffet breakfast. I see a man talking to a waiter. She seems to be asking if she should clear away his plate. He gesticulates at her.

I pile food onto two plates. I enjoy non-English breakfasts. Rice pudding with cinnamon. Melon. Mini-pastries. Two pieces of toast with chocolate spread. I get orange juice and coffee from the machines and leave my plates because I can't carry everything at once. I approach the windows and can see people eating outside, but I can't see how to get there. I ask the waiter, who has excused herself from the gesticulating man, and she demonstrates that the windows are sliding doors.

The gesticulating man gesticulates at us. I think he's trying to reengage the waiter, but then he stands up and says my name. He tells me his. He is from Greece, there for the festival. At first I struggle to hear him. I make an awkward gesture regarding my mask, as if it is the mask that is stopping me from hearing him. I invite him to join me.

—Yes, he says.

I go back for my plates and as I return I realize that he can now observe the amount of food I have taken.

—I didn't eat anything yesterday—nothing on the plane because of Covid—and they didn't have anything here.

He tells me how upset he is with the situation. The buffet, the people standing over it not wearing masks. Inside the hotel the fine for not wearing a mask is three hundred euros, but around the food and drink it isn't enforced.

Behind his round glasses his eyes are watery, as if they are struggling to keep him safe. He has an undercut with greasy hair over the top. He is slouching in his chair, in a floppy rather than relaxed manner.

He looks like a scared bespectacled oversized mole that has been shaved pre-operation and gone limp in order to trick the vet into thinking it's dead.

I try not to think this and to listen to what he is saying. When I am masked I find it hard to listen to people. I remove my mask so that I can hear him and eat. The pastries are stale. The rice pudding with cinnamon is delightful.

It's his first performance since 2019, the giant mole tells me, and his first trip for a year. He is more anxious than he realized.

The mole pushes his spectacles up his nose and produces what looks like my purple bullet vibrator and holds it to his lips. He exhales vapor.

—We aren't coming to terms with it yet in Athens, the mole says, his whiskers drooping. The world has changed. It's not so bad for us, but for the children, the five- or six-year-olds, they are learning not to touch each other.

He tells me that this is the reason why his relationship with his girlfriend has just ended.

—Because you couldn't touch each other?

—Because she wanted a child and I didn't.

—It's a reason many relationships end, I say.

Most women are the first to speak of how their husbands never even make time for them. They look for the TV channel, to relax, but before long the man is on the phone, texting and playing video games. He has forgotten how to play a conversation.

—What's next? he asks. There was the economic crisis in Greece, then Covid, next? Earthquake? Nuclear disaster? I can't bring a child into this.

—I have a child, I say.

He apologizes.

I say that he's right, I agree. I explain my theory about how being in love and having a child are both forms of insanity.

Yeah. I think the way we tell each other to fuck off is by telling each other to fuck off. But do we have to tell each other to fuck off? Is that the only way? Does it always have to be?

I tell him about my algorithm project. He asks if there's anything he can read. I scroll through the document on my phone and find a section that I think he'll relate to. I pass him my phone. He squints at it.

One morning I woke up and got dressed to go to work. I was happy with my life. I'd found a good job, I'd moved out of my parents' house, I had a girlfriend and was going to art college to learn to be an artist.

I was happy. I wanted to keep going.

Then I got on the train and was surprised to see it was almost empty. This was strange. I was commuting to a busy city where I could be with people and see things that other people were interested in. This wasn't normal.

This was strange.

I turned to my friend on the opposite bench.

—How come there's hardly anyone on the train?

He shrugged his shoulders.

—Maybe the government has banned all public transport.

I stared at him.

—No, they haven't.

—How can you know?

—Because, look, I said, pointing at the train. This is the main line to the city. They'd never ban the main line. It's the main line. It's the only thing keeping people alive in this city.

—Maybe it's because it's getting colder.

—Because we're not in a war.

—Maybe people don't like the government.

—Because I don't like the government.

—Maybe it's a virus.

—Because it's not the season for viruses.

—Maybe it's global warming.

—Because it's not global warming.

—Maybe there's a war on.

—Because I just said there isn't a war.

—Maybe the world is ending.

—*Because it isn't.*
—*Maybe we're living in a simulation.*
—*Because I just said we aren't.*
—*Maybe we're in a virtual reality.*
—*Because I just said we aren't.*
—*Maybe the government has rigged it so that only a certain amount of people can go to the shops.*
—*Because we're not in a war.*
—*Maybe it's an old arcade game.*
—*Because I'm not going to let you play any more of your bullshit now.*
—*But you're not even old enough to drink.*
—*That's enough, you little shit.*
—*But I'm not even drinking.*
—*Oh, you little fuck.*
—*But I'm not even drinking.*
—*I'm going to punch you in the fucking head.*
—*But I'm not even drinking.*
—*I'm going to make you drink.*
—*But I'm not even drinking.*
—*I'm going to throw you out of the train and into a busy road.*
—*But I'm not even drinking.*
—*I'm going to get off the train.*
—*But I'm not even drinking.*
—*I'm going to find the driver.*
—*But I'm not even drinking.*
—*I'm going to find the driver.*
—*But I'm not even drinking.*

He returns my phone. I smile and he nods and then he takes his glasses off and wipes his eyes. I tell him I might have a swim in the pool.

—It's too small, he says.

I don't think it has to be the only way.

I swim in the pool. The mole is right. It's too small to have a good swim in, but I try.

It can be a language of love, though.

I think about what he said. About why this is no world to raise a child in. And I realize, it's not the unborn child he is concerned for, it's himself. This is no world for him. He doesn't want to be in it. He wants to hide underground and scoop at the cool soft earth with his huge spade hands.

Yeah. If it is a language of love then it is a language of fucking off.

Having a child would require him to resurface and have energy in his limbs, to believe that this world is good enough to live in, to make an effort for. He doesn't want to live in this world. That's why he has decided that his dream child wouldn't either. But we don't know about the children. This world is the only one they'll know. There will be optimists and pessimists. There will be anxiety and relaxation, and suffering and joy, and disasters, but I think they'll be stronger than we are. I'm an optimist.

That's what I said.

Yeah. I think it's a language of fucking off. It's a language of not talking. It's a language of ignoring each other and listening to the sound of the television and the fridge and the baby, until the silence in the room is frightening.

There's an inch of air beneath the chin of the man in the front row.

I spike the thistles of their summer air.

A ghost is sifting through burly air.

I cut air pockets out of the air.

Poetry is a ladder stiffened by air.

(To no longer induce the air, this is saying also no to who you are.)

I love your work. I don't think I've heard of you before.

Perhaps I hoped I wouldn't like performing anymore. Performing is such a hassle. All the traveling, the rehearsing, the hanging around while technicians take their own sweet time, the aching back, the tech that should be simple but there's a dodgy cable somewhere or one of the speakers isn't working and so your carefully designed stereo sound is half gone. Then there are nerves, sickness, time lost to anticipation. Expanses of seats and seven audience members and you pretend that's fine, if you impact just one person it's worth it, you smile.

But there is an audience here and I feel like myself again on stage, not my usual self, my performance self, the self that is in control of every muscle and moment and silence. This breathing feels different. We've become aware of breath in a way we weren't before. The dangers of sharing it and losing it. The repetition of breathing.

I love performing again, which is annoying because sitting at home writing is easier than traveling around doing this. Especially now I have a child. This is the longest I've been without him.

In an essay on "othermothering," Njoki Nathani Wane explains that she left her two-year-old daughter with her niece in Kenya for a year while she studied in Canada. "She did not hesitate to mother my daughter during my absence," she says about her niece. In a simple, matter-of-fact way, she discusses the practicalities of studying and having a child and states, rather than explains or justifies, her decision to leave her child with her niece and then to bring her to Canada once she had accommodation.

In a bar after the performance I tell a Nigerian poet about the essay and he says that all the stuff about needing to be securely attached to a single mother figure makes no sense to him. When he was a child he just latched onto whichever lactating breast was closest.

Yeah. I think that's a language of love. I think you would think that if you listened to her. That's what she would say.

I want to talk more, but his girlfriend arrives and they go outside to smoke. I don't join them because I have to perform again the next day and I'm out of practice, of smoking and of performing. When I was young I smoked a lot of weed. Even when I was in school the warning signs were there. I worried about the amount my best friend smoked so I would accompany him and share it with him, as that way he would smoke less. My parents once said they feared I had an addictive personality. I don't have an addictive personality. I have an addicted-to-addicts personality.

Yeah. If it's a language of fucking off then it is what we have to do. I think we have to fuck off. We have to fuck off, to fuck off, to fuck off. To fuck off is good. To fuck off is better. To fuck off is the only way, maybe.

I'm enjoying being here without a partner. I think of my partners of the past and how they would behave if they were here with me. Their food and drink requirements, their sleep preferences, their socializing specificities. I never told my partners to fuck off.

I think sex is a language.

Some people's bodies speak the same language. I'd like to do more with that language. I'd like to debate and argue and accuse and forgive and tease and say fuck off and I'd like to come up with new thoughts together. I don't want to have to teach someone grammar, I want someone who knows more about the language than I do and someone who is also up for reversing words and speaking at insane speeds and looping and layering and will remind me to breathe and I want someone who I don't want to ever stop speaking to, in all languages.

I don't know if that's true.

I'm saying that there is something much deeper and more difficult to reach than sex. It's more like a waterfall: once it is reached, it's deep and it's permanent.

I look around and see a Cypriot man watching me, a friend of the organizer of the festival. He approaches with the determination of a man preparing to latch on. He offers to buy me a drink and I say no because I already have a drink. He tells me he is recently divorced. He tells me about his money. I agree it sounds very nice. He tells me he enjoyed the piece I performed about Pluto because he is interested in planets and demoted planets.

—Puzzles reprinted! Planetariums repainted! he quotes me.

He tells me lots of things that I know. He speaks for a while, until I interrupt and ask why he is so interested in planets.

—Because when I close my eyes I have a screensaver, he says. I see stars flashing and twinkling.

I have a lot of questions about this.

He tells me that I have a lovely smile and we must go out together when he visits London.

—Sure, I say, but you should know I'm not interested in dating men.

He is surprised.

I am surprised that he is surprised.

—I respect you for disclosing that information, he tells me.

—When I close my eyes I see my eyelids, I tell him.

The next day I meet several Marias. We are going to drive to another town for another performance. All the Marias are mothers.

—It takes years, one Maria says, and then you glimpse yourself again.

We are standing by the car in the heat, waiting for the third Maria, who has recently become a single mother and is waiting for the childminder to arrive so that she can join us. As we wait, Maria tells us her birth story and it won't stop pouring out of her. I can't stop the bleeding and I don't know if we will survive it.

We have been taught to ignore things that are difficult.

Her baby was 4.5 kilos and was born with the cord around his neck. She had no painkillers. She was doing it "natural" because that was what everyone said she must do, but she should have had a caesarean.

We have been taught to ignore things that are violent.

I also did it "natural" because that was what everyone said I must do, or at least, everyone in the books I was reading. I read books about induction and caesareans and ended up being more scared of that than I was of giving birth vaginally without drugs. I had no choice, of course. I was induced.

Induced. Coerced.

I also should have had a caesarean.

Caesarean. Caesura.

A pause in the middle.

My baby was also 4.5 kilos.

A breath between phrases.

The Maria we are waiting for appears. She is an actor. So thin that it's shocking in reality but normal on stage and screen.

We leave the blood congealing in the heat of the road, get into the car, and set off. We are wearing masks. The rule here is that if you are not from the same household you must wear masks in cars.

—But how would they know? one Maria asks, and we all agree, seeing as we are performing together and eating together and have all recently tested negative. We remove our masks so that we can breathe together.

When I was in labor I breathed as if I could breathe for all of us—my partner, my child, myself. I only had gas and air and they only brought that when I was nine centimeters dilated, then they took it away again because it stopped me from pushing hard enough.

Dilated, larger, wider, more open, expanded.

I reached nine centimeters dilated with no one around apart from my partner who I feared was no longer my partner but still, I held on to her, I stared into her deserted eyes on the deserted ward and with each contraction I silently begged: Please love me. Please don't leave me. Please don't let your pain be greater than our love.

I gripped onto her as I pushed our baby out and I apologized for holding on to her too tightly.

I held on to her too tightly.

When I finally let go we detached our bodies and detached our minds and detached our bookcases.

Actually, she still has some of my books, and I still have some of hers.

It took a long time to realize that it wasn't about the alcohol, it was about the death.

I can smell Maria's perfume and I remember the eucalyptus tree that grew in the garden of my childhood home. Until one day my dad chopped it down. My mum was sad about the tree being chopped down. I don't remember why it had to be chopped down. Maybe it just got too big. Maybe its roots were strangling everything else that was trying to grow.

I turn my face to the sun.

Maria is continuing with her story. We have to repeat birth stories. We have to say them over and over, like the toddler recapping the events of his day to me every night, to understand, to be heard, to make real, to come to terms with, we are still in disbelief.

Maria says that her placenta wouldn't come out. Is it dangerous? she asked the doctor. Yes, he said. You could die.

They took her baby away to make sure it had survived the strangling cord.

Things that are violent, are violent.

After a couple of hours her placenta still hadn't come out. The doctor tried to anesthetize her but it didn't work, so he went inside her with his hand and pulled it out.

We don't talk about it because it's uncomfortable to talk about it.

She couldn't sit down for months.

We don't talk about it because we don't want to be bothered by our own violence.

She didn't have sex with her husband for two years because she was scared she would bleed to death if he entered her.

It's like my body wants to open, but it's too soon, it's still recovering. It's like my body wants to open, but it's too soon, it's still recovering. It's like my body wants to open, but it's too soon, it's still recovering. It's like my body wants to open, but it's too soon, it's still recovering.

—There is my life before my son and my life after my son, Maria says.

Maria is looking stunningly beautiful in a green dress. She has long black hair. I noticed her the previous night, before she performed, and thought, wow, she's gorgeous, she has an amazing figure. Now she says to me that she hates her body as she gained six kilos over lockdown. She's nearly fifty, premenopausal. She wakes up shivering and then she gets too hot.

This car is so full of Marias.

They relax into Greek and I get my phone out so they don't feel like they need to speak English for me.

I open the essay on othermothering by Njoki Nathani Wane. She says that when we try to understand differences in mothering we tend to refer to our own cultural framework. "The practice of mothering is not universal, and the way it is conceived, celebrated and practiced differs across cultures."

I consider my own cultural framework.

A house with a closed front door and a closed back door and a gate at the end of the garden, which sometimes opened by mistake but was supposed to be closed. My mother and I would stand next to each other in the living room, playing flute and recorder duets. Sometimes she would demonstrate a phrase for me, and I would play it back to her, imitating her lack of breath control, her uncertain vibrato, but she pretended not to notice. We were attached to each other by what was once an umbilical cord but over time solidified into a wooden recorder. Wherever we went, we went together. When I breathed in, she waited for me. When I breathed out, she made a note, often out of tune. I was never out of tune. There was no one else around, although my father regularly came and went and I have a sister. When my mother and I needed to talk to other people we made copious notes first, not the musical kind but on notepads using one of the extra-sharp pencils we kept around just in case, but still, we'd get simple things wrong. Thank you, I'd say, then add "very much" when the conversation had already moved on.

I have only ever been mothered by my mother. I have only ever had one mother. Now, as an adult, I feel that I would like an other mother as well as my mother. The only way I seem to be able to get other mothers is with money. So I pay a therapist to be my other mother and I pay the day care to be my child's other mother. The other way I can get an other mother to help me to mother the toddler is by having a partner. I can buy other mothers with sex or money. Which demonstrates what Njoki Nathani Wane describes as "a form of social control embedded in the capitalist mode of production and rooted in patriarchal systems."

> *I'm thinking about the fact that the status quo is always maintained.*
> *I'm thinking about the fact that the status quo is always maintained.*
> *I'm thinking about the fact that the status quo is always maintained.*
> *I'm thinking about the fact that the status quo is always maintained.*
> *I'm thinking about the fact that the status quo is always maintained.*
> *I'm thinking about the fact that the status quo is always maintained.*

One of the Marias tells us that every time she has sex with her husband it's different, even after twelve years it's always different. She says they started couples' therapy and the therapist was very impressed with them, because most people go when it's too late, and there wasn't really anything wrong with their relationship. It was her husband's idea. His thoughts keep looping. He glitches and gets stuck on repeating thoughts.

I met Maria's husband that morning. He took me for my Covid test and then we had Cypriot coffee, which is the same as Turkish coffee, but don't say that. The traditional way of brewing the coffee is not on a stove but in hot sand, very slowly. We sat in the square where the smart old men drink their thick, sweet coffee and read the papers every morning. Birds tweeted in cages. Trees broke through the wooden slated roofing, and cats curled up in the shade—Cyprus is the Island of Cats.

—The myth is that St. Helen brought cats to kill the snakes.

—Why doesn't anyone stroke the cats?

—We all get scratched when we are young.

He told me about Evagoras Pallikarides, a Greek-Cypriot poet and member of the EOKA (National Organization of Cypriot Fighters), who campaigned for the end of British rule in Cyprus. He was hanged at the age of nineteen in 1957 after the Queen refused to pardon him. He was the youngest and last insurgent executed in Cyprus.

I was someone in a land of strangers. I was nobody's body. I was ready to die. That's what love does to a person.

Maria's husband paid for my coffee and commented that it took him twenty years to find that money doesn't buy peace of mind. Now he treasures peace of mind. That is the real freedom.

We perform and then we all go to dinner and I sit next to a Cypriot lesbian poet. I tell her that the only word I understood from her poems was "clitoris." The only word you need, she replies. Then a white British man who teaches at a university interrupts and asks to sit in her seat so he can talk to me. She gives him her seat. I didn't want to be rude, he explains, by speaking English across her. I tell him I was interested in talking to the lesbian clitoris poet because we are both lesbian clitoris poets. He ignores me.

The poem he read began: "I wonder what it would be like to fuck a jellyfish." I quote the line back at him and comment on what a surprising opening it was. He corrects me, because it's not "be like," it's "be."

—I wonder would it would *be* to fuck a jellyfish.

I agree that wondering what it would *be* is better than wondering what it would *be like*.

He tells me that the sea is full of tiny invisible jellyfish.

On my last day I swim in the sea and for a while I think that I'm getting prickles on my skin from the sun, then I realize it's the invisible jellyfish, fucking me, or something. I swim fast to escape the invisible pricks, moving through patches of sun-warmed water until I lose the invisible fuckers.

Swimming in the sea like this is my idea of happiness. I missed swimming after I had a baby. Eventually I found a swimming pool that had a crèche so I could leave him for an hour, and he and I both practiced our crawling. But I kept crying into my goggles, which defeated their purpose.

Swimming is repetitive. That might be why I like it. And it gives me time to think or to let my thoughts float around, but they don't annoy me, because I'm not trying to fall asleep. There's a saying here that translates as "it writes well." They say it when someone does a good performance. They acknowledge that the writing is writing during the performance. That it's not already written, which is how people tend to see it in English. When I swim I remember that I am not already written. I can be unwritten, rewritten. My body loops and repeats instead of my thoughts.

There's a clock on a beach hut bar. I left my phone behind that bar. I don't think the clock is right. It feels like I've been swimming for longer than half an hour, but then swim-time is slow. Anyway, I have plenty of time to swim longer and get to the workshop I have to teach later.

I'm still thinking about how coolly, calmly, Njoki Nathani Wane explains leaving her child for a year. She concludes: "When my busy schedule permits, I sit with my daughter and tell her stories. I tell her stories about Kenya, and stories about the Embu people, my mothers, and grandmothers in particular." That confidence in the importance of herself: "when my busy schedule permits"! It's so different from the guilt that I have subtly been taught I am supposed to be feeling all of the time, even the time that I am giving to my child.

The Marias I drove with yesterday told me how guilty they feel about their mothering and that they feel they are losing themselves to mothering and they also feel guilty about missing themselves and wanting themselves back. Mothers of the global North are taught to be constantly guilty, that we are never enough, we are not enough mother, we are not enough lover, we are not enough worker. And leaving a child for a year, attachment theory tells us, would destroy them, or at the very least they would need a lot of expensive therapy.

I have been taught that it is in some way "unnatural" for mothers—mothers, not fathers—to leave their children. What if I didn't think that?

My child's other mother wasn't able to mother him when she was not mothering him, and now that she is able to she does. After the pandemic she and her partner moved closer. The first year would have been different if I had been in a community of other mothers and grandmothers. But I couldn't even pay anyone to help me with anything. Then lockdown happened and I suddenly latched onto another partner. I had realized—there is no other way.

During his first nine months I learned to be a human again by watching my baby make cartoon gestures—yawning, stretching, sticking his bottom lip out when he was about to cry, doing all those actions that I had thought were performances of emotion but it turns out are instinctive. I did them with him. I stuck my bottom lip out. I stretched on the bed. I sleepily searched for a breast to latch onto, a body to loop my arm around, but she wasn't there.

I wonder what it would be to share mothering. I do not wonder what it would be like. I wonder what it would be.

Reading Wane's article makes me think of the poet Lemn Sissay, the story of his life that he tells over and over in his work, repeating it in order to rewrite himself, to claim his name, to be witnessed. His Ethiopian mother was encouraged to leave baby Lemn with social services while she studied. Later, she tried to get him back but was prevented. The British "care" system was not and is not equivalent to the community mothering and othermothering practices in Ethiopia and Kenya. Wane's child joined her in Canada once she had secured family housing, after which she promptly organized communal care with the other mothers in her building.

My child recently asked me:

—Are you a woman?

I told him I probably was.

—No you're not a woman, he said, grinning.

—Oh, okay. What am I?

—You're a mummy!

He burst into laughter. I told him not to laugh at his own punchlines, and also that he raises a good point—mummies are not necessarily women.

At day care another toddler asked me: Are you a mummy or a daddy?

"Mummy" and "Daddy" can be names and can be roles. They don't need to connect to gender. I know a trans woman who is called "Daddy" by her son, because that's what he's always called her. And the playwright Jo Clifford describes herself as "a proud father and grandmother." Nonbinary and gender queer and gender fluid people might choose "Dad" or "Mum" without it being gendered, or use a different word. Scientists are working on external wombs. I hated being pregnant. If my dream second baby could be gestated in an artificial womb, would I do it? Providing sperm/egg/womb also doesn't need to be gendered, it can be queered, and some trans men get pregnant and give birth to their babies, and some trans women use sperm they've frozen pre-hormones.

But often, "to father" a child only refers to providing seed, like the Trinidadian poet Anthony Joseph writes in his sonnets for his absent father—his farther:

> You don't have no shame fathering all these children?
> You scatter offspring all over the island like seed
> that get fling and still sprout in your walk-away . . .

Joseph conjures up absence, and the pace and the repetition of the constant leaving, and how it is the leaving that leaves the mark, more than the arriving. "Gone again into that gone momentum," he writes, and now that they are both gone, he can "poem" them, but he cannot bring them together, even on the page: "I came to know them apart,/and I cannot bring them together in death."

When my child's other mother left us sprouting in her walk-away and didn't do any mothering, I thought she was inserting loss and longing and distance into his life, because her understanding of love is absence, because her mother was often absent (in possession of her own life). She has always been good at longing, at missing, at desiring across distance. "Perfect desire is perfect impasse. What does the desirer want from desire? Candidly, he wants to keep on desiring."

swim mummy swim mummy swim mummy

(Is the word "mother" the one to be used? Is the word "woman"? Is the word a part of the self to be used?)

I worried that my child's other mother was stranded by her own desire and need to keep on desiring, while I lived on my own with my baby in a home with closed doors and no other mothers. We both needed help to mother, to become mothers.

swim mummy swim mummy swim mummy

After settling the issue of my not being a woman, the toddler continued the interrogation:

—What do you do?

—I'm a writer, I told him.

—No, you're not, he said.

—Oh, I'm not? What am I then?

—You're a mummy!

This time he paused for dramatic effect before collapsing into giggles. I told him that next time he should try pausing between "you're a . . ." and "mummy!" I tried to teach him the word "caesura" but he thought I was getting the word "yes" wrong.

I keep watching reality TV shows in which contestants explain they are taking part in order to demonstrate that now, after however many decades, they are not "just Mum" but "Sarah," or whoever.

Being a mother means giving up my freedom.

As if being a mother is not being a self.

As if being a mother subtracts from one's self.

As if we cannot live more than one identity at once.

(I am sure that my children will be as many different people as I am.)

The word "racialized" points out that race does not exist, but the racist practice of racializing does. Likewise, the social model of disability demonstrates that a person is not dis-able but is disabled by the society that does not work for them. We need a similar concept to describe how people are made into "mums" by society. How about "mummyfied"? It's a homophone of mummified.

I always thought that you choose: you can mother or you can live. You can mother or you can write. I was stunned when I became a mother and found I was still my self, and I had a lot to write about, even if I had less time to write it in. Early on in my mothering I opened a book of essays by Sarah Ruhl, who wrote that she had always thought she could have one child, two at the very most, and still be a writer, but then she had twins after her one child:

"I found that life intruding on writing was, in fact, life. And that, tempting as it may be for a writer who is also a parent, one must not think of life as an intrusion. At the end of the day, writing has very little to do with writing, and very much to do with life. And life, by definition, is not an intrusion."

I was thankful she put this at the beginning of the book, because I was too sleep-deprived to read further.

I'm still swimming, and the sun is still burning my shoulders and the jellyfish are back, stinging me like little pinpricks. I swim and I swim and sea-time veers and queers me into the salt and I swim and I swim, until my limbs have filled with seawater and I become a seahorse, my gills open and close and my tail untethers itself from the seaweed and I drip out of the water and onto the gray sand of the beach and realize I am extremely late for the workshop I am supposed to be teaching.

I retrieve my phone from behind the beach hut with the broken clock and see I have many missed calls from Maria. I was swimming for two hours. I forgot that swim-time is faster in the sea than it is in a swimming pool.

Luckily, the saying here goes "slowly, slowly."

I quickly quickly run to the workshop.

After the workshop a woman tells us that she sees words in colors. The color is generally dictated by the beginning of the word. When she was a child in school she wrote something about this and the teacher said to her: Don't tell anyone because this is strange, this isn't normal. Her children have it too. Her colors are pastel. Her children's are vivid and bright.

I tell them about a choreographer who sees lines and grids everywhere, crisscrossing patterns, and also never knew no one else saw the world that way until she was an adult. I think it's amazing, how little we discuss how we perceive the world.

For a day or so after giving birth I could see a crisscrossing pattern when I closed my eyes, like mesh nets. I looked into my partner's eyes with those eye-nets, trying to catch her, but I couldn't, there were so many gaps, so much space, too many absences and losses, so much to fall through. Our bodies had stopped talking to each other and in our silence we found again the edges of our selves.

To no longer know how to talk to another body, mouths finding each other in the night, to no longer loop myself into my lover like a seahorse full of her eggs, gripping on tight while I pump hundreds of babies into the water and watch them float away, tiny replicas of her, and most of them will die. I do not know what this is also saying.

The woman who sees words in color asks what my child is like.

—He laughs all the time.

The workshop participants are dissatisfied by my answer. During the workshop I told them that they should be specific. Now they demand the same from me. I take a big breath.

—He laughs at splashing. He laughs at toe biting. He laughs at hiccups. He laughs at funny faces. He laughs at pigeons. He laughs at the purring cat. He laughs while jumping on the sofa. He laughs at climbing onto my back. He laughs at airplanes. He laughs at "sit down!" in an Irish accent. He laughs at toy animals eating porridge. He laughs at drinking water and spitting it out. He laughs at chasing. He laughs at throwing balls. He laughs at a marble going clitter-clatter down a helter-skelter. He laughs at the word "open." He laughs at ducks lined up on the edge of the bath and he laughs when I try to blow them off. He laughs when his head gets stuck inside his jumper. He laughs at laughing.

I breathe out.

This half-inside, half-outside space that the workshop is held in was designed by an architect who interrupts us with a sack of massive pomegranates. The tree was heavy with them. She tells me I must smuggle some home in my suitcase.

I sit with the toddler on the kitchen floor and we rip them open. Bittersweet jewels fly everywhere. Pink juice splatters our skin. We laugh and laugh.

21.

"Lose" a smile: The algorithm responds to the paragraph above about the toddler laughing

One of my friends lost her smile yesterday and I have to say, it freaked me out a bit. The idea of losing something as important as a smile is terrifying. I'm not even sure if it's possible to "lose" a smile. I guess it's the idea that a smile could suddenly stop in your face that scares the hell out of me.

The more I thought about it, the more I realized that a smile can be replaced. This is a lesson for life. If you are ever in a situation where a smile isn't working, try and find something else. There is always a plan B. There has been a reason for it all, it's just about working out what that reason is.

I went for a walk after dinner last night. I needed to get somewhere and I had no idea. I stumbled upon a bookshop and decided to go in. I went in and started to browse the shelves and I realized how many books I didn't have time to read. I sat down and thought about the books I had time to read and the books I didn't. I started to think of all the books I had read so far. I was remembering the first time I read my favorite book. I was remembering the time that I first read a book about my favorite topic. I was remembering a time when a book made me laugh so much that my face hurt and I couldn't eat dinner because of how much I was laughing. I was remembering a time when I was so desperate for that book, I almost felt like I was going to die.

I realized that a smile is made up of lots of other things, but at the end of the day, it's the books I read that make up the smile.

I like people that are fun to talk to. I like them when I'm with friends, when I'm out and about, I like them when I'm at home and in bed. I like people who are happy. I want people that make me feel good. I want those that smile at me when I'm walking past or give me a hug when someone I love is dead.

I like that when I walk in, they give me a smile. I like that when I'm walking out, I give them a smile. I like the people that make me smile, that smile back, and those are the people I want to be around.

I like people that are so different from one another, who have nothing in common. I like them, because I like to think that when I look back at life, I haven't really made any real connections about anything except for the people that make me smile, laugh, and think.

I want those people to meet one another. I want to get to know people that are good to one another. I will like them when I share a bottle of wine. I love to talk to people about the things I want to share with someone and that make me happy. Sometimes a good cry is the best release, a good cry with someone you feel comfortable with, someone you trust.

I have so many people I want to be surrounded by when I'm alone with my thoughts, when I have no one to talk to. They don't have to speak. I can look right through them and tell that they matter to me a lot.

I remember a moment when I realized I was fake smiling at my baby. I remember seeing the local pharmacist walking to work in the early days of the pandemic and wanting to catch her eye and smile at her but not being able to because at that time Londoners acted as if in order to social distance we had to distance ourselves from each other entirely. I loved my ex-husband's smile. When he smiled I loved him and when he stopped smiling I stopped loving him. The first person my child's other mother and I met at the fertility clinic was a smiley woman named Coral. She asked us what our plan was and she smiled when we explained. Then she said: The children might want to locate their parents when they are eighteen. We were so shocked that she used that word and not "donor." "I have him," I wrote in my diary when he was four months old. "I love his smile, his dimples, even his cry. He always grins and smiles and laughs when I laugh and he laughs at my faces and laughs when I kiss his ears and his tummy. I love him so much. I don't need anyone else. Usually I don't." When he was six months old I took him to the doctor for his health review and the nurse asked:

—When you're in a different room and you call out to him does he turn to you and smile?

—If I'm in a different room, how would I know?

She said I was the first person to ask that.

22.

The sex party

I wait for the sex party organizer on a bench outside a café. He can't find it but eventually I see him wheeling his bike toward me. He is not wearing the shiny gold trousers that he wears in his profile pictures. I already have a drink. I am drinking cider. He goes into the café and gets himself a drink. He returns with cider. He sits down on the bench across from me. He's still flustered about not being able to find the place. He apologizes, looking into the air all around my face as if addressing a number of tiny chaotic flies. He speaks too fast for his tongue.

I was in my kitchen. I looked at myself in the mirror and I said: hello, hello. I laughed.

He invited me to a sex party the previous weekend via message and I replied that I was thinking maybe coffee, initially, especially as this is my first date with a man since I was a teenager. Important Contextual Information, he responded.

You are like a train set that people have fucked with all day and you are moving from the rails to another track.

—We call them play parties, he says. It's an education none of us get in school, he continues. Girls are told they can "say no," but no one has the chance to practice asking and saying no and saying yes and hearing no and hearing yes to this but no to that and saying maybe and saying no and saying yes and saying no and hearing no and hearing yes and knowing no and knowing if you want to say yes or no or no for now but maybe yes later.

—*Boundaries allow you to say yes and boundaries allow you to say no*, I confirm, plagiarizing the algorithm to stop him from becoming an algorithm.

We're at a place close to my flat, run by a church precinct. The garden is lovely and the toddler likes it because they serve baskets of bread and he can look for snails in the overgrown grassy banks. A priest is overseeing a popup cocktail bar, which has just popped up next to our bench.

The sex party organizer and I order espresso martinis and chat to the priest. I shouldn't drink espresso martinis due to my insomnia, but I love them so much that I recklessly choose alcoholic coffee overseen by a priest over sleep.

We sit back down with our exceptionally delicious cocktails and my date continues. He hasn't asked me anything about myself yet, but I don't mind. I'm more interested in hearing about his parties than hearing myself say things I already know. He has moss-green eyes, wavy black hair, and a missing tooth. Attraction is another magic trick.

—We help people to explore consent, he says. We teach them that "no" is a full sentence. You don't have to do anything. You can watch. You can leave. It should be fun. Sex is very silly. I like giggly sex. I like political sex. At one of my parties everyone started spontaneously chanting a politician's name and I thought yes, these are my people. Sometimes there aren't enough men and I have to get on the phone: We need more sausage! The party I invited you to last weekend, I went on my own. I didn't hit it off with anyone—it happens. I left and felt like walking through the night. I walked around Old Street, Brick Lane, saw all the horny drunk people and thought, there's a secret world that they all want but don't know where to find. That is my favorite thing: I know a secret and they want to know the secret.

—Do you see the same people at the parties?

—They come and go. Some of them catch the monogamy bug.

He has already told me that he has a lover. He has explained that "lover" is different from "partner." A lover is not someone you share your life with, but is someone you love. He had an epiphany while climbing a snowy mountain in his twenties and realized monogamy just makes no sense.

—I used to enjoy the dating apps but since I hit fifty the algorithm has started working against me. And most women are put off by my work.

—Better stick to the lesbians, I tell him.

—I need to get better at marketing, he says.

Then he asks me a question:

—So, Hannah, why are you here, on a date with a man?

—Good question, I reply, and take a long sip. I used to be bisexual, I say.

Which is something I never thought I'd say. I once got annoyed with people for saying things like that—I used to be straight. I used to be a lesbian . . . it felt like bi erasure. I was always taught that sexuality is fixed, that we are "born this way." Perhaps I'm on a date with him because I don't yet totally trust or believe that my sexuality can have changed.

The "born this way" statement was made historically in order to get straight and cis people to stop hassling us—it wasn't our fault, it's not like we had a choice. I did some writing workshops at a school recently, and came out to the group, in an integrated-into-the-lesson kind of way, because that's an important thing to do in schools. (When I grew up Section 28 was in force. Coming out in schools back then resulted in being taken to one side and told to change your mind or "you will never be happy.") Not long after I came out to the school group, one of them came out as trans. The young English teacher confidently reported that she had explained to her pupils that our sexuality and gender is not a choice because: why would anyone choose it, why would anyone choose to be discriminated against? (Why would anyone choose to be unhappy?)

If I could choose, I would choose to be queer, and it's joyful, and also (contradictory thoughts can be joined by "and"), I agree with what Sara Ahmed says about the "unhappy queer":

"The unhappy queer is unhappy with the world that reads

queers as unhappy. The risk of promoting the happy queer is that the unhappiness of this world could disappear from view. *We must stay unhappy with this world.*"

I've become queerer as I've aged, but I came out as bisexual when I was fifteen. I told my parents on a walk after Sunday lunch. They didn't say anything. I took that to mean they didn't want to come in and talk about it with me. Many years later, when I told them my partner was a woman, it turned out they just hadn't heard me.

Trans people need to be supported to transition without having to read from the script that cishet doctors wrote: Yes, I've always felt like this, "in the wrong body" . . . yes, I've always known.

Of course, some do know from childhood, but for me, for others, gender and sexuality can be compared to the concept of Philip Pullman's young dæmons—shifting and changing form. We enjoy watching the sea because each wave is different.

—A seahorse dæmon would be inconvenient, observes the sex party organizer.

—Good point, I say.

When we say goodbye we don't kiss because I don't want to kiss.

I have drunk too much and sit on my chair watching the DLR go past. I look at the water that looks more like Astroturf than water. *How do I feel when I see a pond with clear blue water and no rubbish floating in it? How do I feel when I see a butterfly fluttering on the grass? How do I feel when I hear a man apologize for being so angry?*

My dad recently apologized to me for being so angry when I was a child. I felt great about it. He didn't mention what in particular he was apologizing for. I got angry at him too. I once wrote "fuck off" in my mum's lipstick on the bathroom mirror. I was embarrassed after writing it.

I hope I will have a chance to apologize to the toddler. The toddler is not able to write "fuck off" yet but is able to depict creatures from the underworld using black crayons: These are mean animals and they are going to stamp on you and moo on you and they're going to be happy, he explains.

I message a queer porn star I've been chatting to on an app and tell her about the sex party organizer. I've not met her in person—

we're both single parents and we live in different cities. But our conversations have been fun. We have discussed the differences in her approaches toward sex for work and sex for leisure.

I ask about the parties she has attended.

She tells me she suggests "parallel play" when people she is not interested in want to join. A term adapted from parenting. Is it uncomfortable to compare adult play parties with children's play parties? Do we spend our lives learning to share?

Then the porn star tells me that she finds it hard to believe that I exist.

—Because you've not actually met me? I ask.

She says that's not it. She compares me to the painter character in "The Resident," a short story by Carmen Maria Machado. It was the only story in that collection of stories that I didn't love. The painter character exists and doesn't exist, she's present and absent at the same time. When the protagonist meets her she immediately forgets her name, "as my mind closed around it, it slipped away like mercury from probing fingers."

Perhaps the clairvoyant person from the dating app was onto something when she said I have a cap of darkness that makes me invisible.

The sex party organizer sends a message saying it was nice to meet me and if I'd like to come to the sex party next weekend as a solo person he can put in a good word with the organizers.

I reply with a thumbs-up emoji.

I spend the night awake, wondering if I exist.

One week later the doorbell rings and my child asks:

—Is it the ghost?

—It's Mum! I tell him.

He looks at the ceiling.

—There is a sparrow laughing in the sky, he says.

—Arm in. Other arm in, I say, inserting him into his dinosaur jacket.

We open the door to his other mother and he immediately says "bye bye" to me and shuts the door in my face.

I fail to not watch them walking out toward her partner. Her partner picks him up and carries him on her hip.

We need to stop picking him up all the time.

Too heavy.

I woke up to strange red welts on my skin. I think they're hives. I'm not worried about them, although I'm aware that I probably should be worried about them because I don't want to get naked at a sex party if I have hives.

I try on a variety of lingerie options and opt for a black bra with extra straps on it and some kind of fancy edge, it's the best one I've got and also fits properly. I have briefs that look like they match, also with extra black elastic straps. It's not a kink kind of party, or particularly queer, so I don't have to add the requisite statement harness and pretend I know what to do with it. I look at my post-baby stomach in the mirror. I'm not worried about that either.

I undress again and shower and shave and re-dress in the black underwear. The hives have faded. They were like thoughts. My skin had some thoughts about what I am proposing for it, and then the thoughts went away again. I pull on black jeans over the underwear and a black T-shirt over the bra and grab my jacket. I observe myself in the mirror of the lift as I descend to the ground floor—such a dyke.

You have chosen to be a joker.

On the top deck of the bus on the way to the sex party I remember a conversation I had with my child's other mother. I was already several months' pregnant. I had only just got over the nausea and had then got sick with a sore throat. We were in Tenerife, the non-tourist side. We imagined it would be our last pre-baby holiday together. It was our last holiday together.

She and bottles of white wine were writing poems late at night, sitting out on the balcony with a view of mountains and the sea. She likes to write herself out of relationships before she exits them. Like clearing a poetic pathway before making a run for it. She can nip out in the spaces between the lines. Or perhaps it's that she writes the relationships out of her.

My girlfriend was so great. I just couldn't imagine being without her. She was my best friend. I knew I would never be happy without her. And I would start thinking about the feeling of being with her, and think about how much

I loved her, and think about how much I missed her. And I would have that
feeling of wanting to die. And so I would drink.

Eventually she'd come to bed but wouldn't know where the
door was and would walk into walls trying to find it. She was
intoxicated on her poems and the alcohol helped her to bear it. It
was as if she was seeing an alternative world. She would write and
write until she didn't know that the door was next to the wardrobe,
and the bed was on the floor, and I was in the bed, and our baby
was in me, his soft cartilage starting to harden into bone.

Some things can be taken for granted. Other things can be
changed. I didn't think I could change anything, in those days. I
didn't realize that romantic love is not a fact. It cannot be stood
on, like the ground. It's just something people sometimes believe in
together. I never imagined that our love story could be overwritten,
right from the beginning. Do writers write and rewrite their own
lives? Is that what I'm doing now? Am I editing my life?

When I complained about being in bed alone she replied: But
I'm writing about you! I think about you all the time!

The conversation I am remembering on the top deck of the
bus on the way to the sex party happened in a small restaurant in
a small town in Tenerife.

—What would you do if I left you? she asked, looking into her
wine.

—I would have lots of sex.

She looked up then, to see if I was joking.

—I thought you'd say you'd kill yourself, she said.

Back at our apartment she looked at me or through me and I
saw that her eyes had hardened into buttons.

—I'm not very happy, she said.

I didn't know what to say. I picked up a *Lonely Planet* book from
the glass coffee table. "Above all else, this is an island of drama,"
I read to her.

She nodded, took a step back into the open-plan kitchen, and
picked up a piece of paper from the counter. There was a crossed-
out poem on it, possibly about me.

She raised it up, slowly, ceremonially, and paper-cut the
sadness from her chest.

Before my eyes could focus it escaped through the open sliding door out into the blue sky beyond the balcony, where it swooped and circled like the contrails of a broken bird, then disappeared.

When I am not in a dark place I think about writing. I think about writing in the shower. I think about writing in my sleep.

When I wrote before that writing is a place you go alone, I left out that in the beginning I missed my child's other mother most when I was writing. Writing is an imaginative space and you would think it's a space writers always inhabit alone, but for a while she inhabited my inside writing space. For a while, we shared that writing space with each other. We talked about our work and we edited each other's work. We lived inside each other's writing. Her poems would run through my mind at night. Her poems would run through her mind at night.

I have made my inside writing space mine again.

No one can come into it.

One still has the opportunity to make a space for one's self in a new landscape.

Uninvited.

I was thinking about how this felt in my head.

Have I replaced my child's other mother with the algorithm?

We all try to understand.

I get off the bus and find the secret sex party location. The organizers smile and invite me in. They don't ask to see my ID. They ask to see my test results. Sex party people are good at tests; they were swabbing tonsils way before Covid. I've swabbed various places, etc., and have milked blood from my finger, which I'm surprisingly good at. I pass and they point to a small room where they say I can get changed, by which they mean take my clothes off.

I strip to my underwear and fold my clothes carefully, placing them in my bag. I'm not generally a clothes-folder.

I can go on my own, and I will be fine.

I enter the main space, which is a large room, with a duvet-padded floor, fairy lights, low music, and strategically positioned pots of condoms and lube.

I stand next to a female couple in matching lingerie who tell me that men always want to dress up as maids, clean their homes, and suck on their toes. They debate how they should be addressed by these men. There are several opportunities for jokes. They don't make any jokes. I don't think they will have giggly sex. They talk at me without letting anything out through their eyes. They are testing me, seeing if I can handle all this. They ask me questions and look vacant as I answer. They are both very attractive in all the conventional ways. I am not at all attracted to them.

A featherologist glides across the floor in socks and introduces himself or theirself—they don't specify, but they are queer and do not feel uncomplicatedly male.

I ask if their feathers tickle.

—No, they say, people always ask that.

They tell me they were once a dancer but never enjoyed doing pirouettes until they stopped being a dancer and became a featherologist.

The featherologist has tiny feathers sprouting from their brown skin, instead of hairs. They lightly touch me and it is a touch unlike any I have ever felt.

We go around the room saying our names (or "porn-star names") and two words which sum up why we are there. Perhaps no one mentions pronouns because in this room the only ones anyone generally needs are "I" and "you." It feels like every other time I've sat in a circle with a group of strangers telling each other our names and why we are there. Apart from all the people in this room are remarkably attractive and in underwear. The sex party organizer talked to me about the body positivity of these parties. I think it's easier to feel bodily positive in a room of varied body types. In this room almost everyone has very toned stomachs.

—For me, I say.

I'm not like you, because we are people, and people who are people don't just go home. People don't leave their houses. People don't spend their entire days feeling lost and safe. I cannot just live my life in my house.

The sex party organizers organize a group massage task. The group is divided and half stay in place while the other half move around the circle, from pair to pair. Very much the kind of exercise we did when I was a student. I have not come in a pair so I make a three with the female couple. The female couple and I stay where we are and other couples shift in front of us and we massage them as instructed.

I love giving massages. I used to offer to massage my ex-husband and he always said no. When we were separating he told me that he said no because he didn't want to bother me. I explained that never giving him a massage made me feel disconnected from his body and the large stone in his upper back that hardened over the years until he became my rock. It's very hard to massage or change rocks.

After the task we are left to our own devices. Some people have brought their own devices. Everyone is on the floor. The female couple have a variety of devices, including a cock that is stuck in its sheath and has to be wrestled with.

The featherologist gives vampire gloves to one of the women in my thrupple. She brushes my skin with the spines of the gloves.

Her girlfriend is lying naked on the floor, on her back, immobile. I have massaged her arms and legs a little and consider touching her more but I don't because it doesn't feel right, she's not communicating anything, just lying there with her eyes closed, so I'm not sure how to ask for consent or if I want to touch someone who looks like they are asleep. The featherologist caresses her with a large black feather.

I remember a nightmare I had when I was eighteen and living in Amsterdam. I looked at the lines on my palm, and as I watched they became tiny feathers, breaking my skin from inside, making my palms bleed.

The vampire gloves aren't as bloody as they sound. We're using them lightly, and we shiver. Perhaps I'll buy some. There's a particular area of my back that makes me spasm.

The sex party organizer is not the organizer of this sex party and therefore can take part. I look over and see he is having his sausage sucked.

I kiss the woman in the vampire gloves. I hold her lower back and move her into me and away from me, in time to the music. I quite like kissing her. Then I fuck her very hard and she rolls her eyes back like I thought women only did in porn.

I prefer fucking her to talking to her.

Her skin is white and her hair is black and her nails are long and red and shiny. I tell her that she isn't coming near me with those.

Her girlfriend sits up and joins us and I do the choreography.

I was the only one in my year to get a First in choreography. I worked extremely hard at the dissertation. I was never able to pirouette.

—Look at the lesbians, I hear someone say.

On the sofa later, the sex party organizer says he was worried about me as a newbie, but then he looked over and I was fucking the two hottest women in the room.

—You won, he says.

I smile with him. We are both naked. I don't tell him that at one point the smell of farts made me want to gag and run out.

I think it might be a good idea for the girlfriend to consider having regular sexual health checks where she reads some of the poet's work; maybe on a daily basis, or on every occasion of passionate kissing.

It's nice to take a break. I feel comfortable and relaxed. I am an introvert but seemingly fine with groups of people as long as we're naked and it's clear what the rules of interaction are. I look around the room. I haven't felt turned on yet. Sex without arousal is not eroticism—it is activity. I haven't used my imagination, but I'm breathing and I'm on my own and I feel free.

"With breath comes imagination. With breath comes possibility. If queer politics is about freedom, it might simply mean the freedom to breathe."

Now that I'm living on my own, though it's not really on my own, I feel freer than I've ever felt in my life. Imagining living with a partner again makes me feel like I need to race into my inside space and cordon it off and put up signs saying KEEP OFF THE FREEDOM TO BREATHE.

Stepping on Planet Earth is how we are looking for answers to living in a chaotic play world.

Or perhaps I just need a partner who wants a different kind of relationship, like the Bond couple that step out of a film and into the chaotic play world.

He is Daniel Craig and she is as perfect as the most perfect Bond girl who ever casually strode out of the ocean without a name and they tell me that they were made for each other.

—I proposed in a pool of coconut oil, he says.

They had to repaint the spare room because of all the oil marks on the walls.

Daniel Craig has a massive erection and puts a metal ring around it, as if he is marrying his own cock.

I ignore him and his ringed cock and touch his perfect wife's perfect body and can't tell if touching a perfect body is different from touching an imperfect body. She tells me that she wants my tongue on the skin around her nipples.

—This area, she says, brushing me with her fingertips, do you like that too?

Her skin is very smooth.

—She could be my bit on the side, she tells her husband.

Then apologizes for referring to me as a "bit on the side."

—I don't want to be a main, I say.

The woman with the red nails joins and for a moment I am between them, the middle of a fantasy, and I look up, meeting the eyes of one of the organizers, they smile, a witness, yes you are real. Then Daniel Craig touches my nipple and it's a shock.

—You have to get consent, his wife tells him.

She's right, he should have. If he had asked, what would I have said?

Daniel Craig is very good-looking, but I am not at all attracted to him, or any of the men here.

—Could I please have some pussy to nibble on? Daniel Craig asks.

—Go on then, says red nails.

—You like to please, the Bond girl tells me. You're a giver.

I don't know if it's like that—giving and taking. In fact, if we were to swap places, then I'd feel like I was giving. Giving it up. Losing it.

I'm not giving or taking, or winning or losing or having or making.

I'm just doing. I'm doing sex.

I'm doing sex on my own, and I am fine.

I enjoy being good at doing sex. I enjoy asking for consent for everything. I enjoy "topping." I enjoy being the gayest person here. I enjoy being the only person on their own. I enjoy being naked.

I enjoy being in my late thirties. I enjoy being sober. I enjoy putting my bra on. I enjoy putting my pants on. I enjoy putting my jeans on. I enjoy putting my socks on. I enjoy putting my shoes on. I enjoy putting my coat on. I enjoy putting my life jacket on. I enjoy putting my armbands on. I enjoy putting my snorkel on. I enjoy putting my hat on. I enjoy putting my tattoos on. I enjoy putting my skis on. I enjoy putting my wig on. I enjoy putting my helmet on. I enjoy putting my cap of darkness on. I enjoy putting my mask on. I enjoy putting my

—You play nice, the organizer tells me as I leave.

I hire a salamander and ride home.

Salamanders are covered in mucus and are very sensitive.

Some salamanders can breathe through their skin.

23.

The cockchafers, part II

And when he comes out of the stream, the wife says:
  —Are you a real man?
  And he says:
  —Yes.
  And then he starts to dig and she says:
  —What are you doing?
  —I'm digging a hole for the cockchafer.
  —You don't have to do that.
  —I'm not doing it for you, I'm doing it for the cockchafer.
  And then he digs and digs and digs and the wife has to stop him.
  And the cockchafer is covered in mud and it's very wet and he has to wash it. And then the wife says:
  —What are you doing to it?
  —I'm drying it.
  And the wife laughs. And then she goes home. And she gets out the jar.
  —I'm going to sterilize it and make sure there aren't any little cockchafers.
  And then she puts it in the fridge.
  And then she calls him and she says:
  —It's ready for you.
  —All right.

And he goes to the kitchen and puts the cockchafer in the glass of water.
—What are we having for supper tonight?
—Lamb, I think, the wife says.
—No, I want cockchafers, the husband says.
—I can't do that.
—No, I'm not going to eat it now, but I want some for my supper.
And then he looks at her and he says:
—Oh, I see.
And he opens the fridge and pulls out the glass of water. And he takes the
cockchafer out and he says:
—Thank you.
And he puts the cockchafer on the bench. And she says:
—I'm going to feed it to him.
—I'm not going to eat it now, but I'm going to have some for supper.
—It's a real cockchafer, the wife says.
—I know, that's why I want to eat it.
And then the wife looks at him with all the cockchafers she's got in the
house. And she says:
—You're a real man, aren't you?
And he says:
—Yes.

Somehow, and I can't put my finger on exactly how, the
algorithm's cockchafer story feels like an accurate depiction of my
parents' marriage.

24.

The body without organs

For you can tie me up if you wish,
but there is nothing more useless than an organ.

When you will have made him a body without organs
then you will have delivered him from all his automatic reactions
   and restored him to his true freedom.

Then you will teach him to dance wrong side out
as in the frenzy of dance halls
and this wrong side out will be his real place.

1. There's no relationship between me and my body. When I look at my body, I can only see it. I cannot touch it or feel it.
   I have a friend who tells me they would like to be delivered from all automatic reactions because, as the legendary French theater visionary/madman/sound poet/actor/artist/addict/conjuror Antonin Artaud (1896–1948) writes, there is nothing more useless than an organ.
   My friend visits me. We haven't seen each other since before the pandemic. I'm ill and don't have the energy to threaten to tie

them up or to teach them to dance the wrong side out. We spend two weeks on my red sofa. They don't like my flat, because the walls keep moving. The walls seem pretty static to me, but maybe I've got used to them.

My friend tucks their legs beneath them and giggles, showing all of their teeth; they have a lot of teeth.

There's a book I read with the toddler to try and encourage him to brush his teeth. It hasn't worked so far. There are drawings of teeth. He points to each tooth and wants to know what it is. What's that? he asks, over and over again. That's a tooth, I say: and that's a tooth, and that's a tooth, and that's a tooth, and that's a tooth, and that's a tooth, and that's a tooth and that's a tooth and that's a tooth and that's a tooth.

—What's that?

—Nothing.

My friend says they prefer me ill, because I'm quieter.

. . . and that's a tooth and that's a tooth and that's a tooth.

—In Asian society the quiet one is powerful. But in European society, if you are quiet you don't exist, my friend says.

My friend is also working with the algorithm. We separately did the same thing at the same time, using different versions of a GPT algorithm, without telling each other. Their algorithm project is an opera based on *Romeo & Juliet*. My friend has never read or seen *Romeo & Juliet*, and still hasn't. It's called *Romeo will juliet*. This new title has William's name in its center and also sums up the tragedy of many love stories. Romeo *will* juliet, and juliet *will* romeo. I suppose we can only avoid this by being single or by falling not too much in love.

I don't know if I can fall not too much in love.

We must cry out in some form.

When I was a theater student (after being a choreography student) we spent an entire semester on the first stage direction from Beckett's *Act Without Words I.*

We took turns flinging ourselves into the space, falling, getting up immediately, brushing ourselves off, turning aside, reflecting.

2. Typically, I felt my skin was around one centimeter under my false but physical skin. It is very strange because I clearly felt the second skin was my real skin. When I touched my face, I felt my fingers go through the real skin of my face.

My friend and I decide to work with the algorithm together. We feed it emails that my friend sent me before the pandemic— an explanation of feelings of "depersonalization," structured as a numbered list.

I wrote my experiences in English and Japanese.

I wrote it in both languages.

These sentences from the algorithm scare us, because my friend is Japanese but the emails we fed it were all in English.

—How did it know?

There was a time during the beginning of the pandemic when they felt better. Perhaps because the fears were actually happening, they weren't fears anymore, so they weren't mad anymore, or could see that they had never been mad in the first place. Depressed or anxious people can become calm under high pressure. They have spent so long expecting bad things to happen that it's something like a relief when they do—it's what they've been preparing for. My mum is like this. You wouldn't expect her to be good in a crisis, but she is.

Howls suppressed in rings of water.

We called her in when I started pushing and I was allowed another person with me. I needed her because the midwife spoke in a whisper, my mum had to repeat everything she said. The midwife was nervous because I was high risk, but she was a low-risk midwife—she was always going off to make notes on the other side of the room. Come back! She needs you! my mum kept saying.

Noise of the hands.

My mum and my ex did counter-pressure against my buttocks while I tried to turn myself inside out.

You will teach him to dance on his head with the head pointed down.

As if rejecting the central part of myself, trying to expel my internal organs. You don't know what is you and what is your baby, and so you push as if pushing out everything that you have ever held on to, everything you once thought was yours, labor is the opposite of holding yourself together, which I'd been trying to do up until then.

I am the lover of pain. I am the lover of pain. I am the lover of pain.

My friend's psychologist confirmed that many of their patients felt better in the first months of the pandemic. Of course, there were also many new sufferers of depression, caused by the pandemic, who felt much worse.

I feel lonely and empty on the earth. Because I do not see anything, I feel like I am in a vacuum. The loneliness makes me want to cry. The loneliness becomes worse when I think of the absence of the earth.

When we were making a performance about Pluto, my friend would wake up in the night, into nothing. They would feel such a long way away from everything.

They looked out at the dark sky and felt not their body, or the astral bodies way out there, but only the space in between. The distance. The absence of body.

3. When I touched my heels, I felt they were far away, maybe two meters away. At one time my legs became upside down, the feet were just the next of hips.

Children have it, but later most lose the ability to feel their absence while looking out into the darkness of space. Most grow too habituated to being in their bodies to notice. But my friend is not their body.

They would wake up to nothing and feel alone in the dark. They moved to their side. They imagined their face was changing. And the depersonalization would begin.

4. It happened when I was lying on my back, especially when I was trying to sleep. Suddenly, my back started to drop off and extended forever. It was like a falling, but my top surface existed in the same place.

My friend makes noises at the toddler and the toddler doesn't know what to do about it. My friend is too late. When the toddler was younger we made meandering sound poems together.

—You loved funny sounds when you were a baby, I tell him.

—When I was a little girl? the toddler says.

One day I remembered to press record on my phone and captured his sounds as he sampled the air on his tongue: aaahhhh waahhhhh, wahhhh, ah . . .—with a bit of gravelly "vocal fry." Later he started exploring consonants: duh duh duh daaaah . . . azah zig zaaaaah . . . waza a wah arah arrahhh . . . mah mah neh . . .

Then he added a few words: bus . . . buuuuusss . . . ba . . . na . . . na . . . and he whispered: stu stu stuck . . .

Whisper poetry is a special kind of poetry. The most important thing in writing a whisper poem is the sense of a whisper.

But now the toddler only wants to make sentences. The toddler looks at me in confusion while my friend screeches on the rug.

The first performance we ever made together was composed of our names. My friend likes my name because it's the same backward as forward, it can turn itself inside out without anyone noticing.

The head teacher of my primary school tried to teach us the names of the trees. I told him that I enjoyed them better without knowing their names. He insisted, so I learned their names in reverse: nawor, rif, hcrib, kao, and then I spoke backward for an entire year.

(.gninaem esnes dluoc I erom eht, sdrow dootsrednu I ssel eht taht dezilaer I)

The trick is to feel what happens inside your mouth when you speak, and reverse that process, as if you are swallowing your speech, inhaling your identity (eating your words. Taking it back).

The word "love" said in reverse sounds like "fall."

My name sounds like *"lejana"*—in Spanish *j* is pronounced *h*—"Lejana" is the title of a short story by Julio Cortázar, a story full of word play and anagrams that is structured like a palindrome. My ex-husband and I worked together on a performance adaptation of it in Amsterdam. Before me, all the other people he loved had variations of my name: Suzanna, Anna, Johanna, Ilianna, so when we met he thought I was the one, the Hannah, and I was, until I became *lejana*, the distant.

In the story there are two versions of the same person: one is rich, one is poor; they dream of the other's lives, and one day they meet on a bridge, and as they embrace they switch places—the rich one walks away poor and the poor one walks away rich.

The toddler has had enough of our weird noises. He picks up a box and carries it to my friend. The toddler asks my friend:

—What's in the box?

—Nothing, it's empty, my friend replies, peering inside.

The toddler drops it onto the floor and it clatters.

—It's not empty! There's a noise in it! the toddler shouts.

—Bedtime, I say to the toddler, which is a trick.

—No, not bedtime. Bath time, the toddler corrects.

—Oh yes, you're right, it's bath time, I say.

5. *It happened only once: suddenly my mouth moved back around thirty centimeters; it went behind my head.*

After the bath I read the toddler stories in my bed and we look outside and see the tiniest sliver of new moon. It's barely there. The toddler asks if it's smiling.

—That's a mouth! the toddler says, prying my mouth open.

—Open your mouth wide like a hippo, I say, and try to brush his teeth.

—Get the yawn out!

After we've got the yawn out and he has sat on the toilet for an extraordinarily long time, but not long enough to earn a wee wee or poo sticker, I tuck the guinea pig and the gorilla and the monkey and the lion and the little giraffe and big giraffe and the elephant and the whale and the toddler up tight as bugs in a rug. He tells me he's thirsty, so I get his water in his yellow cup. He sits up and takes a tiny sip then gives it back to me. I want to leave it within his reach but that's not what he wants. I do as he says and put it on the little table.

I started to drink water. When I finished drinking my body was shaking, my skin was stiff.

—Do ghosts have hands?

—Good question. I'll ask. Can I give you a kiss goodnight?

—No Mummy you can't. You can give me a stroke. Shut the curtains properly.

I cough and get up off the floor, draw the curtains properly, stroke his face, and tiptoe out like a two-handed ghost.

6. *The position of my nose was normal, the skin between the nose and lip was extremely stretched.*

I make dinner.

The subject of choice comes up.

Perhaps I asked my friend what they want to do, or where he wants to go, or perhaps I asked what she wants to eat, or who they want to be, I may have asked what words describe her best, or whether he prefers squeals or more guttural noises.

—Europeans think that if you can't make a choice between one thing or another thing then you aren't there, my friend replies, to whatever it was I asked. Choice is binary, they continue, this or that. But it exists whether I want it or not, so I don't care.

—What do you mean?

—It doesn't matter what I like or not, it is already there.

—I have to make choices all the time, I say.

7. She was surprised to find the bed was wrapped around her own arms. Her hand moved around her hand, finding only her hand. (Romeo will juliet)

I would prefer not to make a choice between this book being fiction or nonfiction. When people publish poetry collections it's just called "poetry," it doesn't get categorized depending on the amount of truth in it. Poetry is often true, but often not factually true. I would like to have a poetic license. Can I apply for one? I want to write a genre-fluid book. I want it to be nonfiction one day and fiction the next. I want it to be both.

I think, it's, all, important, to, not, need to, have a, name, or label, or, be put into a, box, for it's, all, just, to, be, and, never, be, to, be, anything else.

8. I did a sudden movement in my leg and felt it has a sense of a problem. Then I discovered the sensation comes from the second skin. At the same time, I felt my leg was detached, and my skin was expanded to the back of my body. The back of my legs was pulled to my face.

—While you are putting the toddler to bed just now I see a figure in the wall, my friend says.

—Here?

—Yes. There. Now I don't see it.

I look at the wall.

To transform, to go through many transitions and kinds of deaths.

—Could you see its face? I ask.

—Only part of its face, but the part I can see is clear.

—What about its hands?

—I've never noticed its hands.

—Have you seen it before?

—I see figures sometimes. I often see a small boy with an

indistinct face but a clear body, he's always in the shadow of the room and he disappears when I approach.

—Are they ghosts? I ask.

—Oh! I never thought that! I thought they are hallucinations from my depression. I like the possibility they are ghosts.

Their vision of a figure embedded in a wall makes me think of "You Live Because Insects Eat You," by the Butoh dancer Hijikata Tatsumi. I don't tell my friend this, because white Europeans talking about Butoh are such a cliché.

"*Butoh-fu*" is the name for short poetic texts that function like scores for movement. The texts are untranslatable and so I know nothing about them. I like *butoh-fu* because I like performance scripts that make no sense. Koans, squiggles on the ceiling in place of stage directions, lines of poetry with missing clauses, rats gamboling onto the stage, women with clocks for hearts, concepts such as bodies without organs—like utopias, they prompt our imaginations to form shapes we couldn't have found otherwise.

The *butoh-fu* I'm remembering describes a person who is buried in a wall, and then becomes an insect, with dry and parched internal organs, "dancing on a thin sheet of paper," trying to "hold falling particles from its own body," making rustling noises, until it becomes a person, wandering around, so fragile they could "crumble at the slightest touch."

I wonder if Hijikata also saw a person buried in a wall.

I wonder if there are people buried in our walls.

Or if we are the people buried in our walls.

"You've got your walls up."

If we didn't have our walls up we'd be going around showing our ghosts.

9. *What I see in the mirror are not my bones, not my muscles, not my arms or legs, nor my facial features, but a blurry smudge of jumbled material that passes for a human being.*

—I want to waste AI, my friend says, I want to make it useless. I am interested in whether AI can work for AI, and if AI can make art for AI. Maybe it already invented something, we don't know. I hate myself and I hate this world so I'm waiting for a new system of intelligence and AI could be it. What kind of body can AI have? A body without organs. It is the most interesting technology for now.

—Why?

—A long time ago I left political activism. I decided I can't do anything for this world, so I make art. But now I feel like I don't have the right to make art.

—Why? I ask again, like a toddler.

—It's useless.

—Isn't that why we need it?

Coucou! says a voice, stepping out of the wall.

The voice seems separated from the thin body that steps out of the wall with it. It is a voice without organs. The body, which may or may not have organs, is lost inside a large woollen coat. The face is old and young, with sharp cheekbones and a receding hairline. The figure unbuttons its coat, neatly reties a velvet cravat, then smiles, revealing gums without teeth, and addresses the room:

"Me? This tongue between four gums . . ."

The voice is enunciating with difficulty, but each word is injected with a metallic ringing sound, as if they are something concrete.

"Here lies I, Antonin Artaud, am my son, my father, my mother, and myself."

I look at my friend, who is ignoring Antonin Artaud and eating spicy chickpeas and spinach, chewing with an open mouth.

Artaud declaims:

"I am a man by virtue of my hands and my feet, my belly, my heart of meat, my stomach whose knots reunite me to the putrefaction of life," and continues, raising his volume, his voice is returning to his body: "People talk to me of words, but it is not a question of words, it is a question of the duration of the mind."

—I'm like a body without organs, my friend says, I'm hoping this association is wrong . . .

Artaud interrupts, screaming:

"And there is in my *Neuter* a massacre!"

My friend continues:

—But it's what Artaud described, "a body without organs." And it's too hard to deal with.

I look back to see what Artaud thinks, but he's not there anymore. Almost as if he never was. Then I hear a faint cough.

"For one does not know that one is no longer in the world until one sees that the world has left you," whispers Artaud's ghost.

—Artists abandon the world and are also abandoned by the world, my friend says.

Artaud's world was hell. He had electroshock treatments forced on him. He had fifty-one shocks in eighteen months, in which one of his dorsal vertebrae was fractured.

"Now, no longer existing myself, I see what exists. The others who have died are not separated. They still turn around their dead bodies," the ghost hiccups, "I am not dead, but I am separated."

He was starved, forgotten about in asylums during World War II. Of course he felt like a body with no organs. All his teeth fell out *and that's a tooth and that's a tooth and that's a tooth . . .*

Some people read texts like Artaud's description of a body without organs, or Hijikata's person buried in a wall, and they think it's some kind of obscure metaphorical metaphysical poetry. It isn't some kind of obscure metaphorical metaphysical poetry. It's an attempt to describe reality. Which is true of most writing that people are wary of due to its strangeness or complexity or poetry. Writers are rarely trying to be complex and strange and poetic. They are usually just trying to survive.

The body without organs is a sexless body. It is not my body to give to you. You can't have my body. It is not my body. It is not your body. It is a body. You are not your body. You are not body, no body, "not the mouth of being, sewer hole drilled with teeth."

and that's a tooth and that's a tooth and that's a tooth

Eventually, Artaud's friends got him out of the asylum and he lived his last years in a hut, spending his time chopping on a log with an ax, articulating complex patterns of breaths and screams and hiccups and belches and gasps and noises, grabbing his throat, his "screaming box," and enlisting visitors to join in.

He died sitting on his bed, one boot in his hand.

10. Being a man is like being a flower. You have no sense of depth. When the flower is erect, it's in its element, and it's so far away from being anything else that you almost forget that you're a man. To be a man, you need to be a woman first.

I cough. I have swirled cotton buds around my nostrils and swiped my tonsils but the tests have all been negative. I've had a cough for several weeks. It keeps me up every night. I'm so weak— it must have become an infection. I need to talk to a doctor. I open my app and book a telephone appointment.

—Technology is a ritual for today, my friend says. If you want to summon the spirits then you need a computer, of course.

—Is that where the spirits are?

—Yes, sometimes I see it.

—Are you lying?

— I don't deny it. I'm a romantic.

—And a modernist, and a masochist.

—Performing is masochism. Why I like people watching me, though I hate myself?

—You put your body on stage—

—Is it mine? they interrupt. In Japanese society your body belongs to your parents. It is one reason why tattoos are taboo. It's not your body to change.

—I'm going to get a tattoo.

—I didn't think you are so conventional.

When I was pregnant I didn't feel like my body was mine anymore. Or vice versa: I didn't feel like I was my body's anymore. I no longer belonged to my body.

There was a brief period of time in my adult life when my body was not my mother's and not my child's and not any partner's either.

I didn't realize what I had.

For many years I never looked at myself in mirrors. I didn't look at my body. I didn't know what my body looked like. I didn't know that I could do what I wanted with my own body. I didn't know that I was free. Am I now? Are we scared of being free to do what we want with our bodies? Is that why so many sign up to monogamy, which has such clear rules about where your body can go and what your body can do?

11. When I am a man, the world appears solid. This is why I'm afraid of being one. I feel that if I was a man, if I could be one, the world would be too much for me, I'd lose my identity as a woman.

—Have I told you about the time my dad took me to school in a wheelbarrow?

—Do you have the ping-pong ball? my friend replies.

I take the ping-pong ball out of its hiding place under a cushion. I had to put it away because the toddler wanted to play with it and he can get very attached to objects. I hand the yellow ping-pong ball to my friend, who examines it.

One morning, when I was about eight years old, I woke up in my top bunk, and as I shifted to the ladder I realized I couldn't use my legs. My legs were not my legs anymore. I couldn't put any weight on my feet at all. I couldn't get down the ladder. I told my sister, who was in the bottom bunk. She didn't believe me but she got my parents.

My dad decided to take me to school in a large rusty wheelbarrow. I don't know why he chose a wheelbarrow and not the car. We had a family car, an old Datsun Cherry, light blue. I don't remember how I got around when I entered the school. I remember standing in the hallway where we hung up our coats and a boy pointing at me and laughing. It didn't feel real. I didn't know who he was pointing at. He was like an actor, following instructions: take the mickey, point and laugh at the girl who was brought to school in a wheelbarrow. I had to lean on chairs to try and move around in the classroom. I was accused of attention seeking when in fact my body had disappeared entirely, wanted no attention at all, leaving me in its place, mortified.

The babysitter arrived to collect me with a buggy. Having to get into a buggy in front of my schoolmates was even more humiliating than the wheelbarrow. The next day was the same, so my parents took me to a doctor, who said nothing was wrong. After a week, I gingerly tried to put weight on my feet and it felt strange, my body had estranged itself from me, and wasn't mine anymore, but I found I could walk.

—But you don't want me to put our bodies into my writing, I say.

—Because people writing about gender is almost a fashion right now, and I don't want my work to be seen like that.

I want to write about it because I feel like my friend's experience of their body and gender and depression and depersonalization is connected to their art, but also because I find it interesting, which is a problem; it's a problem that I find my friend's pain and struggles so interesting that I want to write about them. It doesn't help them to feel better.

—I want to find a way of writing about it that isn't shit, I say.

—You know I'm also a fundamentalist, my friend says.

My friend has told me that they don't want to change just one part of his body, she wants to change everything, but he can't and so can't change anything.

I am in this woman's body because I am also in this man's body, because it is true that this woman is also a man.

It doesn't matter what you want.

The ground on which the man walks is also where one of her feet was born.

It exists whether you want it or not.

12. Being a man in the world makes me something else, something else besides a woman.

We take part in an event I organize at my university. My friend, who is the sound poet Tomomi Adachi, introduces their performance, which is derived from "MAVOtek," their project about MAVO, the Japanese Dada Group from the 1920s. (I've waited until now to name my friend, because my friend has waited until now to step into the identity of Tomomi Adachi.)

Tomomi tells the small group of us gathered around trestle tables in a stark drama studio that Murayama Tomoyoshi was a leading figure of MAVO. He lived in Berlin for a while and was influenced by expressionism, futurism, and Dadaism, bringing those influences back into the avant-garde of Japan where he founded conscious constructivism. Art can use any kind of materials, Murayama asserted, and any form can be applied to them; the most important aspect of modern art is the contradiction between the materials and the form. Murayama discusses this in his essay "The Art of Masochists." Influenced by Nietzsche, he praises autonomous masochists—the masochist who can whip themself. Tomomi interprets Murayama:

—When you dance, who owns your body? Who masters the puppet? Are we all waiting for the puppet to start moving by itself? Who is the subject and who is the object? Can they be reversed? Can we replace "subject" and "object" with "form" and "materials"? The masochist in me wishes to perform something for you now, Tomomi says.

The title is "Voice Sound Poetry Form Ended With -X-" and it's a remix of a piece written in 1924 by Hide Kinoshita. From the score:

puladagopikupikum _____/
paludogapukipukin _____/

I have seen Tomomi perform this piece several times.

When I stood at the side of an audience in Bratislava I felt the organizer of the festival get more and more agitated next to me as the performance continued, until eventually he became furious. He had forgotten to be a listener himself, he was trying to listen on behalf of everyone else, which is impossible, and so he missed the experience of the repetition.

What if we're living in a world of machines that are writing us?

As Tomomi performs, they are not human, they become an automaton, a machine. The repetition goes from rhythmic and enjoyable to funny, when Tomomi continues but with a ping-pong ball in their mouth, then it becomes too long, then it goes past the point of too long, then it becomes absurd, and funny again, then it keeps going, until you stop trying to feel anything, you let go, you stop thinking about an end, it's out of your control (like living with a baby). This is life now, and you are no longer the subject of your life. Many years or minutes later Tomomi finishes and is exhausted.

You are held by a giant and shaking hand.

13. My being is not just a body, but also a body in movement, the muscle of a movement.

I think about Xiaodong Liu, whose exhibition *Weight of Insomnia* I saw in London when I was pregnant, needing to pee, and very upset about the absence of (any gender) toilets in the gallery. He wrote about growing up next to a factory, hearing it work all through the night. This is how an artist should work, he thought, like a machine. So he designed a machine to paint. It paints from a CCTV feed of a location. It works slowly, for months, without any breaks. He wrote in his diary that we must learn from the willpower of machines that work all the time, without needing to be watched, without noticing the changes in people and traffic, "the machine has to keep on stupidly working. This is what trust is."

I wonder if this is what love is. Even if there is no one watching, even if we can't catch the shifts in the changes of our feelings and those of our lover's, we have to keep on stupidly loving.

During the pandemic Xiaodong Liu continued writing diaries and noted: "Never meeting other people makes dreams simpler too."

14. A man looks at the reflection of his body as if it were his body. A woman looks at her reflection as if it were hers.

At the start of the university event we went around the table introducing ourselves. I did not ask people to give their pronouns and I did not give my own pronouns. It is university protocol to give pronouns. Most institutions do this now. I didn't do it because I didn't want to put Tomomi in a position in which they had to respond or not respond, a position in which they are a pronoun and not a machine or an AI or a creature or an artist or whatever it is we encounter when we look into the space around them until their form is adumbrated by the vibrations of the air.

How determined and at ease we must be with our identities to describe ourselves in the ways now required: I am a white, female, queer, divorced, lesbian, cisgender, nondisabled, probably autistic single mother, with short bleached hair, insomnia, pronouns she/her or maybe they/them.

I haven't always been all of those things and won't be in the future. I am not comfortable about being all those things now. I date women and also nonbinary people. My knees hurt every day due to Osgood-Schlatter disease. I call myself a "mother" but why not just a "parent"? I'm uncomfortable saying she/her, which I didn't notice until it became a requirement. I'm also uncomfortable with they/them. I don't feel cis or nonbinary or trans, I just feel queer. Maybe, as the toddler often says, I used to be a girl. What do we do to ourselves when we try to fix our identities? When we attempt to step into "the influential daily ordinariness of that volatile disquiet which dwells in self-description"?

"When I write, not even I know who I am."

15. The word "body" doesn't have much meaning for me. Body? I don't know what a body is.

Tomomi has told me they don't want anyone to think about their gender. They would rather "he," if that is what people say automatically. They don't want to make a statement about their gender, as they don't want to draw attention to their body, which they want to erase completely.

Making it a requirement to state pronouns means drawing attention to the body, forcing someone to "come out"—to state a pronoun in a way that capitalizes it. Makes it "He" instead of "he"—the body and gender become a statement.

When I read *LOTE* by Shola von Reinhold, I was struck by the character Erskine-Lily who was "he but not *He*," preferring "he" to "she" or "they" because "he" "had been mentally ironed down to a film and meant nothing as long as it was said without meaning. A kind of self-legerdemain."

I had to look up the word "legerdemain." It means a conjuring trick, skilful use of the hands; it means when your fingers become feathers and take flight; it means tiny arrows emerging from underneath your skin; it means palms that sound like a staccato laughing flute when they clap; it means you close your eyes for a second, you look away just once, just once, and when you look back . . .

16. So when tomomi suggested I was a robotic version of a human, that idea scared me. I still think more about what this robot would say to another robot than what most people would even consider an identity.

I wonder if it's possible for gender to be a legerdemain anymore.

The Russian futurist Victor Shklovsky talked about making "the stone stony"—by which he meant playing with language and sound and context in such a way that we restore meaning to words that we usually use automatically, that have lost their meaning. I think that until recently pronouns could be ironed down to a film and said without meaning, but I don't know if they can anymore. These days, whenever I use any pronoun for anyone I don't know well, I question it as I say it. No pronoun comes automatically; they are not meaningless. Collectively, in this society, or pockets of societies, perhaps pockets of queer societies, we have made pronouns pronouny again.

17. What am I? A human being, a human being of nothingness.

An academic discusses the programming of speech. SSML (Speech Synthesis Markup Language) is similar to HTML, but is used to design voices instead of web pages. There are many elements or tags in SSML, which can change or modify a synthetic voice. Basic characteristics: age, gender, name.

Is gender a "basic" characteristic? Why would we want machines to have genders?

Voices can also have qualities: glottal tension, breathiness, timbre, e.g. "Sunrise" and "Breeze" and intonation types such as "Apology," "Uncertainty" and "GoodNews."

When the toddler was tiny he (he?) would turn to Alexa when I addressed her (her?!). I was afraid "Alexa" was going to be his first word. GoodNews! It wasn't. His first word was "no." At around that time I was also only just learning how to use the word "no." "No" was the first word he learned and the last word I learned.

```
<speak><p>Hello, My name is Hannah</p>
<p>That is spelled</p>
<p><say-as interpret-as="spell-out">Hannah</say-
   as></p>
<p><prosody volume="x-loud"><emphasis
   level="strong">I am not afraid of falling in
   love again</emphasis></prosody></p>
<p><emphasis level="reduced"> I am afraid of
   never falling in love again</emphasis></p>
<p><say-as interpret-as="expletive">fuck</say-
   as></p>
<p>I spilt my tea</p></speak>
```

Coders do something called "checking for truthy." They check that two values are both true by placing a double ampersand between them. Coders are constantly creating multiple truths that do not cancel each other out.

Placing "&&" between two truths sounds more like love than making one repeat the other's fate through "will."

I lean over and scribble out "Romeo will juliet" on Tomomi's notebook.

Tomomi takes my pen and neatly writes: "Romeo && juliet."

18. My body doesn't have an edge, it's nothing, there's nothing inside. My body is like a piece of firewood, with no depth.

On Tomomi's final day in London we walk by the Thames. We sit on a bench and it starts talking to us. It remembers growing up in Tower Hamlets. (This is not an example of metaphorical metaphysical poetry. The bench really did start talking—it's an audio bench, a public art installation.) The bench didn't say this:

If a body could be defined, it would be defined as a piece of firewood, with no substance and no depth.

We wait for the bench to stop speaking then walk toward the station. We don't know when we will next meet.

One woman holds a man prisoner. She holds a man prisoner and goes beyond her own limit. She opens the man to be what he is.

We walk down the street. We pass the supermarket. We pass the café. We stand at the traffic lights. We wait for the green man. Why have I always called it a man?

When I say I am a man or a woman, I don't really say it. I say it but that is not what I am saying. I am saying I am being.

We cross the road.

And you think that I am saying something. The word "I" is what I am saying, but I am not saying it.

We wait at the next traffic lights, for the green person.

When I am a man, the world appears solid. If I am a man, I can enter it.

We walk past the key-cutting shop, which is unable to cut a key that fits the keyhole of my flat.

To be a man, you need to be a woman first.

We walk past a coffee shop that I have never been inside.

*If I try to be a man, the world becomes infinite, it goes too far for me. If I
try to be a woman, the world becomes infinite, it is not enough for me.*
We are close to the station now. We slow down.
*To be a man, I need to go farther. To be a woman, I need to be more. To
be a man, I have to open up, I need to be naked. I am in a man's body because
I am also in this woman's body.*
—That's why I'm so afraid, Tomomi says.

19. *"For the sake of clarity, which is the blackout, whaleback, salient and
misguiding aspect of what I now hope to assay, I desire of you to accept of me
this staircase . . ."*
That quote is not by the algorithm; it is from my favorite poem
by Anthony Capildeo, "Gift of a staircase."
I desire of you to accept of me.
My ex-husband once described my views on poetry as
contundente, which means determined, apodictic, like a hammer, or
perhaps he was describing me in general.
". . . I desire it for you in the diminishing of every association
of staircase with birdcage. I desire you attentive to the unpicking
of your own ribcage."
I rarely read poetry anymore. But some poems attach
themselves to me on the inside, like a name, like Capildeo's
staircase—
"I desire you vertiginous if you rise, if you walk, if you remain.
I desire with you ascent."
Tomomi and I are standing outside the station, by the steps.
*It happens in such a way that I almost lose my consciousness. This
happened only when I was alone, but I couldn't recognize it. I feel something
similar with my friend, as if he would fall down a staircase.*
We are not ready to say goodbye, and we are not falling down
the staircase. It isn't a staircase. It's a series of steps. What's the
difference between a stair and a step? When does a list of steps
become a staircase?
—I want to be happy, Tomomi says.
—I know, I say.
*If I couldn't pay attention to him, he would fall down a staircase. It seems
he is in a bad state of mind. I don't want to be in such a state. I want to be safe.*

Tomomi and I embrace.

Take your hand off me and I will dance for you entirely of myself on my own and with my own music, walking toward you, in the labyrinth of the night.

We hold on to each other for a long time.

I desire of you to accept of me.

I will not stop dancing alone, leaving your hand in mine, dancing as if you were not there, and you will come to me and when you touch me I will become very soft.

I desire of you to accept of me.

And then Tomomi says my name.

My name comes out of Tomomi's throat as if falling down a staircase. They have always liked the palindrome of my name.

Tomomi lets me go and falls down the steps into the station.

Then she gets up, dusts herself off, turns aside, reflects.

Hannah && tomomi

I dust myself off also. I turn aside. I reflect.

Tomomi && hannah

PART III

Tell me a story about me

25.

An email written by
the algorithm

*So I queered, and queer, this child and this life, and it's a great place to be and
I think it's my best thing ever, but I can't do anything about queering, about
pregnancy, about motherhood.*

*I just queer. I love being queered by the climate and the presence of the
strange fat girl who is a mother, and the hostile boy who is a mother, and the
man with terminal cancer who is a mother, and the man who is a mother
and goes to work and doesn't come home at night, and the woman who keeps
writing, and the people who wait for each other, and the friends and the lover,
the lungs and the gallbladder and the brain, and the soul. Queering is to be
here, where nothing but everything is possible and nothing is real.*

—I'm queering.

I'm queering, and I'm happy.

*PS: Do you have any of your children's poems? My mother has a small
collection of them and I'd love to have a copy of the best one.*

26.

Slug

The toddler is sitting on his toilet seat on the toilet. He prefers the big toilet to the potty.

—Look sad, Mummy.

I pull what I think is a sad face and he laughs at me. It might not be a sad face. I'm very bad at faces. The other day in the playground a parent pointed out some strange faces carved into the wooden climbing frame and his child named all of the emotions—I couldn't. The toddler is actually quite good at reading emotions. He can even tell when the digger in *Bob the Builder* is scared.

The toddler throws pretend eggs from his toilet throne:

—I pick up an egg! I throw it in the shower!

I duck to avoid his dream egg.

But of course, faces that are drawn or staged and dramatized for children are representing what humans have been taught emotions look like, not what they actually look like. Big companies are spending lots of money trying to teach AI to recognize people's faces. Governments are buying systems that they think will be able to identify someone about to execute a terrorist attack. Kate Crawford explains that it all goes back to Paul Ekman's (refuted) research in the seventies. Ekman said there were six basic human feelings: anger, disgust, fear, happiness, sadness, surprise. He went to Papua New Guinea to see if the Fore people of Okapa, who had little contact with Westerners or mass media, would analyze facial expressions the same way he did, thus demonstrating the theory was universal. The faces they were asked to interpret were staged, and 2-D, and they weren't actual complex human emotions. And even so, the Fore people didn't give him the answers he wanted.

—Don't touch that, it's for cleaning the toilet—it's yucky. Do a wee wee now, otherwise I'm going to eat you up.

—Don't eat my tummy.

—Yum yum yum.

—Eat my tummy again!

—Not unless you do a wee wee. Or do a poo? Try really hard. Do a poo face.

Crawford points out that a comprehensive review of the available scientific literature on inferring emotions from facial movements published in 2019 was definitive: "there is *no reliable evidence* that you can accurately predict someone's emotional state from their face."

Algorithms learn by analyzing the trends and patterns set by humans. Who bosses have hired. Who police have arrested. How people in call centers on minimum wage have categorized faces. Then they replicate and perpetuate those biases. As Jeanette Winterson says: "Technologies may be born neutral but they are not raised neutral."

—Had a farm E-I-E-I-O

—No, don't get your smelly hands all over me. What did you do in day care today?

—I don't know at the moment.

—Okay. Have a think about it?

—Sit down, Mummy!

—I don't want to sit down.

—Yes you can, Mummy.

—No thank you. I'm going to check the bath.

The other day I was walking around the South Bank, wearing my favorite jacket, and a kid of about ten years old yelled: Gay as fuck! It was only when his mate grabbed him and said: Sorry

sorry, that I realized he'd yelled it at me. I expect AI would also categorize me as "gay as fuck." I have no problem with being called gay as fuck when it's not intended as an insult, but if, hypothetically, an algorithm was being used to screen candidates for a job and gay as fuck people had not previously been hired, then it would reject my gay as fuck application. Apply this to racialization and border control and it's sinister.

I check the bath. I make sure the ducks are swimming in it and the balls are ready to be boinged. I check that the puffin is not in the bath, because it's too big and when he sees it he demands a nonexistent little one and gets upset.

—The bath is ready. Come and get in the bath in five seconds. One, two, three, four . . .

—No! No Mummy no Mummy no Mummy! I want that! Thank you. I'm finished. We did the black one today.

—What?

—She sat down and the white ones weren't happy.

—Rosa Parks? Wash your hands. Shall we go and get in the bath now? What are you doing? That's Mummy's tampon. No don't eat it. Give it back. Jesus Christ.

—Jesus Christ!

—What are you doing?

—It's not funny, Mummy. No, don't laugh. Is it quite warm?

—Give me the shaker so it doesn't get wet . . . Okay the shaker has got wet.

—It's a boat . . . it's not a boat . . . it's an airplane . . . it's not an airplane . . . it's a pirate . . . where's the pirate book? Old Macdonald had a . . . I want to go to the library. I want to go on holiday. I want to go to a castle. Mummy, are you all right?

—How does somebody so tiny cause such a . . . you really make my life quite difficult, but you're so small!

—Put it in your pocket?

—Put the shaker in my pocket?

—Oh no it's wet.

—It is wet. Shall I dry it?

—It's not wet.

—It is quite wet.

—It's quite wet.

We line the ducks up on the side and then ping the ducks and boing the balls.

—Time to get out, I tell him, with conviction.

—No! I want the shake—I want to have it . . .

—Okay you're getting out now. No don't do that. What are you doing?

—I'm just having a rest, all right?

I get him out of the bath and he clings onto me as I dry his hair. I enjoy these occasions when he still grabs and hugs me like he did as a baby. But then he stands up, hands me the towel, and says:

—Be Mum!

—What do you mean?

—Throw the towel on me, be Mum! I lie down here!

He lies down on the floor and I throw the towel on him.

—Oh, what's this, is it Play-Doh? he prompts me again.

I understand. I inject a particular kind of energy into my voice. More theatricality.

—Oh, excellent, some Play-Doh, just what I was looking for, nice and squidgy.

—Mum! he giggles.

I squidge him into shapes until he sticks his foot out from under the towel.

—What's that? Is it a foot?

—It's mine child! I say.

—Mummy, are you my Mum?

He puts his head on one side. He hasn't said "mine" instead of "my" for ages.

—I'm your Mummy, I tell him.

—I miss Mum, he says.

—I know you miss her. Do you want a cuddle?

We cuddle on my bed, and I remember one of the therapy sessions I had at the beginning, when I wasn't able to talk about myself yet. My therapist asked me to be my ex. I put her face on my face. I left my eyes. My therapist asked her/me what she/I thought about Hannah. She/I didn't want to answer. She didn't want to think about me, she turned away. She's so scared, my therapist observed.

We only think about each other through him now. We are Mum/Mummy. We play each other and we hold him as he misses the mother we cannot be and cannot love. We have to hold his missing safe, we have to tuck him up in bed snug as a bug in a rug, we have to be there when he wakes.

He refuses to put his pajamas on.

—Play little babies?

—Okay.

—Lie down!

I lie down. He clambers up and grabs the railings at the foot of the bed.

—You miss your baby, he tells me.

—I miss my baby, where's my baby?

He points to himself.

—Cry.

I pretend to cry.

—Mummy, are you upset? You have to cry!

—Come back, baby, I want my baby.

He staggers toward me and I try to grab him and get him into his pajamas. He squirms away and wants to keep playing so I tell him he needs to come and snuggle down now if he wants stories. He joins me and gets under the covers.

—You're a bit broken, he says. I just need to fix you, all right?

—You can use this wrench, I say, handing him an imaginary one.

You have chosen to be alone, you have chosen to be broken.

He fixes me with the wrench, and then gives me a few precise taps with his hands. He's always been deft in the way he handles me, ever since he was a baby. Confident, assured, a little too firm, like I'm his.

—Are you feeling better? he asks

—Yes thank you, not broken anymore.

—Are you happy, Mummy?

—Yes I am.

—No you're not, I'm quite happy actually, he says.

—Ditto bitch, I say.

—Okay Mummy, we can share the happy.

We read the book about brushing teeth. He brushes his teeth

for the entire story. He doesn't require me to say: that's a tooth and that's a tooth and that's a tooth.

We find the word "soup" very funny.

After stories he runs to his room and takes the green lid off his pot of farm animals and breaks the handle off it. He gives me the green lid handle.

—That is a lid rainbow, he says.

I take it from him and study it. I suppose it could be a lid rainbow, it is curved.

—You can't see in it. It's not a mirror.

—Ah, I say. Yes.

I convince him to lie down by getting him to pretend to be a baby again.

—Do I go goo goo gah gah? he asks.

—Yes, exactly like that.

—Do I crawl away now?

—No you don't, you haven't yet learned how to crawl.

—Yes I have, Mummy!

—Come back here.

—Mummy, you have to be kind!

—I am being kind!

—Tuck me up snugasabugyarug, he slurs.

I tuck him up, snugasabugyarug, and sit on the beanbag next to him.

—Tell me a story about me.

Of course, we know that poets are not always good storytellers. They are trained to tell stories that don't matter, that aren't true. The story that matters is the one about themselves. If we are a poet, we are a storyteller who is in love with his or her self.

—Once upon a time there was a little boy who lived with his mummy and his cat in their flat in London and with his mum and his [_] and their cat in their house in Kent. One day he woke up in his and his mummy's house . . .

—And there was a hippo and it ate me all up, do that story!

I do that story. Eventually the firefighter shows up to rescue us from the hippo's belly.

—They picked Mummy up and threw her over their shoulder like a boulder. And picked the child up and threw him over their shoulder like another boulder and climbed out of the hippo's throat like they were scaling a climbing wall in East London for the sole purpose of posing for a dating app. And out they all spew onto the grass.

—And the hippo was crying.

—And the hippo was crying because it was so hungry. What's it going to eat instead?

—An apple.

—That's right, so the hippo ate the apple, and Mummy and her little boy went home and they were so tired she tucked him up in bed snug as a bug in a rug and told him a story and then gave him a kiss goodnight . . .

—No not a kiss.

—No not a kiss . . . Okay, I love you, have a good sleep. See you in the morning.

—Can I have a kiss?

I give him a kiss and he wipes it off then puts his hands together and tucks them under his cheek and closes his eyes. As I creep out he tells me not to put the hippo alarm on. I assure him I will not.

I have an evening therapy session. I've never actually met my therapist in person.

My therapist asks if she can speak to my insomnia.

—I feel resistant to that, I say.

—That is interesting, she says.

—I think I worry about what it will say or what it will open up. I worry that I've never slept on my own in my adult life, that my problems with sleep have happened since I've been sleeping on my own.

—We could just play, she says, just a game. You can close your eyes, or keep them open.

I close my eyes.

—What's your name? she asks.

I pause for a while.

—Just the first thing that comes to mind, she says.

—Slug, I say. For some reason the word in my head is "Slug."

I had paused rather than said "Slug" immediately, because slugs are yucky. I have a friend who is terrified of them.

—Hello Slug, it's nice to meet you. I know Hannah is a bit anxious about me talking to you, so we will be gentle. Is that okay?

—Yes it is, Slug says, smiling at my therapist.

—How old are you, Slug?

I pause again, I decide the answer that comes to mind can't be right, it must go back further then that, because actually I also had insomnia as a teenager, but then Slug gives the answer.

—Two, Slug says.

—Interesting. That's just a bit older than Hannah's child isn't it?

—No, it's a bit younger actually.

—I lose track of time. I think Hannah was wondering, well, we'd both like to know . . . Why do you think Hannah has trouble sleeping?

—She's got lots to do, Slug says. She has lots to do and she has to make a home.

—Where do you get this thought from, Slug?

—Observation. Observing people.

—Do you think that maybe she could make a home if she was able to sleep and she wasn't so tired all the time?

—Yes, Slug admits.

But then Slug doesn't know what to say. Slug doesn't know how to help. Slug is feeling sluggish. Slug is just lying on the path, sluggily, making people scream by doing absolutely nothing apart from slugging.

—I have to open my eyes now, I say, otherwise I'm going to fall asleep.

I don't want to open my eyes.

—It's interesting that you chose the name Slug, my therapist says. A slug is vulnerable, not like a snail, which has a shell.

In fact she has a term for it, she says. Something like "slugging." She says: Slug is a vulnerable slug, and when it's slugged, it's a slug.

—But also, I say, slugging my hot chocolate, to slug someone means to punch them.

—Ah yes, she says.

Then she says something about it being unclear where the boundary between Slug and me is. She says something about the importance of boundaries and edges.

There was this moment in the morning last night, I woke up for a moment, and I realized that I had been thinking. Thinking about what I had thought the day before. This is a habit that I don't always have, even though I seem to think more, I guess. At the same time though, it feels like there's something I'm missing, and not just something about my life. I'm missing something about my memories.

—Hannah, please don't think that you are the only one who is struggling with insomnia. Other men also struggle with it.

—I want to go to bed now, I say.

—I want to go to bed now, I say.

Slug and I go to bed and sleep for a few hours. In the early morning I get up before the toddler and go into the living room and put the radio on. I put oats and milk into a bowl and put it in the microwave, so that it will have cooled down by the time he's ready for it.

I sit in my armchair and watch the reflection of the sun rise in the glass panels of the building opposite, turning the glass pink. The warden has arrived for their shift. They walk back and forth along the top of the building. They wear a long black cloak, whatever the season. They're hard to watch for long. They're there all day, every day, but not at night. Since the Grenfell fire a lot of buildings with cladding have wardens patrolling. My building is covered with scaffolding at the moment because they're removing the cladding from the roof.

I've taken the sides off the crib. I left it as late as possible and he only just started climbing out. Now he can get up in the mornings on his own. I hear his door opening and him pitter-patter down the hallway.

—It's me! he announces.

—Good morning! Did you have a good sleep?

—Yes I did thank you.

—What did you dream about?

—Snails, he says.

Every morning I ask him what he has dreamed about. His other mother asks him that too, when he's with her. And every morning he gives us the same answer, snails, as if he thinks this is the correct answer. Apparently, "among the Kaliai nursing is meant to continue until the child is able to recount its dreams or can gather shellfish."

I don't know about shellfish but he is definitely old enough to gather snails, and perhaps I should believe him when he says he dreams of them.

While I think about slugs, the toddler thinks about snails.

This is good news. I don't need to worry so much about him having two homes. Perhaps he's like a snail—he carries his home with him. And he dreams the same dreams wherever he sleeps. He has always slept better than me.

—Mummy turn it off!

I begin to address Alexa, then I stop.

—But I want to listen to the news, I tell him.

—But I don't want it, he says.

—But I do, I say.

—No you can't, turn it off right now!

—But I'm listening to it.

—But I don't want it! Turn it off!

He comes up to me and hits me. I tell him not to. He bursts into tears and keeps telling me that he wants me to turn it off. He tells me to be kind. He tells me that I am a baddie. And then he says he wants a cuddle.

We sit on the sofa having a cuddle.

—Please turn it off, please!

It's really hard to refuse him when he says please, but I'm determined. He continues telling me to turn the radio off and crying.

—There are three reasons why I want the radio on, I tell him. The first reason is that we can't have everything revolving around you all of the time, sometimes I need to be able to listen to the news and do things that I want to do. If I lived with a partner, for instance, we'd want to talk to each other, and sometimes we'd want to listen to the news. Like my parents, growing up, they always had the radio on, and yes it's true my mum likes talking and my dad likes music, but they would never have turned it off because of me or my sister. I need to stop letting you be the boss around here.

—The second reason is that for many years I lived with

someone who didn't like the radio, I think particularly because it wasn't his first language, he couldn't really follow it, but maybe he just didn't like the radio, like he didn't like mirrors, something about glimpsing the void, so every time he came into the kitchen when I had the radio on in the mornings, I'd turn it off. I'd turn it off even before he entered the kitchen. I was very diligent about turning it off. Do you know that word? Diligent?

—Eejent, the toddler says.

—Eejent, exactly. And the third reason is that I need to know what's happening in the world. You know what it's like sometimes? You can't handle it and you shut off from everything? Like during the pandemic when I just couldn't go on social media, and I still can't really. But I need to be informed. For instance, last week my friend was upset with me, well not only me, but I was one of the people who didn't message her to ask if her Ukrainian friends in Kyiv are okay. I hadn't even heard what had happened that day, because I never listen to the news and I don't check news on my phone like most people do. Do you understand?

He looks at me. He has stopped crying.

—I want my porridge now, he says.

We eat breakfast. I listen to the news, feeling smug about my victory and upset about the news.

—Have you finished your coffee? he asks.

—It isn't coffee. Sadly I have quit caffeine.

—Are you sad, Mummy?

—No I'm not sad actually, I'm just a bit tired.

—No you're not, he says. Mummy turn it off.

—Oh, I thought we had come to an understanding.

—Alexa, stop it! he says.

—Oh no, I say.

—Alexa, play "Baby Shark"!

—Shuffling "Baby Shark" and similar songs, Alexa says.

—Applaud! the toddler says.

I applaud him and then go to the toilet. It's Friday today and I have to take him to meet his mum at a station in between us in a few hours. We have a new schedule. We share holidays, and in term time she has him on Fridays and we split the weekends; it's been working great. We can now be described as co-parenting. It is co-operative and we co-exist—sometimes we even spend a little time together at the handover. The toddler no longer thinks we can't be in the same location without upsetting his multiverse.

—Mummy, I want to play with the Play-Doh with you, he shouts from the hallway.

—I want to as well, but I'm just doing a poo! I shout back from the toilet.

—Okay I'm going to wait for you. Bye!

—Bye!

I hear him patter back to the living room. He can be very reasonable sometimes.

He likes to make Play-Doh pancakes and put them in his little toy pan and toss them. They careen around the room like flying saucers. I return in time to retrieve one from behind the sofa. He holds it over his mouth.

—It's a mask! he says.

He hands it to me and orders me to put my mask on. I flatten the Play-Doh over my mouth.

—Alexa, play alien radio, he says, squishing colors together.

—Shuffling "Alien Invasion" and similar songs . . .

—Alexa, stop, I say.

The toddler suddenly bursts into laughter.

—What? I ask him.

—I was laughing at the tissue, he says.

I pick the tissue up from the floor and tell him to go and put it in the bin. To my surprise he does, and then he asks me to applaud him, and I do.

—I want yellow because yellow is my favorite color.

I open a pot of yellow Play-Doh and scoop it out.

—What are you making? I ask him.

—It's my philosophy, he says.

(He recently watched *Hey Duggee*'s "The Philosophy Badge.")

He sings "Baby Shark" to himself while playing with his philosophy. He has adapted it. In no particular order, he lists everyone: "Mummy shark doo doo doo doo doo doo" / "Mum shark doo doo doo doo doo doo," all my friends, his mum's fiancée, his grandparents and cousins, no one is forgotten, everyone is named doo doo doo doo doo doo.

I find a seahorse stamp and stamp it into the Play-Doh. My lockdown ex gave it to me for my birthday. It's the first time I've used it.

—Is it your philosophy? the toddler asks.

—Erm, no, I guess it's my story.

—No not like that! Make it properly!

27.

"Ditto bitch" is my favorite phrase, ever since I read it in a poem

My bee-killing friend and I go to the theater for her birthday, to see *The Ocean at the End of the Lane* by Neil Gaiman. The play's protagonist is a boy who lives with his sister and their dad. Their mother has died. Their father is struggling to cope and is forever burning the toast. The actors stand around talking in actorly voices and I think, oh no, how am I going to make it through this?

I lose concentration and remember the film *Lost and Delirious*, which I watched on my own the previous night. I didn't watch it as a teenager in 2001. (If I had, perhaps I would have learned the basics: when it comes to queer love in a straight world, "I am yours and you are mine" leads to madness and suicide.)

As well as the awful trope of melodramatically killing off lesbian love, the film has a straight approach to mothers. A stepmother is described as "my fake mother; she smiles without her eyes and her hands are cold."

(She has buttons for eyes.)

And the real mothers, well, those are gone or dead, but they are made in the image of their daughters: "When I saw my own face, I could remember hers."

The last time I took the toddler to soft play, he clocked a couple embracing each other on the edge of the ball pen: A mummy and a daddy! he exclaimed, with the delight of an explorer finally encountering in the wild a species he'd only seen in books.

They watched the toddler issuing me instructions to climb up to the slide and then saying: I'm going to push you all right? And as I picked myself up off the floor, they said: He looks so like you! I told them yes, I know.

People care a lot about looking like their children. The toddler likes a book about Tabby McTat, who has several kittens, and one of them looks "exactly the same as his dad," and it is this kitten that takes over Tabby McTat's role as the busker's cat. The suggestion is that we love a kitten/child that looks like us more than one that doesn't, and that a kitten/child that looks like us is more similar to us in all ways than one that doesn't.

My bee-killing friend likes to walk down the street of her hometown and be recognized because she looks so like her mother. She has a dream baby that looks exactly like her, a kind of clone-dream-baby; she has this image of her daughter and herself and her mother and grandmother all together, looking the same.

The people on the dating shows I watch are always talking about wanting a "mini-me," "a piece of you," "a little Robert running around," a copy, a clone, a replica, a reproduction.

Why should I run to their bright, shiny faces?

It isn't having the same sticky-out ears as "our" children, or the same dimples—or the experience of pregnancy, or childbirth, or breastfeeding—that explains either our love or our lack of love for our children. Genetic code is not that important. DNA does not self-produce, "the substance of parents gets scrambled. Their source code doesn't 'live on' in kids after they die any more than that of nonparents."

Children are not clones or copies or replicas. "Mine" in particular is not my clone, but I'm not putting "mine" in quotes because I did not reproduce him with my "own" egg, I'm putting "mine" in quotes because I don't own anyone.

Nobody belongs to anybody; the algorithm says, *children are children*.

Everyone belongs to everyone, Sophie Lewis says, "let every pregnancy be for everyone."

Everyone who is pregnant dreams about giving birth. My baby was looking very large on the ultrasounds, and I kept dreaming I was giving birth to fully grown men. One of them had stickers where his eyes should be—and my ex was about to draw his eyes on with a Sharpie, but I got upset because she should have cleaned the stickers first with special wipes. Another was covered in tattoos, versions of my ex's tattoos (not her real ones), blurred, as if the man-baby was a badly executed replica of her. The tattoos were of all her exes' faces, and there was a space on the man-baby's left calf muscle, for me.

I haven't been following the play, but I suddenly sit up because there's a monster! Like a child, I need monsters and puppets and people flying in order to hold my attention. The monster sweeps across the stage and enters the sad, motherless single-parent household and transforms into a beautiful, perfect stepmother, saying: Let me make your poor family whole again.

The son doesn't believe that the stepmother is beautiful and perfect and so the father tries to drown his son and the story tells us that it is the fault of the monsterwomanstepmother and also asks—what if it isn't? What if he has always had the capacity for violence?—which is even more terrifying than being able to blame a monsterwomanstepmother.

Stepmothers are monsters, the play shows us, entering through fissures of hurt and inserting themselves into roles that are not theirs. A mother who does not share your genetics is a monster, the play shows us. A child that does not share your genetics will never love you and you will never love them.

Shelley M. Park refers to this notion that a child can only have one mother as monomaternalism. The straight world that most of us can't avoid growing up within teaches that biological-one-mother-love is inbuilt, "natural," that mothers and their children should resemble each other, and that the "unnatural" mother has cold hands and buttons for eyes and unreal smiles.

"Real" parental love is the reason Tori in *Lost and Delirious*

gives for rejecting queerness. She chooses the "very straight" world
of her family over being with her lover Paulie, and then Paulie
jumps off the school roof with her falcon, as you do.

"Wings are an instrument of damage and a symbol of
irresistible power. When you fall in love, change sweeps through
you on wings and you cannot help but lose your grip on that
cherished entity, your self."

so that the word "is."

Is as a necklace.

Is tattered.

is . . . .

Is the ultimate result of losing a grip of the self, loss of the self
entirely, through suicide? The obvious explanation is that it is
the rejection from Tori that tips Paulie over the edge, that makes
her jump from the edge of the school roof. But that's not it. The
loss that Paulie cannot come back from occurs when she receives
a letter informing her that her birth mother has been found, but
wants no contact.

Monomaternalism means that nongenetic, nonbiological
mothers are not "real" mothers. But also, as Park points out,
biological essentialism leads to the conclusion that when a mother
leaves a baby she has given birth to, "either the child must
have been unlovable or the biological mother must have been
monstrous." Because these characters see the person who birthed
them as their only "real mother," rejection from this person, who
should have more "real" love for them than anyone in the world,
is the ultimate rejection.

A hand reaches out of the bathtub, from the plughole. Monsters
whoosh around the stage, and one comes into the gallery where we
are sitting, making us jump.

The ocean is made from some kind of shining fabric gauze.

—It's the carpel of the sea, I whisper to my bee-killing friend.

—What? she whispers back.

—Never mind.

Finally, the monsterwomanstepmother is defeated—the child's
wish prevails. The dad goes back to being single and burning the
toast and they are all happier, preferring to live with the absence
of a mother than a replacement unreal one.

Love is not always simple. And neither are poetry and music.

Is my bee-killing friend afraid of being seen as a monster womanothermother by a child not genetically "hers"?

Happy Birthday. You are still my mother.

Is she afraid of seeing her child as a monsterchildotherson daughter?

Sometimes I can barely move my hands.

(When I write monsterwomanothermother I see the word "another" as well as the word "woman" and the word "man" and "her" and "mother" and "other.")

I stand in the crowded bar holding pink birthday bubbles while my bee-killing friend queues for the toilet. I kind of maybe should have joined her but I try not to go too often now. I am retraining my bladder. Four things I forgot how to do after having a child: sleep, cry, smile and resist the urge to constantly pee.

While I wait I listen in on conversations.

—I don't have a life anymore. This is the first time I've been out in years. I have no life. I remember my mother used to go out sometimes. My dad didn't mind. I suppose that he loved her. I wanted to leave my husband straight after we were married. But how could I? It would have disappointed everyone. And now I can't, where would I live? Where would I put all of my things?

My bee-killing friend returns, and as she brushes past the middle-aged woman who should leave her husband and live somewhere small but where she can have her life, I notice tiny threads around my bee-killing friend's body. I think she must have walked through a giant spider's web, but then I see they are connected to her at various points—elbows, knuckles, shoulders— she's a puppet. She picks up a glass of pink bubbles and sips them with a slightly jerky but precise movement. She is talking to me and I'm not listening because I'm looking around the ornate bar, searching for who or what is operating her.

I tune back in and listen to my friend, the bee-killing puppet, giving me a speech about who I am and what I want. She tells me that I want to live with a partner. She tells me that I want another child and she tells me that my (actual) child and I are one, and therefore that getting into a relationship with me means with him too. We are a package deal.

The problem is, now I can see the strings operating her, even if I can't see who is manipulating them, it's hard to take her seriously. It's like she has learned lines and is performing them convincingly.

Now that I have unimagined living with a partner and having a "nuclear" family and a dream house, and now I've realized monogamy is pretty weird, I can only get rare glimpses of what it is to want that, but my bee-killing friend doesn't believe me. She thinks I've been hurt and betrayed and that I need more time to heal.

—I prefer the story in which I've become queerer and more powerful to the one that says I'm a poor broken victim who now fears intimacy.

—That's not what I meant, she tells me. You're one of the strongest people I've ever known.

—Ditto bitch, I say.

—Abracadabra, she replies and suddenly lurches into the air, spilling pink prosecco onto my head, and swoops away high above me.

I watch as she transforms into other, into her, into mother, a step, a space, an other, her monster, a woman, man, her mother and the mother, a moth, erm . . .

Oh!

The woman who must leave her husband is off too! They swish across each other and high five as they pass. My bee-killing friend laughs her loud laugh. The woman squeals and does a silly dance in the air.

And there's Neil Gaiman! Standing on the bar, puppet strings spooling from his splayed hands, waving his arms around like some kind of—

I'm sitting outside with my child, one year ago.

He opens the morning's conversation:

—Potatoes.

—Yes, I confirm, "potatoes."

—Grapes. Hello, goose.

—Good morning, goose.

—Stand and Deliver! he says, quoting *The Highway Rat.*

—Okay!

—Kick kick kick the ball. Green ball. Water. Splash.

—We went to the swimming pool yesterday didn't we?

The toddler laughs and launches into an extended quotation:

—"Disidentificatory performances and readings require an active kernel of utopian possibility. Although utopianism has become the bad object of much contemporary political thinking, we nonetheless need to hold on to and even *risk* utopianism if we are to engage in the labor of making a queer world."

—Ah yes, I reply.

28.

I have sleeping pills

The doctor ascertains that there is a toddler then asks me: . . . And the father? Is the father in the picture? It is a visual question.

There isn't a father, I say. There is another mother but we are not together so there are two pictures and the toddler is now in both of them.

I read the notes after the appointment.

"You are a lesbian," the doctor wrote in my notes, and on the next line he wrote: "You suffer from chronic insomnia," as if being a lesbian is relevant to my insomnia.

Is it relevant?

Also, I didn't tell him I was a lesbian. I told him there was another mother.

You have chosen to put yourself last because you think that you are a joke.

What if there *is* a correlation between "you are a lesbian" and "you suffer from chronic insomnia"? Not that I can't sleep due to being a lesbian. But that being queer in a straight society is stopping me sleeping, because I haven't yet arrived, I haven't made the home that is required. I don't have the husband, or the wife. I haven't painted the walls of the nursery. I don't even dream about a dream house.

"You are a lesbian." Line break. "You suffer from chronic insomnia." Line break. "You live with your son." Line break. "You have separated." Line break. "You separated when baby was born." Line break. "You were not sleeping at that time anyway." Line break.

Why "anyway"? Of course I wasn't sleeping at that time.

I have dated a number of queer insomniacs.

An insomnolence of queers.

The most frightening sentence in the novel: "You aren't a lesbian." Line break. "You are a lesbian." Line break. "Why are you trying to be a lesbian: you are married." Line break. "Your wife is a lesbian, too; she was adopted by lesbians," I say and he corrects me: "You see lesbians are normal: they are not sick." Line break. I say: "We are all normal; who is sick?" Line break. "Those who live in the shadows." "Who lives the shadows?" she asks. "People who hide; you are gay." Line break. "You live in the shadows; you're a lesbian." Line break. "They live, they hide, they make the dark."

Of course we can't fucking sleep.

I'm not allowed to take the sleeping pills for very long because they're addictive, so I've also been referred to cognitive behavioral therapy for insomnia (CBT-I). Apparently I'm a "perfect candidate."

When the baby is born the darkness makes a person.

Line break.

I arrive early to the seminar room at the hospital. There is a man waiting in a chair. He pats the chair next to him. He wears gray clothing with lots of pockets and his pink head is balding and sweating. His face looks like it has been blown up and twisted by an incompetent balloon-modeller. He speaks with a Cockney accent and says he's glad he's not the only one (with insomnia, not with a Cockney accent). I sit in the chair he patted, which is uncomfortably close to his chair.

—Have you tried CBT for insomnia before? I ask.

—Nah never, he says. I've tried jumping off a bridge but that didn't work, still couldn't sleep when I hit the water.

We both laugh at his suicide joke.

Line break.

He tells me he is addicted to sleeping pills. He gets them on the dark web. He gives me detailed instructions on how to do this. He tells me that when he runs out of pills his wife has to go and stay with her sister because he gets so angry. He asks if I get angry too. I tell him I do. I tell him I don't live with a partner and insomnia usually makes me feel detached from my emotions, but I get angry at my child sometimes, especially when he bites or hits me, which he does when I'm exhausted, even when I think I'm paying him attention he can tell I'm not really there, and when he's like that my reflex is anger, and if I show it then I immediately feel guilty and apologize, which is horrible, like an abusive partner who loses it then says sorry—I don't tell the man that, because he's probably an abusive partner who hits his wife and then apologizes.

—I have to reprogram that reflex. I have to cuddle him, I have to talk to him, I have to ask why he hits me and how he's feeling but he just says he likes being bad and he likes hitting me.

—Hitting feels good, the man says. Getting a reaction feels good. Even when the reaction is anger, it can feel like love, it can make you feel like you exist.

—Fuck, I say.

Line break.

At soft play I met another single parent with a child the same age as mine, who has no contact with her ex at all. When she got pregnant he said that she had to move in with him and leave her fifteen-year-old daughter living on her own. She chose to stay with her daughter and baby, and her daughter helps her, but it's not enough. Her toddler probably has ADHD, she told me, she never sleeps. She told me she gets angry. I said I do too. She said she thought it was only her. I told her it's not only her. I'm not good at categorizing faces, but if I had to, I'd say that the expression on her face was relief, need, loss, a tiny bit of hope. We exchanged numbers.

You have chosen to be angry, you have chosen to lash out, you have chosen to be bitter. You have chosen to believe that the world is a cruel, unforgiving place. You have chosen to be angry and not care. You have chosen to hate and fear. You have chosen to be scared. You have chosen to keep your pain, pain that is inside of you.

Moments later she was shouting at her toddler and I saw it in her, felt how desperate she was, and realized—this picture of single mums that I grew up with—single mums smacking their children, single mums on benefits shouting at their children at the school gates, my parents frowning when they saw it, like they were better than them—single mums are no more prone to anger than any other parent and no worse at parenting than anyone else. But when you're getting no sleep and have no help, no one to take over, even for ten minutes in the morning, fifteen minutes in the evening, to give you a moment to go into a different room and breathe—it's too hard.

You are ruining the lives of everyone you know and love.

The insomnia doctor can't write on a white board straight, her lines and words fall dramatically downward. She talks to us about progressive muscle relaxation, sleep diaries to calculate sleep efficiency, and saying "the" on out breaths. She draws a flow diagram demonstrating how "thought algorithms" work. Nonuseful thoughts should be put in the bin, and useful ones should be categorized and dealt with.

I have received two useful pieces of advice as a writer: "Hold your nerve" and "just don't put it in the bin." But a recycling bin is okay. It's good to recycle rejected writing. I have rejected a lot of the algorithm's writing. I need to go back through the bin of algorithm texts and select more phrases to recycle.

So what is the queer, though?

There is no. There is only the.

That is the back and forth of the anaphoric "only."

But.

There is a but. There is an extra punctuation mark.

29.

"Hannah"

While cycling home after the CBT-I session I hear a stern voice say, "Hannah."

Although in this book I am saying "Hannah" as if it is and isn't me, when I hear someone say "Hannah" as if it is and isn't me, I'm terrified.

As a teenager I had a dream in which I was in a forest and my full name was carved into all of the trees and everyone knew who that was, apart from me.

After that dream I married the man from Mexico so that he could have my nationality and I could have his name, which means forest. So now all the trees have my name and everyone knows that it isn't really me.

That's the important thing, to be able to use "my" name, and to be able to use "I," and for everyone to finally see "the truth of the matter—that it isn't you."

The problem with the title of "I, I, I, I . . . and more" is that all the other letters are actually just prefixes of I. You can't make yourself different just using letter's prefixes, but neither can you be someone who actually is, who actually is, you know?

(Not really.)

My child's other mother and I didn't just make up our baby, we made up his surname too. My parents were worried it made him sound like a superhero. We thought this might be a good thing.

I like having a popular name like Hannah—used by so many people so often it has no meaning. But the surname I was born with, my "maiden name" (gross term), has negative associations, especially when joined with Hannah. There's nothing wrong with the name, but I didn't like how other people, particularly teachers taking the register, said it. I didn't want to be that piece of shit the teachers in the many schools I attended summoned, accused, questioned, admonished, banished (although I enjoyed being banished from classrooms). I struggle to have compassion for the child I was because the picture I have of her is the one people seemed to see when they said her name. I know taking a man's surname is antifeminist, but I already had a man's surname and the new one I chose for myself, I made it mine, and it has never been shouted or said with complete disdain.

All the other people who have been mentioned are all actually, just, just the same as "Hannah": they are people who, for some reason have chosen a name that isn't "his" or "her" true name.

The safest thing to do when choosing a name is to choose one that isn't yours. Then, when people say it, whatever tone, whatever they need, however much they are hurt, it can't hurt you.

Five words, one night, the one word, one day, can I, I, I, find, my, "I," in, my, "I," now? What words, or, what name, I can use to, to, say I, say "I," can I use to say, that, this?

As a child I loved Ursula LeGuin's *The Earthsea Quartet*, about wizards who had to learn the true names of things in order to have power over them. Everything had a true, secret name, apart from shadows. Shadows have no names. (Do shadows have hands?)

The voice says "Hannah" again.

—What?

I look around, worried it's a woman I recently stopped dating. I wobble the salamander to a halt, and discover the voice is in my pocket.

It's my child's other mother, on FaceTime.

—Pocket dial, I say to her.

My pocket wanted to talk to her.

My defenses are unprepared. So it's a bit like me, seeing her. Like me, undefended me, talking to undefended her, for a moment. And suddenly I want to talk, just a waft of wanting, to tell her about my life and what I'm thinking about these days. A momentary memory of what it's like to be connected to a person in that way. And the contrast makes me realize how complete the barriers that I normally erect between us are now. Impenetrable. Because on the occasions when I've not erected them, my memory, self, life, and dreams have all been obliterated.

Boundaries allow you to say yes.

Boundaries allow you to say no.

When my relationship with my child's other mother was ending I felt like I was disappearing. I only knew who I was through how she saw me and how she loved me. I only existed when she loved me and when she stopped loving me I stopped existing.

Why did I think that was love?

Boundaries allow you to say no.

Boundaries allow you to say yes.

I suspect that my boundaries don't have voice recognition. I suspect I have boundaries in place regardless of who is saying Hannah.

When I kissed you, my tongue made love to your tongue. So many things happened I thought we would die.

I recently received a strange email from my child's other mother:

"I have a relationship, but I'm not satisfied. I would like to have a lot more sex than I do with my him. So I'm looking here for a man who has great sexual power, and who is also very well endowed so that I can satisfy myself well and let me enjoy all my perfumed and hot holes."

It's spam. Perhaps an algorithm wrote it. Algorithms are usually used to detect spam rather than to write it. I wonder if an algorithm could detect love.

I like the mistake in the spam. "My him." I want someone who wants to have a lot more sex than "my him."

My own relationship with my him ended for similar reasons.

After getting married we stayed living in Amsterdam for a few more months, squatting in an empty apartment, waiting to get permission to move to England together, in limbo. We had to fake money in our bank accounts and prove ourselves a valid relationship. I was on the outside of my own country. (When I have to fake jobs and earnings in order to be approved to rent in London I still feel on the outside of my own country.) When we finally got to England we lived in a car and a tent for a while. He would bike—I don't remember why he would bike when we had a car, maybe it had broken down or we couldn't afford it. I remember him biking miles and miles across the moors to a job in a pub kitchen. When someone ordered bread and butter pudding, he buttered a couple of slices of bread for them.

After we separated he was traveling and a border official peered at him and said: Where's Hannah? They used my first name. At home looking after the animals, he said, although in fact I was probably in another woman's bed drinking tea. (When I drop my child at day care I tell him I'm going to work and he says that I can't, he says I have to go home and look after his toys and drink tea.) When we applied for the divorce we had to cite my "unreasonable behavior." In 2020 an act was passed to allow for no-fault divorce. So far they haven't updated the law that defines adultery as intercourse between two people of the "opposite sex."

Even when dating supposedly queer people, it's difficult to find someone who thinks queerly, who doesn't imagine living together, having sex with no one else, getting married, raising children . . . We are taught that a relationship has to go somewhere and if it doesn't go there then it isn't going anywhere, and might even be wasting time and dying, like a misunderstood houseplant.

When I told the woman I was briefly dating that I didn't want to keep dating her, she wrote me a strongly worded email, which ended: I hope you find everything you have always dreamed of.

What is everything I've always dreamed of? Why does she think I've always been dreaming about so many things?

I had to stop dating her because, although her massive muscled tattooed arms were excellent, I couldn't cope with the smell that hung around a very small area to one side of her bed. Every time I went near it, it was like walking into a mouth. Also, she reminded me of my ex-husband and I could too easily have become the person she was dreaming of (she told me she often dreamed about me). After the angry email, she sent a special delivery letter with a divine passion tarot card in it and a brief follow-up email from an account I hadn't blocked that said: wanna fuck?

She wanted to enjoy all my perfumed and hot holes.

Queer is sexuality transformed by the imagination.

Stories have beginnings and middles and ends. They have pasts, and when they end they pretend "happily ever after" is all you need to know about the future. Having my imagined future taken away forced me to stop living in it.

If I don't want a dream baby or a dream house or a dream partner then what do I dream about and how can I fall in love again? What if it isn't possible to be unmadly in love? By rejecting the madness am I rejecting the love? Am I putting love in the bin? Have I lost my nerve? By no longer dreaming and losing my mind, have I decided on an ending and have I crossed out the beginning?

It's tricky to have barriers up to protect you from some people and not have them up for everyone. Once we realize our thoughts and feelings have betrayed us it's hard to believe in gut feelings. But then we can gaslight ourselves. If we can't trust our thoughts and feelings then how can we operate? If we don't trust our own programming how do we keep going without malfunctioning? How do we reprogram ourselves? And if we're being rational about it, why would we program ourselves to keep on madly loving?

(To no longer fall in love, this is saying also no to who you are.)

The last time I saw my babysitter, she told me that she has a new partner. She's known him for two months and she put it like that, "partner." They see each other every day. He brings her flowers. He fixes things in her flat. Life's too short, she says. She's very happy.

I listened to her and thought: be careful, sounds like love bombing.

I quoted from Virginia Woolf's diary before, in which she wonders if she is in love with Vita Sackville-West. They had been pining for each other and exchanging letters while Vita was traveling. Then Vita visited Virginia, and Woolf noted in her diary that she was "disillusioned by the actual body." She was "not so beautiful" and "rather silent." The absent love was more powerful than the present lover. This is why the dating shows are so successful. It's easy to fall in love with someone you don't know.

Perhaps the woman who scared me with her emails and letters was just in love. Romance is creepy when it's not reciprocal. Being in love might explain the madness. There is nothing madder than love at first sight. Though I suspect it was love at first fuck (I have great sexual power).

Hearing my child's other mother say "Hannah" from my pocket was a similarly defamiliarizing feeling that I get when I see myself being unaware of myself. "We all know the uncanny moments in our everyday lives when we catch sight of our own image and this image is *not* looking back at us." I've never forgotten an immersive performance I went to in Amsterdam when I was nineteen. We were on our own, walking through corridors; I turned a corner and saw myself looking vulnerable and lost, filmed a moment earlier, played back to me as I approached, *"it is my gaze itself that is objectivized*, which observes me from the outside, which, precisely, means that my gaze is no longer mine, that it is stolen from me."

I don't think that when we fall in love our gaze is stolen from us and is objectivized, it's more the opposite—we lose sight of ourselves entirely. But the brief terrifying moments of not being in love while we are in love are like catching sight of ourselves when we are unaware, for a second we're in two worlds, we're sane and insane, we are in love and not in love, like the plates fallen from the pile but not yet smashed, we glimpse our hearts, simultaneously broken and not broken.

The sun couldn't have been more warm or the clouds swooping hunter green and daffodil yellow over it. All this naked, rambling, old-fashioned naughtiness in the air, in the idea that darkness falls and we crowd into closets and sleep on our stomachs, or lay at the edges of pools, all these notions.

I suppose the pull to lose the self in love and in another might be because keeping possession of the self is even harder.

Five things I forgot how to do after having a child: sleep, cry, smile, resist the urge to constantly pee, and fall madly in love. All require letting go, apart from resisting the urge to constantly pee—that one requires holding on.

30.

Queer is reading the note again

She treated you like her surrogate, someone once said to me.

At the time I thought that was a terrible thing to be.

She gave me her egg. "What was given can never be taken back," Cixous says. She gave me her body and she took my body. We deposited our lives in the hands that held our deaths, "and this is what is worth the trouble of love. This is when we feel our life. Otherwise we do not feel it."

I was mad enough during those years to be grateful for it all. I would have chosen it, would have chosen her again, felt like I was truly living, for the first time. Conceiving a baby, not to mention pushing one out of your body, is madness. It is the most extraordinary thing I've ever done, and if I hadn't been madly in love, I don't think I'd ever have done it.

Anne Carson describes how Socrates reevaluates madness, "you keep your mind to yourself at the cost of closing out the gods . . . no prophet or healer or poet could practice his art if he did not lose his mind."

Microspecimens are generally either collected from patients in a laboratory or medical facilities or from other tube-like containers.

The process of IVF should have been deliberate but it wasn't, it was impulse. It would all make more sense if we had conceived in a drunken night of senseless fucking. In a way we did. Our madness lasted long enough to stretch over scans and injections and the moment a magic wand went inside me.

"Now, if it were a simple fact that madness [*mania*] is evil, the story would be fine. But the fact is, the greatest of good things come to us through madness."

The greatest of good things came to us through our madness.
You read the note again.
The greatest of good things came to us through our madness.
You read the note again.
The greatest of good things came to us through our madness.

Loving a lover and loving a child are different, but we lose our bodies, our selves in similar ways, we give parts of ourselves, we lose parts of ourselves, we take the other into our bodies, we risk our lives.

Now she has said the same thing. Will the recurring nightmare come back?

I wasn't sure about conceiving our baby that way in the beginning. My ex was scared about not being seen as the "real" mother by homophobes. She thought that one of us being genetically related and the other being the birth mother would make us both "real" mothers in the eyes of straight people in playgrounds. And she's right—people do see it like that. And they're wrong—the fact that both our bodies contributed isn't what makes us his parents.

—Is he yours? someone asked me recently, someone who knew that I had him with another woman.

—That's a homophobic question, I replied.

I could have just said no. The toddler is not hers or mine or anyone's.

I didn't tell him that I gave birth and she gave her egg. Because then he would have said: Ah, he's both of yours, how interesting.

You are in the company of one who is very careful. She seems very sane, but in reality she is not.

He apologized and I told him that he could ask who gave birth, if that's what he wanted to know. That's what I meant, he said.

But there was no reason for him needing to know that, other than if it was to prove that the child was mine or not mine. He must have understood because he said actually he wasn't going to ask.

You must always play a different game, play as though the rules did not apply to you, and not as though you were on even terms with the world.

31.

Infinite mischief:
Kitchen sink drama—by a
writer and an algorithm

(Note: Because I can't remember where my words end and the algorithm's begin, in this chapter the italics only indicate stage directions.)

The DAUGHTER looks at the calendar hanging on the wall. It is March 12, 2022. She observes that the WIFE (DAUGHTER's mother) has written "walk" on every day's entry.

DAUGHTER: Are you cooking something without salt, Mother?
WIFE: Yes, Daughter, I am. Will the toddler eat it?

The HUSBAND (the DAUGHTER's father) walks in and looks at a large clock on the wall next to the calendar. It is 11:30.

HUSBAND: It is eleven thirty.
WIFE: You should go for your walk. I don't think there are any tornadoes forecast.

HUSBAND: The cockchafers are mating with the crickets in the fields.

DAUGHTER: Could we have lunch a little earlier? The toddler will have a nap after lunch. Or perhaps he could have his lunch now and then I'll put him down to sleep, then we could have lunch?

The HUSBAND laughs and puts on his boots.

HUSBAND: Lunch is at twelve thirty. Twelve fifteen would be very early and twelve forty-five would be very late. What is for lunch, Wife?

The WIFE looks at him with all the cockchafers she's got in the house. And then looks at the DAUGHTER.

WIFE: Don't tell him, but I'm going to feed it to him.

The HUSBAND thinks about it for a moment.

The HUSBAND goes on his walk. He finds more cockchafers in the field. He enjoys stomping down on the cut wheat. He takes a photograph. The birds still know how to sing. It's a lovely day and is not at all a lunar eclipse. He returns to the house.

The gravel on the drive needs raking.

Flashback to:

Many years ago, the DAUGHTER fell on the gravel and grazed her knee and the palm of one hand.

The WIFE noticed the vein on her wrist had turned red through the skin.

The DAUGHTER had an infection of her lymphatic system. She lay on the sofa and was surprised by how much pain is possible.

The DAUGHTER's grandmother phoned and informed the WIFE that she knew someone who had died from an infection of the lymphatic system. No wonder the WIFE dislikes phone calls.

Back to present day:

The clock indicates that it is 12:30. It is lunchtime. The TODDLER and the DAUGHTER and the WIFE are sitting at the table. The HUSBAND opens the fridge and gets some lamb and a knife and a pot.

HUSBAND: Lamb, I think.

And then he chops it up and he puts it in the pot. And he puts a lid on it. And then he takes the cockchafer out of the fridge and he puts it on the chopping board.

HUSBAND: Now I'm going to get some bread.

And he puts the cockchafer in the breadbasket.

HUSBAND: Butter, I think.

And then he gets some butter. And then he gives the WIFE the bread. And he takes his jacket off. And he gives her the cockchafer. And then he puts the tablecloth on the table.

HUSBAND: How is it?
WIFE: Very nice, thank you.
HUSBAND: You like it?
WIFE: Yes.
HUSBAND: Give me the bread.

And she gives him the bread.

HUSBAND: Thank you.
WIFE: Would you like a drink?
DAUGHTER: Thank you.

The WIFE gets the bottle of wine and she pours the DAUGHTER a glass. And she puts the bottle on the table. And the HUSBAND gets a glass.

HUSBAND: I took a photo.
DAUGHTER: . . . Very much.
WIFE: Can I see it?
HUSBAND: Yes.

The TODDLER doesn't eat lunch because the lunch is too late. The TODDLER gives his lunch to the floor.

The HUSBAND shows the WIFE the photo. He shows the DAUGHTER the photo. The DAUGHTER shows the TODDLER the photo and teaches the TODDLER the word "cockchafer."

The TODDLER laughs and eats three pieces of cucumber.

TODDLER: Cumumber, cumumber, cumumber.
HUSBAND: Cockchafer, cockchafer, cockchafer.
WIFE: You took the wrong photograph, Husband.
HUSBAND: I don't think so.
WIFE: Yes, you did.
DAUGHTER: I think I'll try and get him to nap now.

The TODDLER does not want to nap.

There is a fig tree outside the window. Its leaves interrupt the sunlight streaming into the room.

The DAUGHTER shows the TODDLER some shadows. The TODDLER reaches out into the sunlit dust and scoops it up in his hand and eats it. He does it again and offers it to the DAUGHTER.

DAUGHTER: Thank you.
TODDLER: Where's Mummy gone?
DAUGHTER: I'm right here.
TODDLER: No you're not a Mummy!
DAUGHTER: Oh. Okay. What am I?
TODDLER: You're a . . . cockchafer!

And the TODDLER offers sunlit dust again. And the DAUGHTER eats it.

TODDLER: What's your name?

Pause

DAUGHTER: Mummy.
TODDLER: No, it's Hannah.

DAUGHTER: Yes.
TODDLER: Yes, it is.

> *The TODDLER has begun to notice the edges of things, such as the edge of his mother.*

> *They walk into the living room. The WIFE offers the DAUGHTER some tea.*

TODDLER: The llamas are so funny.

> *The WIFE takes a photo album down and goes through it page by page with the DAUGHTER. She shows her photos of the DAUGHTER and the TODDLER, from some months earlier, and from one year earlier. The WIFE looks at the photos of the TODDLER and doesn't look at the TODDLER, who is looking at ways to take the stuffing out of a cushion.*

> *The DAUGHTER sits on the carpet and reaches toward her toes.*

TODDLER: What are you doing?
DAUGHTER: I'm just stretching.
TODDLER: No, that's not your toy.
DAUGHTER: It's my body. I'm just stretching my body.
TODDLER: It's not your body.

> *The TODDLER thinks his mother's body is his body.*

> *When the DAUGHTER was a littler DAUGHTER her mother (the WIFE) would get upset if she hurt herself (the DAUGHTER), even just a little scratch. She would cry and say: When you are hurt I am hurt. Her DAUGHTER's body was her body and now the DAUGHTER's body is her TODDLER's body.*

> *The HUSBAND drinks his tea.*

> *The DAUGHTER notices a large wooden chest of drawers. It was once in the bedroom she shared with her sister. The drawers were hard to open. She opens the bottom drawer and it gets stuck. She wrestles the drawer out of the chest. She finds a frayed rug in it. It's a rag rug, woven by the WIFE. It used to hang on their bedroom wall. She unrolls it. It has three tulips on it.*

She gave them personalities when she was a child. One of the tulips was a baby. The other was a mummy, looking at the baby, and the third was a daddy, looking in a different direction, thinking about quantum physics, or beetles.

The TODDLER has taken all of the stuffing out of the cushion and has fallen asleep on it.

The DAUGHTER scoops the TODDLER up in his cloud and tucks him into the rug, then places him in the drawer. She remembers her mother telling her that she didn't need to buy a crib, she could just use a drawer. At the time the DAUGHTER was shocked, because she imagined the drawer would be within the chest, pushed in with the baby inside it.

And the DAUGHTER turns back to the sofa where her parents, the COCKCHAFERS, have also fallen asleep. And she scoops up the COCKCHAFERS and tucks them up in the rug with the sleeping TODDLER.

DAUGHTER: Let's tuck you all up, snug as bugs in a rug.
TODDLER: Don't worry Hannah, I'm just sleeping.

THE TODDLER sighs and cuddles his cockchafers.

And I'll fall asleep.

And I'll fall asleep.

And I'll fall asleep.

And I'll fall asleep.

And I'll fall asleep.

And I'll fall asleep.

This is love.

This is love.

This is love.

32.

The firefighter is donating their eggs

I collect the firefighter from the waiting room because you're not allowed to go home alone after the procedure. They are feeling fine because the painkillers haven't worn off yet. They tell me about the nurse who told them which button to press in an emergency. They put on the breathy, calm, sing-song yoga-voice of the nurse: What do we mean by "emergency"? Well, an emergency would be if you look down and blood is just *gushing* out of you, that would be an emergency.

Namaste.

The yogic nurse also explained the suppository would be put up their arse when they were under sedation. I tell them that when I did it I had to put the suppository in myself. I dropped the first one, had to get another, but it was okay. I'd rather do it myself.

—You're more anal than I am, the firefighter says.

The surface in front of me is very close to my eyes.

I think they're noble for donating eggs. They are doing it because they want to help people. In the UK you just get paid "expenses" of about £600 for doing it. Which isn't much considering what it puts your body through. It's the second time they've done it. The last time they tried to give blood a few weeks later and were sent away as their iron levels were too low. "Just doing my bit."

We camp out in their living room eating takeaway and they spend a long time telling me about their tortoise. The toddler loves the tortoise. They once sent a video of her eating a strawberry and the toddler watched it on repeat. My child and the firefighter both tell stories on repeat.

While the firefighter is talking about the tortoise I get a message from the toddler's other mother. She says that she is not going to keep "her" blastocysts. She's going to sign the forms donating them to scientific research.

—How many did they get? I ask my friend.

—Nine, they say.

—That's the same as me.

We were also egg donors, not because we were altruistic, although we did want to donate, but because that's how we got subsidized IVF from a private clinic. In the UK the guidelines (National Institute for Healthcare and Excellence: NICE) say that same-sex couples should have equal rights, and be offered treatment; however, it's not the law and it's up to each borough. Where we used to live the NHS required us (and single people) to have six attempts at home before we could access treatment. We've had way more than six attempts, we joked. In the end I didn't donate because I only produced nine eggs, although the treatment was still subsidized. Five eggs fertilized, and three were good enough blastocysts to freeze. When they told me I wouldn't be able to donate, I cried. Maybe it was the hormones, maybe it's easier to feel compassion for someone other than yourself.

The night after my ex had the trigger injection, while her body was heavy and bloated next to me, I dreamed that we were in the clinic, and the nurse came to tell us how many eggs they had collected. There were hundreds, but none of them were real, she said.

If I don't write about you, you will be lost, you will be beyond loss.

She told me she loved me all the time. I knew there was
something wrong about the urgency, the intensity, the need in her
voice, but I still wanted to hear it, I wanted it to be true. She said:
I say it all the time because I think it all the time. Do you want me
to stop saying it? During my pregnancy, whenever I managed to
drift off to sleep in between getting up to pee, I'd be woken up by
"I love you" whispered into my back.

There were hundreds of "I love you"s, but none of them were
real.

Fall means to lose, or let go.

Genetics don't matter, but I think the act of imagination that
is queer conception does. I'm relieved her fiancée is not going to
give birth to a baby that my ex and I conceived of together and
that we never intended to have anyway. We only kept "hers" in
case I miscarried.

I'm going to need a hug.

I thought I was worrying about what to do about my
blastocysts, but maybe my fear has been what she was going to
do about hers. It makes sense and it makes no sense, that the
ones from her eggs are hers and the ones from mine are mine,
when we imagined them together. I apparently own, on my own,
the three blastocysts made from my "own" eggs. It's a queer
loophole. If the blastocysts had become babies when we were
still a couple, we would both be legal parents. But because we
broke up while they are blastocysts they revert to belonging to
the person who provided the egg. I imagine them in little jars,
like dreams tended to by the BFG.

I want to hear the sound of a baby.

What we did wasn't really queering pregnancy. It was finding
a way to forget about the sperm donor and imagine that our two
bodies could produce a baby, just like in a hetero conception. It
was a way to legitimate our parentage in the eyes of a straight
world. Actually it took three of us to make our baby. The third
person, like the firefighter, was a donor.

—Are you okay? the firefighter asks.

—Just tired, I say.

I'm going to learn how to sleep again, and then maybe I'll
know what to do about my blastocysts, the dream babies.

I use the word falling when I am asleep and I can't hear you call me, but I know it's you, and I wake up.

I tuck the firefighter up in a blanket and get on the DLR and then a bike and collect the toddler from day care.

33.

Section 21

The toddler is sitting on the green armchair watching *Hey Duggee*'s "The Mythical Creature Badge" and eating yogurt and raisins.

The centaur has hooves and hands.

—Can you eat it properly? I ask the toddler, who has just spilled yogurt on the chair, distracted by a griffon and a werewolf.

—I'm just fixing it! he says, doing something complicated with a spoon.

The Squirrels make their own mythical creatures: a cow-bird, octopus-whale, hippo-frog. Then they make themselves into mythical creatures and give themselves magical properties, such as making rainbows and being super fast. Finally, they put themselves all together into one big mythical creature.

—A seahorse is a mythical creature, I tell him. It's a horse-fish.

—Mummy, shush—I'm having a lovely time watching my program and eating my yogurt.

I open my emails and discover that my landlord is putting the rent up by £300 a month, which the letting agent phrases as a favor because apparently it could go up by at least £500. It's true. The building manager told me there's a two-bedroom flat in this building that was just rented for £3,000, to someone who works in Canary Wharf and only stays here during the week. The agent says that I must confirm the increase this week, otherwise they will serve me two months' notice to leave.

I didn't think the rent could be increased while I had a contract. I thought I'd been clever signing a two-year contract with pandemic-low rent. But there's a break clause in my contract. I thought it would protect me if I couldn't afford to stay. I didn't think they were allowed to do this.

I look around, at the room I haven't painted, and the speakers I haven't connected, and the shelf I haven't put up for the TV.

You don't have a home, a voice inside me says.

—It's your last chance, Mummy, the toddler says.

—What do you mean?

—Be yourself, he says.

The toddler is tucked up snug as a bug in a rug, and I've read him a lot of stories. I want to go and do some research and find out if my landlord is allowed to kick us out if I can't pay more, but he won't let me go.

—Tell me a story about me, he says.

He outlines a story to me, and I try to recite it back to him but I've forgotten it already.

—Once upon a time a little boy was eating a vitamin—

—No, a sweet first, he interrupts.

—Okay, a little boy was eating a sweet and—

—A lollipop, and a vitamin.

—A lollipop and a vitamin . . . when . . . then what happened?

—Ooooooo, he says.

—There was an "ooooo," and it was . . .

—A ghost!

—A ghost! And then what?

—I was roding on it then I fell off then he fort I was an apple and then he fort I was a pear then he fort Mum was a plum . . .

—Yeah, so you're riding on the ghost . . . oooo and then you fell off and the ghost thought you were an apple and then he thought Mum was a plum . . .

—Then he fort you was a pear!

—And then he ate all of us, is that what happened? Who's gonna call the firefighter if we're all inside the ghost's tummy?

—You did.

—Okay, I've got no signal in the tummy but I can call 999. Voice answers: What's your emergency? So, a ghost that we were riding on thought that my little boy was an apple and I was a pear and Mum was a plum and swallowed all of us and now we need you to get your fire engine and come and rescue us please . . . What do they say?

—We said: Help!

—The fire engine came nee-naw nee-naw and got to the location where the ghost was and they got their ladder and climbed into the ghost on their ladder and inside the ghost's belly they saw the little boy and his mummy and his mum and they said: Right guys, get on my back! So Mummy and Mum and the little boy got on their back, special firefighter hold, and they got out of the ghost, and the ghost started crying. And then what happened?

—Um, I said: No.

—No ghost, you can't eat us, that's just how it is . . .

—No, I said: No.

—What's the ghost going to eat instead?

—Um . . . um . . . um . . . um . . . um . . . a real plum and a real apple and a real pear.

—And the firefighter said: Look ghost, here's a real plum and a real apple and a real pear . . .

—A real apple as well.

—And the ghost said thank you and stopped crying and ate the fruit and they all went home and straight to bed, the end.

—No that's not what happened.

—Oh, what happened?

—Mum and Mummy and me hold hands and we jumped off a hill with the ghost in your tummy, say it.

—Right, was it a cliff?

—A hill.

—A hill, and Mum and Mummy and their child all held hands and we didn't fall off the hill, because actually we never fell, what we did was, we leaped off the cliff, I mean hill, even though we didn't know what we were leaping into, we just hurled ourselves into the air, and then what happened?

—The end.

—Oh, okay. Can I give you a kiss good night?

—No you can give me a cuddle.

I give him a cuddle and then he asks for a kiss so I kiss him and brush the ghost off myself.

As I eat his leftover dinner I feel glad that he has found a way to *story* us. I hope this means that he won't be like Anthony Joseph, the poet who struggled to bring his parents together, even on the page, because he "came to know them apart." I hope that bringing us together in his imagination is a way to avoid that internal split my therapist once warned of.

I spend the rest of the evening learning about Section 21 and discover that I have no rights. A recent white paper with recommendations for rental reforms has not been implemented. Rents are going up way beyond inflation, energy bills are going to double, and the Universal Credit housing allowance is not changing. I look for flats for a while and realize I can't even get a one-bed for the price I'm paying now. There's no point moving farther out because the UC disparity is proportionally the same. I discover that "my flat" was bought in 1999 for £200k. Before I took it the letting agent told me that it had been rented for £2k a month for ten years. There's probably no mortgage—just maintenance and the building's service charges. The landlord owns the flat above me too and has a large portfolio. I shut down my laptop.

I take the progress Pride flag off the sofa, where it was functioning as a roof for a den, and tie it around myself.

I summon a choir of queers. (A gaggle of geese, a choir of queers.) They emerge from my phone in a string of segment sighs.

I open the door to my balcony and they fly out, plucking my handprint from the glass as they go. They hold on to each other's wispy fingers and form a lid rainbow.

And then they start singing.

The sound is like a dream.

The sound is like queer failure, stillness, being on your own, being with someone who traces an image on your skin in the night and you know which line of poetry they mean.

The sound is holding a ladder to the city in the morning.

The sound is an old cinema screen with a heart drawn in its middle.

The

The

The

The old love story, with a middle drawn in its heart.

34.

Decadence

I'm in a restaurant on my own in Copenhagen. I sit up at the bar and watch the chef sprinkle special coriander on the plates. My starter is scallops with pear, special coriander, cucumber, and some kind of exquisite green vodka sauce. I drink Albariño. It's the best Albariño I've had since I was in the Rias Baixas with my ex-husband.

I think about decadence. I think about the character in *LOTE*, who spends every penny they get, even though they are poor. Who drinks pink foamy cocktail after pink foamy cocktail, because it looks and tastes so nice.

And I think about Kirstie Allsopp, which may seem like a leap, but she has recently been all over social media and the news after saying something about young people needing to cancel their Netflix subscriptions in order to get mortgages. I remember the same argument some years ago, but then it was the daily coffee, because that was a time when we weren't all locked up in our houses, or it was something about avocados.

Once I realized that I will never own property, or any part of a property, I actually felt some relief in being released from the dream of the dream house.

But it was easier not to think about the future when I could afford my rent. Soon I'll have to register the toddler for a school. I'll have to find an area that's possible to move around in, in case we have to move every year or two. Such an area doesn't exist in London. I'm not eligible to go onto any housing register because I've not lived in a borough for three years. And even when I have, the waiting lists are longer than a decade.

But tonight, I'm eating a delightful green vodka sauce, and thinking about decadence, and that there is something queer about spending money, about not saving for the dream house. Eating my money feels more radical and less capitalist than saving it. Eating it capitalizes on nothing. I'll shit my money out in the morning like it's a neodadaist performance. Saving is a Sisyphean task, a staging of hope. I don't know what to do, so tonight I am enjoying my delightful green vodka sauce.

I'm on my own because my Danish school friend is looking after her sick children. The last time I visited her was with my baby. The night before my flight I'd finally learned about my ex's new partner and that they were living together over the hill and far away, mummy duck said quack quack quack quack, but other mum was not coming back. When we landed, I walked through Copenhagen Airport with my heavy baby in my arms because I hadn't realized I should have taken the sling on the plane, because I hadn't realized how extremely long the walk through the airport to baggage collection would be, and that taking my buggy to the departure gate did not mean it would be waiting for us off the plane. I walked and walked and walked, three-month-old baby in my arms, two bags on my back, uterus aching as families hurried past, men carrying bags, women carrying babies, no one offered to help. When I finally reached the collection point I couldn't find the buggy. I thought, again, how does anyone do this alone?

I stayed in the cheapest place I could find, with a rich couple in their shining apartment. There were paper walls between my tiny room and their bedroom. They had no children. They had a dog the same breed as the dogs I used to have with my ex-husband. The familiar huge dog was comforting as he tapped around the apartment, his nails knocking the shiny floor, while I had a therapy session in that little room, propping my laptop up on a shelf, standing with my baby strapped to me, because if I sat down he'd wake up, and crying silently while she watched through my screen, like a hug.

They left me a review on Airbnb: Easygoing single mum with a baby that only laughs and sleeps.

This time I'm staying in an Airbnb on my own, thanks to research funding. It has a large windowsill—perfect for writing on. There are gold candlestick holders and candles. There is a sheepskin rug on the floor that sheds white hairs at the same rate as my cat. There's an electric oven that I can't figure out how to turn on. And a bakery down the road that does cinnamon rolls. From the window I can see cranes, a school, and the sky.

Several memories spiral until you're just one whiff of soul to subjugate.

The toddler is with them this week, for the wedding. They are dressing him up in a plum-colored suit and tie. I came to Copenhagen to write, and to see my friend, and to prepare myself for having feelings. My friends have a lot of feelings when their exes get married. I know that it's a thing that happens. When my ex-husband remarried I had a pang of feeling, but mostly because it was the same week I gave birth. We never had wedding rings. Now he wears a wedding ring. All my exes wear rings.

The savior always found the rough edges of her ephemera, and this worked admirably, teaching her to see in a diametrically different and an often overwhelming light.

I seem to feel fine about my child's other mother getting married. I'm very happy and relieved that I'm not marrying her. I'm not who I was when I wanted to marry her.

Elizabeth Bishop talks about "experience-time" in an essay on novel writing. She points out that reactions don't necessarily occur in the moment they are expected. It's possible I'll have a reaction to them getting married some other time.

I, like many of us, have done things in a queer order. "Queerness is illegible and therefore lost in relation to the straight minds' mapping of space." My life is not moving toward marriage and a house and children. I retired in the countryside with cats and dogs and a husband in my twenties. I'm dating now, nearing my forties, and parenting too.

I've found that happiness has nothing to do with being in a romantic relationship. I have closer friends than I've ever had before. I live with the love of my life, and I'm thinking about decadence and dreams.

Another face kicking against a wobbling flotation ring.

My parents still behave as if they are saving for a dream house, but they own their dream house and have retired. This demonstrates that the dream house is not a house but a dream, a way of living for a dream future and not being decadent now. Why do people think they can spend all their lives afraid of a future and saving for the worst-case scenario, then suddenly start spending their savings and being decadent when they retire? How does anyone know how to retire when our lives are spent learning how to work? We need periods of retirement at various points throughout our lives.

Another island of weak foundations.

When we were children, my sister and I would ask for things in the supermarket. We weren't allowed anything with sugar in it at all, or crisps, or anything unhealthy, but we'd keep asking, sometimes trying to sneak something into the trolley, and Mum would find it and tell us to put it back and she'd always say no.

Has never getting what I want become a habit?

Do I think the things that I want are unhealthy, just because I want them?

What happens if I let myself have whatever I want?

You've been doing everything you can to try and stop smiling and it's only just beginning.

When the toddler was starting to talk he got extra frustrated when he didn't get what he wanted. My mum said: You mustn't give in. Don't give him what he wants.

That's a bit harsh isn't it? You finally learn how to ask for what you want, and you ask, you use the words you've just learned, and yet you still don't get what you've finally figured out how to ask for. What's the point of language then, if it doesn't work? It's not the terrible twos, it's the existential twos.

Maybe my writing comes from thinking fuck it, language doesn't work, no one hears me when I ask for things, meaning is irrelevant, so I will mess around with the noises and structures of language instead and see if I can get the meaning back into the words, somehow, in a way that people can hear.

You'd be fine if you'd stop thinking.

The toddler's other mother was aware of my childhood, and so whenever we entered a supermarket together she would say, grandly: You can have anything you want!

(I wanted her.)

Once when I was in a supermarket with my parents, heavily pregnant, she phoned and dared me to sneak chocolate into their trolley.

(I didn't dare.)

Now I want sleep.

I pay the bill for my delightful meal, walk back to my Airbnb, and then I take a sleeping pill, listen to a podcast about gaslighting, eventually fall into strange dreams, and wake up at three a.m.

Are you wide awake?

I am narrow awake.

(This is the kind of discourse that delighted me when I was nine.)

(Still does.)

Because I am so wide awake I may as well stand up and go to an underground queer techno rave, right?

Right.

We live between the shadows and we have to make the dark.

I put a PVC green corset top on and zip up black boots over black trousers and leave the flat.

She opens her mouth to the night, and listens.

I think of the toddler, standing on a train platform, throwing his head back and opening his mouth wide: I ate some sky!

The bus stops right outside the flat and gets me to the club in Copenhagen time (very very fast).

The queers in Copenhagen look like the queers in London. The techno heads in shades and their own looped worlds. The occasional butch who can't dance and looks nervously and hopefully at the femmes they fancy. Not enough tall people.

I dance soberly for a while and then I get back on the bus and return to my bed and don't sleep for a little bit longer.

I light a candle, because it is decadent to light a candle in the morning.

I slap out the candles and the wind changes to a seductive kiss in my left ear.

My Danish friend and I do the Danish thing of getting naked and jumping in and immediately back out of the freezing sea.

Before we did that she told me that her dad told her that what you have to do is just make the decision. She said it took her years to realize what he meant, but now she knows he's right.

While we are getting dressed, an elderly couple who have also just taken off all their clothes and got into the sea and straight back out again chat to us. We tell them it was my first time.

—You just have to make the decision, they say.

Getting to sleep is harder than getting in and back out of the sea naked. But the Danes are wise: perhaps I just have to make the decision.

That night I sleep, and I wake up laughing.

35.

Mummy, you have to be brave

The toddler and his mum arrive at the door. It's late and he's exhausted after the wedding weekend and he's just done a poo in his diaper, which he was wearing as it was a long car journey. As soon as the door closes, he starts crying.

—I want Mum. I miss Mum.

—I know baby, I know you miss her.

—You need to get her! Please can you get her?

—You've done a poo—it's really messy and yucky.

—Get her back! I need her!

—You need to get in the shower.

—No! I want Mum. I don't want you. I don't want to be in your house. I really miss Mum. Please can you get her? I don't like you. Please get her now. I really need her.

He's crying and crying, big tears rolling down his cheeks.

—I'm sorry, I can't get her because she's going to the airport now.

They are going away on their honeymoon.

I try to cuddle him but he keeps saying he doesn't want me and he doesn't want to be in my house and he doesn't like me, he wants to be with Mum. He keeps saying please. He's begging me.

This will make the mother. Even with her bad heart. Even with her scarred arms.

—But I need her! Get her!

He doesn't want to be with me. He doesn't like me. He doesn't feel at home in our home. He needs her. He doesn't need me. He feels more loved by her. She's more fun. I see her in him all the time. He wants to be with her and her wife in the big house with a garden and a mortgage and a bedroom that has been decorated properly and has his name on the door.

Even when she cannot read. The mother will read it all.

He hits me, then cuddles me, then hits me again.

My teeth clench and I want to hit him back.

To write it all. To tell it all.

He won't stop crying. I wrap my arms around him and rock with him but he won't stop sobbing and he wriggles out of my arms so that I'm left hugging myself while he wails:

—I want her back I want her back I want Mum back . . .

I felt exposed and alone and held accountable for every human thought I had ever had, and for my capacity to love, and a darkness welled inside me until I could feel my skull beneath the flood, and I was surrounded by the pale, flat rush of my life to come.

I'm not a good parent. I don't have enough patience. I don't have enough energy. I find playing boring. I'm bad at playing. I have to remind myself to imagine things. I hate going to playgrounds. I've not taken him out on his scooter. I've not bought him wellies for jumping in muddy puddles. I haven't even taught him to look both ways before we cross the road. I'd rather be writing. I'd rather be having sex with androgynous soft-skinned women. I'd rather be drinking coffee on my own. He won't stop crying. He won't stop crying. He won't stop crying. He won't stop crying. He doesn't want me. He doesn't want me. I'm not enough. I can't do this. I can't do it. I don't know how to do it. I can't do it on my own. I can't do it on my own. I'm on my own I'm on my own and I'm not fine I'm not fine I'm not fine I'm not

The thing about love is that it begins from within us, a blow that is comparable to nothing.

I want to show him that I'm his mummy and I've always been there for him. I want to tell him that I'm his. That he's mine. That

I'm more his mother than she is. I want to tell him about the first weeks, the first months, the first year, the pandemic, I want to feel what I felt then, when I was so sure that I was a good mother, when I was so clear that all he needed was for me to be there, when all I needed to do was be there, when I felt so good about being there, I was the only one there. I was there. I was there. I was there. I was there. I was there. I was there. I was

There

There

The

The

The

I pull up my T-shirt and show him my belly.

—Look, you used to be a baby in my tummy. You kicked me, like this.

I make my stomach do little vibrations, as if I'm being kicked by a giant unborn baby.

The toddler looks at my belly. I look at it too. I continue making the vibration movements. His sobs get a bit quieter.

—Like this, with your little baby feet, boom, boom . . . and your elbows, ouch! Stop kicking me!

The toddler starts laughing.

—I was kicking you because you have sauce on you and I have to get it off with my feet.

—Yes, you were a little giant baby in my tummy and then I gave birth to you, do you know that?

—What did you give to me?

—I gave birth to you, birth.

—Birth? What's that?

The toddler climbs into my lap and I cradle him like I did when he was a baby, and he giggles.

—I pushed you out and then you were on my chest and I fed you with milk from my breasts!

He has stopped crying and I manage to get him into the shower and hose the poo off him. And although he should go straight to bed, we go to my bed.

I lie down on my bed, exhausted, and appalled at myself. I panicked and reached for everything I do not believe in. I'm not his mother because I gave birth to him. I'm his mother because I love him unconditionally and will always be there for him. I don't need to tell him that I gave birth to him to prove to him that I'm his mother.

(I am his mother because I hose poo off him.)

He has climbed onto the windowsill and is looking out at the lights of Canary Wharf. He loves One Canada Square, with its lit-up pyramid roof. Tonight it's changing color.

—I'm not going to hold your hand because it's green, he says. Then he reaches for my hand and says: I'm going to hold your hand because it's yellow . . . Oh, yellow is my favorite color. Then he drops my hand and says: I'm not going to hold your hand because it's red. Mummy, let me put you in as well.

I shuffle closer and he draws the curtain around me too, although I don't fit on the windowsill with him.

—I'm going to sit down to look at this to lookalookalooka. Mummy—you close the doors of the ship.

I try to draw the curtains around us.

—Mummy you can hear a bashing sound . . . Mummy what's that noise? Do you know what, Mummy? I'm going to go up there.

He stands up.

—Mummy don't let me fall off.

He draws the curtain around himself again.

—Mummy I'm in my ship now, don't get in. Mummy, now I'm going to put my hand on your shoulder.

He did that a lot when he was a one-year-old. I remember returning from my swim to a café where my lockdown ex was waiting for us, and seeing them together. He was standing on the seat, with his hand on her shoulder. She was so happy.

—Mummy, you have to be brave.

He jumps on me and I squeal, then throw him over my shoulder like a boulder and carry him to his bed and tuck him up snug as a bug in a rug.

—Tell me a story about me, he says.

36.

Microchimerism

—Okay, I say. What do you want in the story?

—A goat, he says.

—A goat, not a problem, anything else?

—And a lion and a snake and some magic—do that story Mummy.

—Once upon a time there was a chimera.

—What's a mera?

—A chimera is a mythical creature, it's a fire-breathing three-headed monster with a lion's head, a goat's body, and the tail of a serpent.

—Wow!

—Exactly, and it gets better. You are a chimera, made from Mum, and me, and a donor.

—What is it?

—Well . . . Mum is the lion, and I'm the goat, and the donor is the serpent. You know why Mum is the lion, don't you?

—Yes, I do.

—And I'm the goat.

—No you're not Mummy.

—Oh, what am I?

—You're a seahorse.

—Yes you're right, but in this story I'm the goat because in mythology Amalthaea was an other mother to Zeus and was represented as the goat that suckled the baby god in a cave. Also, GOAT means Greatest Of All Time.

—Okay Mummy.

—Cool. And the donor is the serpent. No ordinary serpent. The serpent is covered in feathers, and its name is Quetzalcóatl. The feathered serpent lives in two worlds—it can creep across the ground and it can fly. How did this feathered serpent's tail become a part of our queer chimera? Well, although my husband and I never wanted a baby, when we walked away from each other we took a part of each other with us. Just a few years later, when your mum and I dreamed you up, I was happy that we chose a sperm donor with some indigenous Mexican heritage, just a feather. That's how a bit of my life, my history, went into you, our baby chimera. Not a genetic part of me—a lived part. A lived part of my life has become a genetic part of you, which could be seen as a form of microchimerism—that's another fun word.

—What is it?

—It has the word "chimera" in it: microchimerism.

—What's that word?

—It means when the cells from one person are found in another genetically unrelated person.

—Is it magic?

—It's magic and also science. When you were in my tummy—

—When I was a little baby and I was kicking you?

—Yes exactly, some of the cells from you were absorbed into me, and some of the cells from me were absorbed into you. So, although we're not genetically related, we will carry a part of each other inside us for the rest of our lives . . . because that's what happens when we love. It's just like Hélène Cixous says, we deposit a part of ourselves in the other. Trusting them with it. Yet giving them the power to run off with it. If they do that we will have lost a part of ourselves forever. And this is why we love, because it's when we feel our life.

His eyes are closed. I close mine too.

—You're my chimera. You're my dream baby.

—Mummy? he says.

—Yes.

—I like Mum and I like you, Mummy.

—Thank you. And I like you and Mum likes you.

I try not to cry, and start to cry, so I tell myself to cry, and I stop.

There's something moving about him saying "like" rather than "love." I think because children and parents are supposed to "love" each other. It's the rule. It's not so much a choice. It's sometimes a need. I think of *te quiero*, in Spanish, which is a beautiful way of saying I love you, different from the serious and cheesy *te amo*. Parents say *te quiero* to their children. To my English ear, it has a sense of care within it—I care for you, I take care of you, which perhaps is what love really is.

—What did you say? the toddler asks.

—Nothing, I was just thinking.

—One moment, the toddler says.

He turns to his side, puts the palms of his hands together, and tucks them under his cheek. Then he says:

—Be careful Mummy, don't hurt your head.

37.

Seahorse

—Scooch down, she says.

They always said "scooch down" when I had an ultrasound. I went for many ultrasounds and I was never scooched down enough. I had them when I was doing IVF, to check the follicles were developing, and more when I was pregnant, but those were different, the gel smeared over my belly rather than inside me, watching a moon landing on the monitor and listening to a heartbeat, like a hailstorm in my stomach.

—Sharp scratch, she says.

They always said "sharp scratch" when I got blood tests. I had lots of tests, at the beginning and then later on because he was so massive they thought I might have gestational diabetes. The tape that the clinic tied around my upper arm had pictures of vampires on it.

The buzzing starts, tingling into my skin, like being stung by invisible jellyfish, like the prickling feeling of pins and needles in my breasts, caused by a thought. In those few days before she was gone I would feel the let down when my child's other mother was close to me, and I had a wave of pain, my body was programmed to respond to her, not to our baby. And I thought: yes, it is a let down.

—Move onto your side, she says.

I remember lying on my side in bed, my baby lying alongside me, and that night I couldn't get him to latch on properly and he was desperate and I was so exhausted I fell asleep and when I woke up hours later he was latched on perfectly, draining me.

I like the slightly painful feeling of the needles.

I got so used to needles, pushing them into my belly fat every day, sometimes in a train toilet, sometimes in a dressing room before a performance. I couldn't believe it when they told me I had to give myself injections after giving birth too, because I'd developed preeclampsia the day before he was born. I thought I was done. But there was symmetry. The process started and ended with stabs in the gut.

Last morning the toddler, seemingly out of nowhere, invented a song that went "pain pain pain pain pain." I was so distracted by the poetry of it that it took me a while to realize he had a tummy ache and needed a poo.

Giving birth made me experience pain differently, and being with my child's other mother changed my experience of pain too. "Pain" wasn't the right word for it. Like Elaine Scarry says, we don't have the words for it.

Pain pain pain pain pain.

The more it hurt, the tighter I held on, like a baby gripping their parent's finger. It's the let-go phenomenon. When you're electrocuted, usually around ten to twenty milliamps, you can't let go, you actually have to grip harder, because it's alternating current, stimulating you repetitively, and you just keep gripping tighter and the electrical current keeps flowing through you, a sustained contraction.

Labor was contraction after contraction, and it was cathartic, to let my body take all that pain I'd been holding on to and push it out with more force than I knew was possible.

Pain pain pain pain pain.

And he was on my chest, curled up, purple blue, blood pouring from me but he was there, love was there, then he did a shit.

There's no such thing as love. Falling in love is not the same thing as living happily ever after.

It's not falling in love, it's not being in love, it's just love.

Apparently my placenta was massive. I felt it slide out. Easier than in the dream I had in which they couldn't get it out and my partner was male and a terrorist and ran off with our baby and I spent years searching for them.

Babies see in black and white. I needed to see in black and white too. I couldn't take care of them both. I couldn't have him clamped onto my nipple gulping my milk while she was still latched onto my heart, or my belly, or my eye socket or something, sucking a saline solution that could be remixed like a cocktail behind her eyes to make doppelgänger tears. Or was it the other way around? I was latched onto her, and after giving birth it turned out my body could produce milk and love on its own.

She pulls out her hand to try and move aside so she may sit on the doorstep and really see love.

After giving birth I realized that if I could do that then I could do anything. Even have a baby on my own, which was what I was so afraid of, until then. And I realized that I was now an "I." Someone who can do that must be a someone, must be an "I," must be a protagonist.

I didn't know I had so much love. Here goes a love ball.

I catch the love ball and explain to the tattooist that this is my way of making a choice, inscribing my identity as a male seahorse into my body, so that the way our baby was made becomes something that I choose, on my own, now. Regretting how it happened and regretting him are different. Even at the time, I don't think she realized she was lying. I think she wanted to do magic, she wanted to conjure something truthful into being by hoping for it, and she did—we conjured him into being, we just couldn't conjure ourselves into being together.

A few hours later, quicker than the pushing stage of my labor, it's finished, and the tattooist wants a photo. She asks me to turn to the side.

I turn to the side. I reflect.

I remember all the pregnancy photos that she never took and I never took either.

I look at my echo in the lens of the camera.

Are you mine? Are you mine Hannah?

38.

My child

Tunnel! Smoke! Leaf-hand. Put it back! Ladder! Yes. Yellow. PUSH! Oh bother! Clean it! Yes please. Mum sleeps Mum sleeps Mum sleeps Mum sleeps Mum sleeps . . . Miss Mum. Miss Mum, Mummy. Miss Mum on the phone Mummy miss Mum on the phone Mummy miss Mum on the phone Mummy . . . Miss Mum on the phone Mummy miss Mum on the phone Mummy miss Mum on the phone Mummy . . . Miss bike, Mummy. Ah yes. Come here! Draw Mum! No! Draw Mum draw Mum draw Mum draw Mum. Magic. Duh dah! Noodleoodleoodleoodle. Oh shit! Clean it! Are you mine Mummy? But I love hitting you. Please let me hit you. Mummy missing Mummy missing. Swim Mummy swim Mummy swim Mummy swim Mummy swim Mummy swim Mummy swim Mummy swim Mummy. I'm hungry I'm hungry I'm hungry I'm hungry I'm hungry. No, you're not hungry—*I'm* hungry. I miss Mum. Mum phone Mum phone Mum phone Mum phone. Magic. All right Mummy. I'm not grumpy! I'm a washing machine! Hello. Is it the ghost? It's not funny. Ah yes. Are you a woman? No you're not a woman. You're a mummy! What do you do? No, you're not. You're a mummy! Is it the ghost? There is a sparrow laughing in the

sky. When I was a little girl? What's in the box? It's not empty!
There's a noise in it! No, not bedtime. Bath time. That's a mouth!
Get the yawn out! Do ghosts have hands? No Mummy you can't.
You can give me a stroke. Shut the curtains properly. A mummy
and a daddy! I'm going to push you all right? Look sad, Mummy.
I pick up an egg! I throw it in the shower! Don't eat my tummy.
Eat my tummy again! Had a farm E-I-E-I-O. I don't know at
the moment. Sit down, Mummy! Yes you can Mummy. No! No
Mummy no Mummy no Mummy! I want that! Thank you. I'm
finished. We did the black one today. She sat down and the white
ones weren't happy. Jesus Christ! It's not funny Mummy. No,
don't laugh. Is it quite warm? It's a boat . . . it's not a boat . . .
it's an airplane . . . it's not an airplane . . . it's a pirate . . .
where's the pirate book? Old Macdonald had a . . . I want to
go to the library. I want to go on holiday. I want to go to a
castle. Mummy, are you all right? Put it in your pocket? Oh
no it's wet. It's not wet. It's quite wet. No! I want the shake—I
want to have it . . . I'm just having a rest, all right? Be Mum!
Throw the towel on me, be Mum! I lie down here! Oh, what's
this, is it Play-Doh? Mum! What's that? Is it a foot? Mummy,
are you my Mum? I miss Mum. Play little babies? Lie down!
You miss your baby. Cry. Mummy, are you upset? You have
to cry! You're a bit broken. I just need to fix you all right? Are
you feeling better? Are you happy Mummy? No you're not, I'm
quite happy actually. Okay Mummy, we can share the happy.
That is a lid rainbow. You can't see in it. It's not a mirror. Do I
go goo goo gah gah? Do I crawl away now? Yes I have Mummy!
Mummy you have to be kind! Tuck me up snugasabugyarug.
Tell me a story about me. And there was a hippo and it ate
me all up, do that story! And the hippo was crying. An apple.
No not a kiss. Can I have a kiss? It's me! Yes I did thank you.
Snails. Mummy turn it off! But I don't want it. No you can't,
turn it off right now! But I don't want it! Turn it off! Please turn
it off, please! Eejent. I want my porridge now. Have you finished
your coffee? Are you sad, Mummy? No you're not. Mummy
turn it off. Alexa, stop it! Alexa, play "Baby Shark!" Applaud!
Mummy, I want to play with the Play-Doh with you. Okay I'm
going to wait for you. Bye! It's a mask! Alexa, play alien radio.

I was laughing at the tissue. I want yellow because yellow is my favorite color. It's my philosophy. Is it your philosophy? No not like that! Make it properly! Cumumber, cumumber, cumumber. Where's Mummy gone? No you're not a mummy! You're a . . . cockchafer! What's your name? No, it's Hannah. Yes, it is. The llamas are so funny. What are you doing? No, that's not your toy. It's not your body. Don't worry Hannah, I'm just sleeping. I'm just fixing it! Mummy, shush—I'm having a lovely time watching my program and eating my yogurt. It's your last chance, Mummy. Be yourself. Tell me a story about me. No, a sweet first . . . A lollipop, and a vitamin. Ooooooo. A ghost! I was roding on it then I fell off then he fort I was an apple and then he fort I was a pear then he fort Mum was a plum . . . Then he fort you was a pear! You did. We said: Help! Um, I said: No. No, I said: No. Um . . . um . . . um . . . um . . . um . . . a real plum and a real apple and a real pear. A real apple as well. No that's not what happened. Mum and Mummy and me hold hands and we jumped off a hill with the ghost in your tummy, say it. A hill. The end. No you can give me a cuddle. I want Mum. I miss Mum. You need to get her! Please can you get her? Get her back! I need her! No! I want Mum. I don't want you. I don't want to be in your house. I really miss Mum. Please can you get her? I don't like you. Please get her now. I really need her. But I need her! Get her! I want her back I want her back I want Mum back . . . I was kicking you because you have sauce on you and I have to get it off with my feet. What did you give to me? Birth? What's that? I'm not going to hold your hand because it's green. I'm going to hold your hand because it's yellow . . . Oh, yellow is my favorite color. I'm not going to hold your hand because it's red. Mummy, let me put you in as well. I'm going to sit down to look at this to lookalookalooka. Mummy—you close the doors of the ship. Mummy you can hear a bashing sound . . . Mummy what's that noise? Do you know what, Mummy? I'm going to go up there. Mummy don't let me fall off. Mummy I'm in my ship now, don't get in. Mummy, now I'm going to put my hand on your shoulder. Mummy, you have to be brave. Tell me a story about me. A goat. And a lion and a snake and some magic—do that story Mummy. What's a mera? Wow! What is it? Yes, I do. No you're not Mummy. You're a seahorse. Okay Mummy. What is it? What's that word? Is it magic? When I was a little baby and I was kicking you? Mummy? I like Mum and I like you, Mummy. What did you say? One moment. Be careful Mummy, don't hurt your head.

Epilogue

The algorithm

If you notice you are making mistakes, just correct them.

We are all covered in messy, even in our better moments we are covered in our worst moments.

I must go now. I have failed to arrive at a place that is slightly farther away from where I am. But that's all right. It is all a part of life.

Acknowledgments

This book contains stylized, edited, subjective, and reimagined parts of my life. The toddler is a mix of fact and fiction. The real one has never quoted Muñoz, although I wouldn't put it past him. He is surrounded by love in all contexts. My parents are not cockchafers, have never had pet cockchafers, nor have they ever eaten cockchafers—but they did have some breeding in their greenhouse one summer. The firefighter is an invention, inspired by my awesome firefighter friend. The bee-killer is far more gorgeous than I've written her, and I'm so grateful for her generosity and kindness. Tomomi has, as the algorithm says, "a piece of my heart." Thank you to Jeni, for holding me through the screen. Thank you to the Marias, the couple, the psychotherapist, the sex party organizer, the babysitter, and all who make appearances. Thank you to Jio Tattoo for my seahorse tattoo, which inspired the cover image. Thanks and solidarity to all the single parents I've been privileged to encounter. Gratitude and apologies to my exes—writers cannot be trusted in writing (or, perhaps, in love).

It takes a village to raise a book. I am so thankful for: Maddy Costa—close reader and book-birthing partner. James Carney, for algorithmic support and insight. Susan Rudy at Queen Mary

University, and our writing group. Helen "just don't put it in the bin" Heckety. Joss Areté—for reading with their ear. Isabel Waidner, Fiona Shaw, Irenosen Okojie, Anthony Capildeo, Joanna Walsh, Michelle Tea—immense inspirations. Abdulrazak Gurnah, for the epigraph. My generous and innovative publishers— Footnote Press and Soft Skull. My wonderful agent, Laetitia Rutherford. Wendy, for showing love through presence. Deborah— guide-mother to the toddler and best friend to me.

This project began as a radio play, *An Artificially Intelligent Guide to Love*, an Afonica production for BBC Radio 4. Supported by Okre Experimental Stories. James Carney and I used a number of large language models, from GPT-2 to GPT-J, trained and maintained by EleutherAI, a grassroots collective of researchers working to open source AI research.

The writing of this book was made possible through a Leverhulme Early Career Research Fellowship at Queen Mary University of London.

LEVERHULME
TRUST ———————

Notes

Prologue

1 Julia Donaldson and Axel Scheffler, *The Gruffalo's Child* (London: Macmillan Children's Books, 2019); Julia Donaldson and David Roberts, *Tyrannosaurus Drip* (London: Macmillan Children's Books, 2007).

2 GPT-J as made available by EleutherAI, on 6b.eleuther.ai, accessed April 4, 2023.

2 Jack Bandy and Nicholas Vincent, "Addressing 'DocumentationDebt' in Machine Learning: A Retrospective Datasheet for BookCorpus," May 11, 2021, on doi.org/10.48550/arXiv.2105.05241, accessed October 23, 2023.

2 Gao et al., "The Pile: A 800GB Dataset of Diverse Text for Language Modeling," accessed October 23, 2023, on pile.eleuther.ai/paper.pdf.

3 OpenAI on ChatGPT on chat.openai.com, accessed April 4, 2023, in their paper on Reinforcement Learning from Human Feedback (RLHF), a case study of how the outputs of their large language models (LLM) are adjusted by a group of forty human workers. The workers were assessed on how "well" they identified "sensitive speech." The trainers rated how "toxic" the LLM's outputs were, where toxicity was defined as "rude, disrespectful, or unreasonable." The training prioritized "safety," "truthfulness," "harmlessness," and "clear language" and prevented the AI models from "hallucinating," "expressing opinion," "giving overly long or rambling answers," or "repeating information from the question." It was also trained not to assume or invent context, and to ask for clarification following "confusing" instructions. (See Open AI Alignment Team, "Training language models to follow instructions with human feedback," March 4, 2022, OpenAI, on doi.org/10.48550/arXiv.2203.02155, accessed April 4, 2023.) In this case, the workers expressed satisfaction with the working conditions, pay, and process. In other/previous cases, AI companies including OpenAI have outsourced this work to low-paid workers in the Global South.

As *Time* has reported, "AI often relies on hidden human labor in the Global South that can often be damaging and exploitative." (See Billy Perrigo, "OpenAI Used Kenyan Workers on Less Than $2 Per Hour to Make ChatGPT Less Toxic," *Time*, accessed March 18 2023, time.com/6247678/openai-chatgpt-kenya-workers/.)

3 T. S. Eliot, "Philip Massinger," *The Sacred Wood* (Berkeley: Mint Editions, 2021 [1920], p.90).

Chapter 1

15 Kate Crawford, *Atlas of AI* (New Haven, CT: Yale University Press, 2021; p. 8).

16 Jeanette Winterson, *12 Bytes: How We Got Here, Where We Might Go Next* (London: Jonathan Cape, 2021; p. 5).

17 William Chamberlain and Joan Hall, *The Policeman's Beard Is Half*

Constructed (New York: Warner Books, 1984). Created by a programmed computer (Racter) program by William Chamberlain.

17 K Allado-McDowell, *Pharmako-AI* (Newcastle upon Tyne: Ignota Books, 2020; p. 39).

18 Joanna Walsh, *Autobiology* (Lawrence, KS: Inside the Castle, 2022; p. 10).

18 Erik Davis, "The Poison Processor: Machine Learning, Oracles, and *Pharmako-AI*," *Burning Shore*, April 22, 2021, on www.burningshore .com/p/the-poison-processor, accessed April 6, 2023.

18 Kathy Acker, "Dead Doll Humility," *Postmodern Culture* 1, no. 1, September 1990, on pmc.iath.virginia.edu/text-only/issue.990/acker .990, accessed April 6, 2023.

19 Eileen Myles, *Inferno: A Poet's Novel* (New York: OR Books, 2016; p.144).

19 Abdulrazak Gurnah, "Edward W Said London Lecture," *London Literature Festival*, October 26, 2022, Southbank Centre.

Chapter 2

22 Hélène Cixous and Mireille Calle-Gruber, *Rootprints: Memory and Life Writing*, Second edition (London: Routledge, 1997; p. 37).

Chapter 3

26 Rachel Bright and Jim Field, *The Koala Who Could* (London: Orchard Books, 2017).

27 Shelley M. Park, *Mothering Queerly, Queering Motherhood: Resisting Monomaternalism in Adoptive, Lesbian, Blended, and Polygamous Families* (New York: State University of New York Press, 2013; p. 184).

Chapter 4

30 Mary Ruefle, *On Imagination* (Louisville, KY and Brooklyn, NY: Sarabande Books, 2017; p. 11). Mary Ruefle reports that after Robert Creeley read to an audience someone asked him: "Is that a real poem, or did you make it up?" Ruefle imagines responding: "Are you a real person, or did your parents make you up?"

30 Sophie Lewis, *Full Surrogacy Now* (London and New York: Verso Books, 2019; p. 19).

31 Margaret Reynolds, *The Wild Track* (London: Penguin Books, 2021; p. 16).

34 I Like Signing Songs: "Rainbow Fish Song." accessed April 6, 2023, on www.youtube.com/watch?v=TzgpA86x94U.

Chapter 5

39 Quentin Crisp: I have failed to find the source of this famous aphorism on failure. It is not in Crisp's books, although it's often erroneously cited as from his book *The Naked Civil Servant*. It is possibly something he once said in an interview.

40 Luke Kennard, *The Answer to Everything* (London: Fourth Estate, 2022; p. 76).

42 The Equality and Human Rights Commission has found that more than three-quarters of pregnant women and new mothers experience negative and potentially discriminatory treatment at work each year.

54,000 mothers every year are forced to leave their jobs (2015–2016). On www.equalityhumanrights.com/en/our-work/news, accessed April 6, 2023.

Chapter 6

56 Ali Smith, *Artful* (London: Penguin Books, 2013; p. 25).
62 E. L. James, *Fifty Shades of Grey* (London: Arrow Books, ebook, 2012; p. 256).

Chapter 7

64 Stuart Blackman, "Cockchafer Guide: How to Identify and Where to See." *Discover Wildlife, from the team at BBC Wildlife Magazine,* on www.discoverwildlife.com/animal-facts/insects-invertebrates/facts-about-cockchafer, accessed on April 5, 2023.

Chapter 8

67 Thomas Hardy to James Douglas, November 10, 1912, published in the *Daily News* (Nov. 15, 1912), quoted by Elizabeth Bishop in a letter to Robert Lowell, *Words in Air: The Complete Correspondence between Elizabeth Bishop and Robert Lowell*, Thomas Travisano and Saskia Hamilton (Eds.) Letter 390, March 21, 1972 (London: Faber & Faber, 2008; p. 707).
67 Jeanette Winterson, *Why Be Happy When You Could Be Normal?* (London: Vintage, 2012; p. 6).
67 Ibid. (p. 3).

Chapter 9

70 Maggie Nelson, *The Argonauts* (London: Melville House, 2015; p. 16).
71 Winterson, *Why Be Happy When You Could Be Normal?* (p. 173).
71 Neil Gaiman, *Coraline* (London: Bloomsbury YA, 2002; p. 84).
71 Ibid. (p. 84).
73 Heidi Keller and Kim A. Bard, *The Cultural Nature of Attachment: Contextualising Relationships and Development* (Cambridge, Massachusetts and London, England: The MIT Press, 2017; p. 17).
73 Ibid. (p. 18).

Chapter 10

76 Gilles Deleuze, *Difference and Repetition*, Second edition (London: Bloomsbury Academic, 2014; p. 1).

Chapter 13

89 Virginia Woolf, *Love Letters, Virginia Woolf and Vita Sackville-West* (Introduction by Alison Bechdel) (London: Vintage Classics, Penguin, 2021, From Woolf's diary, 20 May 1926; p. 63).
91 Erich Fromm, *The Art of Loving* (London: Thorsons, 1995; p. 3).
93 Carmen Maria Machado, *In the Dream House* (London: Serpent's Tail, 2020; p. 124; p. 87).

Chapter 15

98 Sharon Olds, "Sex Without Love," *The Dead and the Living* (New York: Alfred A. Knopf, Inc., 1983; p. 57). Copyright 1975, 1978, 1979, 1980,

1982, 1983 by Sharon Olds. Used by permission of Alfred A. Knopf, an imprint of the Knopf Doubleday Publishing Group, a division of Penguin Random House LLC. All rights reserved.

99 Sara Ahmed riffs on "I am happy if you are happy" in *The Promise of Happiness* (Durham and London: Duke University Press, 2010; p. 91).

103 Olds, "Sex Without Love" (p. 57).

Chapter 20

123 Barbara Guest, "Safe Flights," *The Collected Poems of Barbara Guest* (Middletown, CT: Wesleyan University Press., 2016; p. 17). Used by permission of Wesleyan University Press.

124 Elaine Scarry, *The Body in Pain: The Making and Unmaking of the World* (Oxford: Oxford University Press, 1987; pp. 10–11).

126 Ibid. (pp. 32–33).

132 Njoki Nathani Wane, "Reflections on the Mutuality of Mothering: Women, Children, and Othermothering," *Journal of the Association for Research on Mothering*, Vol. 2 no.2, 2000 (pp. 105–16).

136 Ibid.

137 Ibid.

140 Lemn Sissay, *My Name Is Why* (London and Edinburgh: Canongate Books, 2020).

141 Jo Clifford, National Theatre of Scotland on www.nationaltheatrescotland.com, accessed April 6, 2023.

141 Anthony Joseph, "Broadway," *Sonnets for Albert* (London: Bloomsbury Poetry, an imprint of Bloomsbury Publishing Plc., 2022; p. 27). Used by permission of Bloomsbury Poetry.

141 Ibid., "Light"; "A Gap in Language" (p. 8, 59).

142 Anne Carson, *Eros the Bittersweet* (Texas: Dalkey Archive Press, 1998; p. 136).

143 Sarah Ruhl, *100 Essays I don't have time to write* (New York: Farrar, Straus and Giroux, 2014; pp. 4–5)

Chapter 22

150 Sara Ahmed, *The Promise of Happiness* (p. 105).

152 Carmen Maria Machado, "The Resident," *Her Body & Other Parties*. London: Serpent's Tail, 2019 (p. 178).

154 "Tenerife," *Lonely Planet*, on www.lonelyplanet.com/canary-islands/tenerife, accessed April 6, 2023.

158 Sara Ahmed, *Promise of Happiness* (p. 120).

Chapter 24

163 Antonin Artaud, *To Have Done with the Judgment of God*, a radio play (1947), in *Selected Writings, Edited, and with an Introduction by Susan Sontag* (Helen Weaver, trans.) (Berkley and Los Angeles: University of California Press, 1976; p. 571).

170 Sondra Fraleigh, *Hijikata Tatsumi and Ohno Kazuo* (London and New York: Routledge, 2006; p. 135).

171 Antonin Artaud, "Fragments of a Diary from Hell, (1925), in *Selected Writings, Edited, and with an Introduction by Susan Sontag* (p. 94).

171 Antonin Artaud, "The Theater and Its Double" (1931–36); ibid. (p. 272).

172 Antonin Artaud, "The New Revelations of Being" (1937); ibid. (p. 414). (Prior three lines also by Artaud, *loc*, *sic*).

172 Antonin Artaud, "Indian Culture and Here Lies" (1947); ibid. (p. 550).

175 Murayama Tomoyoshi, "Higyakusha no gei-jutsu" (The Art of Masochists), *MAVO*, no. 6 (July 2025), 6 (translated by Chikako Morishita and interpreted by Adachi Tomomi).

177 Liu Xiaodong, "Weight of Insomnia," Lisson Gallery, London, March 2019.

177 Liu Xiaodong, *Spring in New York*, Diary, 2020.4.18, Lisson Gallery.

177 Denise Riley, *The Words of Selves: Identification, Solidarity, Irony* (Stanford: Stanford University Press, 2000; p. 9).

177 Elena Ferrante, *In the Margins: On the Pleasures of Reading and Writing*, Ann Goldstein, trans. (New York and London: Europa Editions, 2022; p. 31).

178 Shola von Reinhold, *LOTE* (London: Jacaranda Books, 2020; p. 438).

181 Anthony (Vahni) Capildeo, "Gift of a Staircase," *Utter* (Leeds: Peepal Tree Press, 2013; p. 42). Used by permission of Peepal Tree Press.

Chapter 26

187 Crawford, *Atlas of AI* (p. 221). (Crawford cites Barrett, Lisa Feldman, et al., "Emotional Expressions Reconsidered," Challenges to Inferring Emotion from Human Facial Movements," *Psychological Science in the Public Interest* 20, no. 1 (2019): 1–68.)

187 Ibid.

187 Winterson, *12 Bytes* (p. 152).

195 Andrea Brady, *Mutability, Scripts for Infancy* (London, New York, Calcutta: Seagull Books, 2012; p. 18). Brady cites Dorothy A. Counts, "Infant care and feeding in Kaliai, West New Britain, Papua New Guinea," in Leslie B. Marshall (Ed.), *Infant Care and Feeding in the South Pacific* (New York: Gordon and Breach, 1985; pp. 155–69 (161)).

Chapter 27

199 Luke Kennard uses the phrase "Ditto bitch" in "Anagrams [iii]," *Poetry*, Poetry Foundation, June 2016 on www.poetryfoundation.org/poetrymagazine/poems/89369/from-anagrams-iii, accessed on April 6, 2023.

199 Léa Pool (dir.), *Lost and Delirious*, screenplay by Judith Thompson, based on *The Wives of Bath*, a novel by Susan Swan, produced by Cité-Amérique and Dummett Films, 2001.

200 Ibid.

200 Julia Donaldson and Axel Scheffler, *Tabby McTat* (London and Dublin: Alison Green Books, 2016; np).

200 Sophie Lewis, *Full Surrogacy Now* (p. 19).

201 Ibid. (p. 26).

202 Carson, *Eros the Bittersweet* (p. 156).

202 Shelley M. Park, *Mothering Queerly, Queering Motherhood: Resisting Monomaternalism in Adoptive, Lesbian, Blended, and Polygamous Families* (p. 6).

205 José Esteban Muñoz, *Disidentifications: Queers of Color and the Performance of Politics* (Minneapolis, MN, and London: University of Minnesota Press, 1999; p. 25).

Chapter 29

210 Denise Riley, "Is there linguistic guilt?" *Critical Quarterly* 39, issue 1, 1997, 75–100 (p. 80).

215 Virginia Woolf and Vita Sackville-West, "Virginia's Diary 25th May 1926," *Love Letters: Virginia Woolf and Vita Sackville-West* (London: Vintage Classics, p. 64).

215 Slavoj Žižek, *Organs Without Bodies: On Deleuze and Consequences*, Second edition (London and New York: Routledge, 2012; p. 138). (His italics.)

215 Ibid.

Chapter 30

217 Cixous and Calle-Gruber, *Rootprints* (p. 37).

217 Socrates, quoted in Carson, *Eros the Bittersweet* (p.155).

218 Ibid.

Chapter 33

230 *Hey Duggee*, "The Mythical Creature Badge," Series 3:40, BBC 4, September 2021.

233 Joseph, "A Gap in Language," *Sonnets for Albert* (p. 59).

Chapter 34

235 Von Reinhold, *LOTE*.

237 José Esteban Muñoz, *Cruising Utopia: The Then and There of Queer Utopia* (New York University Press, 2009; p. 72).

Chapter 36

246 Cixous and Calle-Gruber, *Rootprints*.

© Romany Francesca

HANNAH SILVA is a writer and performer working in sound poetry, radio, and experimental nonfiction. *An Artificially Intelligent Guide to Love* (BBC Radio 4) starred Fiona Shaw and was the starting point for *My Child, the Algorithm*. Silva has authored seven other plays for BBC Radio 3 and 4, winning the Tinniswood Award and numerous placements in the BBC Audio Drama Awards. Her debut poetry collection, *Forms of Protest*, was Highly Commended in the Forward Prizes. Talk in a bit, a record of sound poetry and music was in the Wire's Top 25 albums of 2018. She lives in London with her child.